JUDAISM:
Development and Life

Belmont, California

Leo Trepp

JUDAISM:

Development and Life

DICKENSON PUBLISHING COMPANY, INC.

L.C. Cat. Card No.: 66–23587

Printed in the United States of America

Third printing: July 1969

PREFACE

THIS basic introduction to Judaism is for beginners. It has been written in the hope that it may be of interest both to the student pursuing a basic course in Judaism and to the general reader in search of a survey. It is of limited length, general in character, not too involved, and self-contained, requiring no additional interpretive material. I hope that it may convey an understanding of Judaism as a living faith, a feeling of its sweep, and an awareness of its abiding contribution to mankind— and that it may equally portray some of the warmth, the emotional appeal of Jewish faith and life, and of the compelling power of the Jewish heritage upon its adherents.

My presentation had to be both descriptive and interpretive to meet the need of those readers who may not be able to turn to a more detailed work on Judaism. The interpretation is my own responsibility, for Judaism has no official body affixing an imprimatur on any work. In general I have followed the rabbinical interpretation of Scriptures as found in Talmud, Commentaries, and Codes, for the rabbinical view has shaped the outlook of the Jew, including his understanding of Scriptures. The results of scientific research have been kept in mind, however, and the decision whom to follow—the rabbis or the scholars—has often been difficult. I have also tried not to take any position in favor of or against any of the modern denominations of Judaism and their philosophies.

The book opens with a definition of the Jew and the fabric of which Judaism is woven in Chapter 1. Chapters 2 through 5 deal with the essential external developments of Jewish history into which is woven its spiritual and intellectual evolution. A historical knowledge is indeed essential for an understanding of an evolving historical religion such as Judaism. These historical and intellectual strands were combined after a great deal of soul-searching to avoid repetition and duplication in the presentation. Chapter 6 is devoted to the relationship between Christianity and Judaism, especially in contemporary life. Chapters 7 and 8

v

offer a brief analysis of the wellsprings of the Jewish spirit, especially
Torah, Talmud, and Codes; followed, in Chapter 8, by a short description of concepts, beliefs, practices, and symbols that have sprung from
these sources. Chapters 9 through 14 deal with contemporary expressions
of Judaism in worship and life. A balance sheet is drawn in Chapter 15.
Glossary and index are appended to facilitate study.

My appreciation goes to those who have helped me with information
and suggestions: to Dr. James Diemer, President of Napa College, who
also adjusted my teaching schedule to allow me time to write in the
midst of a full teaching program; to Bishop James A. Pike; to the
Vatican for current information when the Ecumenical Council was in
progress; and to the Most Reverend Leo T. Maher, Bishop of the
Catholic Diocese of Santa Rosa, California, and his staff for additional
information rendered in the spirit of friendliest cooperation.

Permission to quote is gratefully acknowledged. *The Holy Scriptures*
(Philadelphia, Jewish Publication Society, 1917) was generally used
for biblical translations, unless I chose my own. Judah Halevi's "Ode
to Zion" was quoted in the Nina Salaman translation from *A Book of
Jewish Thoughts* (New York: Bloch Publishing Company, 1943).
Reinhold Niebuhr was quoted from his work: *Pious and Secular America* (New York: Charles Scribner's Sons, 1948, pp. 107f. and 111ff.)
Life Magazine permitted me to quote from its edition of December 17,
1965 (© 1965, Time, Inc.) in connection with the Ecumenical Council.

My sincere gratitude is expressed to Mrs. Jean Phinney for her editorial work, and to Miss Sara Hunter for seeing the book through the
press; both worked with care and dedication. My most heartfelt thanks
go to my publishers, Dickenson Publishing Company, its president, Richard Hansen, and its editor, Richard J. Trudgen, without whose great
friendship, support, and encouragement this book could not have come
into being.

Leo Trepp

TABLE OF CONTENTS

In memory of my parents,
Maier and Selma Trepp ז״ל
foremost of my teachers,
who sealed their faith by their lives.

INTRODUCTION: THE JEWS AND THE FABRIC OF JUDAISM

THE uniqueness of the Jew is revealed in the very problem of definition. At best he may be defined as a person who considers himself a Jew, having cast his lot with that of the Jewish people. But how shall we define the Jewish people? They are not a race. Innumerable racial components are found among Jews. There are Caucasian Jews, Negro Jews, and Japanese Jews. From the very beginning of Jewish history there has been a constant influx of the most variegated racial groups. Some of the leading Jewish personalities—as far back as the most ancient past and including even Israel's greatest king, David—have traced their ancestry back to non-Jews.

This mixture of races has continued to our own day, and goes on still. Are they a nation? In Israel, they proudly call themselves a nation. In Russia, they are so regarded, and—as a nation with "foreign ideology"— are condemned to second-class citizenship. Harassed in their desire to maintain their faith and their traditions, they are to be wiped out by attrition.

American Jewry, in contrast, considers itself primarily a religious group, and certainly not a national group. But religion also must fail as a clear-cut definition. It fails to take into account the deep sense of responsibility which Jews feel for their brethren all over the world and overlooks their pride in the State of Israel. What then are the Jews?

The Scripture speaks of the Jewish people as a "household"—*Bet Yisrael,* the House of Israel. We may well accept this definition. A household creates a specific atmosphere through the love its members hold for one another, the common tradition that has molded them, and the experiences they have shared and continue to share. This spirit encompasses those who dwell within the family home, and those who are spread abroad, those born into it as well as those who have joined it. A family has certain common ways of expressing this spirit in custom and practice; but even those who may not share the forms of expression partake of the spirit, the love, even the conflicts, and are tied to each other by a sense of kinship, which is not the same as a political union.

1

Thus is the House of Israel, molded by its history and hopes, its traditions, trials and triumphs past and present, the spirit of commitment of its members to their heritage and to each other, its creative forces and contributions to mankind, its aspirations for itself and all humanity.

The Torah

The character of the Jewish people has been fashioned by its tradition, the *Torah*. "Moses charged us with Torah; it is the heritage of the congregation of Jacob" (Deuteronomy 33:4). These words are learned by the Jewish infant in his earliest childhood, to be recited daily. They reveal to us the meaning of Torah. The word itself means *instruction,* for the Torah is more than law; it is the compendium of instruction, the guide for life. In the narrowest sense the term Torah applies to the Scroll of the Five Books of Moses, found in every Synagogue. In a wider sense it refers to the teachings contained in it, and in the books of Hebrew Scriptures. But from the very beginning, explanation accompanied the written word. Some of it was later laid down in the Talmud, but much of it continued to evolve right down to the present. Torah stands therefore for the evolving body of teachings; it is the "heritage."

Torah addresses itself to the needs of every generation of the congregation of Jacob, and each generation adds to it out of its own experiences. Thus Torah mirrors the whole Jewish destiny; it has guided it, and with every Jewish child is being enlarged. Moses charged us with it—Moses, who is considered the greatest of teachers, but is a human being. Thus it is both divine and human: out of human experience, in man's confrontation with God, Torah evolved. Out of Jewish history, God is made manifest.

This does not mean, however, that the actual text of Torah, the Five Books of Moses (i.e., Genesis, Exodus, Leviticus, Numbers, and Deuteronomy) and the entire *Tenakh,* is of minor significance. On the contrary, the masters and rabbis considered every word, and even every letter, to be of the greatest importance. The explanation of the written Torah, once transmitted orally, and therefore called Oral Torah, later laid down in the Talmud, is based on a minute study of every detail of the text, every intended meaning. To the modern Jew—knowingly and unknowingly—the text of the Torah is understood in the light of Oral Torah, which may lead him—quite unconsciously—to an interpretation or understanding different from those which a simple reading of the text may suggest. We may find this interpretation in this book. Thus we have indeed a living Torah. A creative tension has been fashioned between

God as the Giver and the people as the respondents, who in responding fashion it. The Torah, in Jewish tradition, is traced back to the desert, Mount Sinai, which was no-man's land. It is thus tied to no specific territory. It is eternal and universal, applying to all lands and conditions. It is the heritage of the "congregation" wherever it may be found. It has fashioned the congregation.

God

The Torah speaks to us of God. He is its source. Torah tells us that He is the Creator of the Universe, that He is the Master of History, that He is One. Ultimately, He remains hidden to the human mind, which cannot encompass Him, yet He becomes manifest in nature as in the events of life. Moses, who wishes to "see His face," is given the answer, "you cannot see My face, for man may not see Me and live" (Exodus 33:20). "You will see My back (that which God has wrought), but My face must not be seen" (Exodus 33:23). Then God recites His divine attributes to Moses: that He is "God, compassionate and gracious, slow to anger, rich in steadfast kindness, extending kindness to the thousandth generation, forgiving iniquity, transgression, and sin; but clearing the guilty, *He will not do*" (Exodus 34:6-7). The rabbis, in their interpretation, chose to read the passage in such fashion that the words in italics here were not included. Thus God is acquitting even the guilty. More is revealed in this change than merely an example of an evolving Torah. The rabbis mean to say that God is understood and found in "imitation." This includes acquitting those who have wronged us. What God truly is, we do not know. That He *is,* we know as we survey history when it is passed, and cannot fail to recognize His presence in seeing His "back." In our lives we become aware of Him as we imitate His attributes.

This does not mean that the Jews did not ponder the character and attributes of God. His Oneness is reaffirmed daily by every Jew: "Hear, O Israel, the Lord our God, the Lord is one" (Deuteronomy 6:4), a statement that is theological in character. But even this Oneness, as the great Spanish rabbi and philosopher Maimonides explains, is so absolute that nothing in our experience compares to it.

In their search, other theologians have come to various interpretations, all of them facets, perhaps, of the unfathomable totality of God. To the average Jew, His presence is both the source of our being and the rationale of our survival.

Some modern Jews, such as in Israel, may have considered the Jewish people as just another national entity or as simply an ethnic entity. Ultimately, they cannot refer to Torah either as Jewish tradition or as creative expression of the mind without confronting God. The Jewish atheist wrestles with Him, acknowledging Him in denial. All Jews have at least tried—inadequately as may have been the case—to imitate His attributes in the life of society. Without God, the existence of the Jewish people is ultimately meaningless.

The Jews saw God in anthropomorphic terms. This is natural as the average person is not a philosopher. Thus God became to them the loving Father in Heaven, their King, their Judge. In His *hands* they have placed their body and their spirit (Psalm 95:4; II Samuel 24:14, etc.). There is nothing wrong with that, it simply expresses God's personal concern and love as understood by the Jew. He is their shield and buckler. The Torah, as tradition tells, speaks the language of simple people. Thus love could be asked and given. Only a truly loving God could say, "Thou shalt love the Lord thy God" (Deuteronomy 6:5). He has always been their Sustainer, and is recognized as their Redeemer. A truly personal relationship may then exist between every individual Jew and God. But the Jew also knows that God, being all of these, is infinitely more, and thus is beyond human understanding and comprehension.

Being more, He could never be less, hence He can never assume any form, nor can He be portrayed in any form. The form is static and God is dynamic; the form—any form—is temporal, God is eternal. The form destroys the divine unity, for form is composed of many parts. The Jewish God concept thus stands in fundamental opposition to the Christian concept, of God having assumed the form of man.

It is possible for a Jew to see God in naturalistic terms, thus bringing the concept in accord with scientific thinking. He is the Power that makes for ideals and their realization. Mordecai Kaplan, the leading thinker and spokesman in modern American Jewry, has taken this position.

Hermann Cohen, another modern Jewish philosopher, sees in Him the creator and capstone of the universe, guaranteeing that the realm of nature and the realm of ethics are perfectly adjusted to each other, for He fashioned both, allowing man to influence nature through ethical conduct.

All these are human efforts to pierce into the unfathomable otherness of the immutable God, and—rather than diminishing Him—throw light upon some of the effects of His being.

The Land

From the very beginning of history, Jewish destiny has remained inextricably linked to that of the Land of Israel. To the Jew, his history starts as Abraham is bidden to migrate to the Promised Land, for only there can he fulfill himself as the servant and herald of God. The Land is promised to his children, who never left it entirely, not even during the centuries of Israel's sojourn in Egypt. The Land of Israel always remained the Promised Land. Only there could Torah be translated freely into the life of an independent nation.

In conflict with the alien, heathen ideologies of surrounding peoples and of conquerors, Jewish identity was forged. National independence became linked again and again with the renewal of spirit. Only on the soil of the homeland of Israel could the faith of Israel develop into a religion with a universal message. A homeless person pleading for universality of ethical conduct and principles may not be sincere, nor is he so recognized; being dependent on others, he may be pleading for understanding and compassion. Not so the free man on his own soil, who may be chauvinistic. In sharing his insights with mankind and in including mankind among the beloved of God, he shows true magnanimity and brotherhood. Rooted in the soil of their land, the prophets encompassed all of humanity equally in their rebuke and in their comfort.

When the Land was taken away, it forced the people to find new justification for their continued existence. People on their soil need but live; people away from it must find a rationale for survival. One of these was that they would return to the Land when it was God's will; hence, they must deepen their religious life in order to survive and to be worthy of a return. In this manner did synagogue and liturgy develop. This hope —of freely living on their land, shaping their destiny under God—gave impetus to the messianic ideal. Out of the certainty of return, enshrined and expressed in every prayer, they found the strength to endure humiliation and persecution for centuries. Through the Land, unity was forged among the widespread community of the House of Israel throughout the world. The polarity of land and the *Diaspora* (the Jewish community dispersed throughout the rest of the world) stimulated creative thought in philosophy and poetry, for ever again the meaning both of dispersion and of their land—which they did not at the moment own—had to be made clear.

In the nineteenth and twentieth centuries, religious yearning for the coming of messianic times was translated into concrete and political terms: the Land would gather in those whose life had become intolerable under persecution, and it did—not all of them, but millions who would have died otherwise.

Some Israelis today want all Jews to return, a physical impossibility. Nor does this desire meet with the feeling of Jews in free countries, especially America. American Jewry feel proudly American; here is their home. But they look with pride and in kinship to the newborn state of

Israel and its people, helping them, and deriving from the Land of Israel spiritual uplift and inspiration. The meaning of the Land is understood by American Jewry as spiritual. To interpret the position of American Jews in any other manner—especially as involving any kind of political allegiance—would be a gravely mistaken and harmful distortion.

Mitzvah

Mitzvah means commandment; it implies action. Through Mitzvah the Jew responds to God. At Mount Sinai the people promised, "All that the Lord has spoken we will do and hear (understand) it" (Exodus 24:7). The understanding comes in the act, provided it is performed as a service to God and undergirded by the true intent of the heart (*Kavanah*); empty performance carries little value, and neither, by itself, does the affirmation of "faith." Only both faith and action constitute service, as *Kavanah* enters every thought, prayer, and act. In living, man becomes God's co-worker.

There are two kinds of *Mitzvot* (plural of Mitzvah) in Torah: those of religious observance (between man and God), and those between man and man. A term sometimes applied when speaking of the Mitzvah speaks of God as *Makom,* He who fills and sanctifies every *place* of the universe. Mitzvah thus is affirmation of God; in this sense, those duties we owe our fellow man are equally Mitzvot of God. "Love thy neighbor as thyself" (Leviticus 19:18) is thus the basic Mitzvah, and was rightfully proclaimed by the sages as the cornerstone of Judaism.

Social justice is Mitzvah, it dignifies the doer and the recipient as children of God. Hence Judaism has placed paramount importance on social justice. Through it we establish God as truly *Makom.* Through Mitzvah the Jew attains self-identification. But he must know the source and intent of the Mitzvah, hence the study of Torah in itself becomes a Mitzvah. Here lies the foundation of the Jew's concern with education: study is Mitzvah, and in all study God is somehow made evident; it is His creation which we contemplate, and penetrate.

Of the 613 Mitzvot traditionally seen as handed down to the Jew, 365 are prohibitions and 248 are calls to action. The number of prohibitions corresponds to the days of the year; every day's activity must be limited and must be confined within God's domain. The number of positive actions corresponds to the parts of the human body. Every one of them must be ready for duty in promoting His Kingdom.

There were many Mitzvot that were related to the Land, to sanctify it and the people who dwelt on it. When the Land was taken away, new rules and the conscientious, detailed performance of the other Mitzvot were substituted to unify the people. This has led even to proliferation of injunctions, a psychological defense against spiritual and physical erosion. In the sixteenth century, Rabbi Joseph Karo, searching for a unifying bond which would forever keep the people together, decided on a Code of Mitzvot, the *Shulhan Arukh,* which became the authoritative work and did keep Jewry together.

Time and forces may prevent the people from full performance of Mitzvot, but there has been the hope that the day would come when both Israel and all mankind might no longer be impeded from freely fulfilling the Mitzvot in freedom, love, and justice toward each other, redeemed from war and persecution. This is the time of the Messiah. Many a modern Jew has abandoned religious practices, but the Mitzvah of social justice is practiced by all, though they may not know that it is their tradition that compels them. And all Jews yearn for the messianic times at least in the sense that they hope for the day when "they will beat their swords into plowshares" (Micah 4:3). All are prepared to toil for this day.

The Covenant

These major forces of God, Torah, Land, and Mitzvot interact, each of them evolving from the other, each of them leading to the other. We cannot separate them. On this basis, the Jew understands his relationship with God: it is a covenant. To be in the world as fighter for Him or as His suffering servant is the mission of the Jew. In Exodus 19:5–6, we hear of this covenant:

> Now if you listen and listen again to my voice [in study of Torah], and keep My covenant [in action], you shall be My treasured possession among all the peoples. Indeed, all the earth is Mine [as the universal God], but you shall be to Me a kingdom of priests [in fulfilment of His commandments in the sphere of religion, which testifies to God] and a holy people [in setting an example among all the peoples, that they may follow Him as well].

Jews have not been permitted to see themselves as "the favored son." On the contrary, they have been told that their distinction, if there is any, consists in higher responsibility. "You only have I known of all the families of the earth; therefore will I punish you for all your iniquities," says Amos (Amos 3:2). The uniqueness of the forces that have fashioned the Jewish people must lead to a uniqueness of obligations. God-Torah-Land-Mitzvot impose responsibilities which must be met for the sake of all of mankind under God.

Failure begets punishment. Once again we find some modern Jews, with Mordecai Kaplan as their leading spokesman, do away with the concept of Israel's chosenness. They may well lean on the Prophet Amos, who addresses himself to all the nations of his world and sees for Israel only the distinction of special punishment. This does not mean, however, that with the denial of chosenness the forming forces are denied; on the contrary, they are affirmed. It does mean that we must conceive of every people as being singularly chosen by its endowment, its gifts, its history, its land, and its culture. And being chosen, they have the responsibility to utilize their endowment in Mitzvah. The chosenness of Israel through the forces that have fashioned it thus serves as an example to mankind to consider itself chosen for duty and held divinely responsible for its performance.

THE LOOM OF HISTORY I

2 THE BIBLICAL AND TALMUDIC PERIODS

To write even an outline of Jewish history would go beyond the framework of this book. In the following pages we shall endeavor to trace the evolution of Jewish history as a guide and framework for the beginner who has no knowledge of it. It may enable him to put men and ideas into their historical setting and to follow the ever-changing tapestry of Judaism as the elements of God-Torah-Mitzvot-Land are woven in ever new patterns by the Jewish people.

Early History

Toward the first quarter of the second millennium, Abraham migrated from "Ur of the Chaldees" (Genesis 11:31) to Canaan. This may be called the beginning of Hebrew history.* In search of the One God, Abraham could find Him only in the Land; and in earnest desire to respond to Him through Mitzvah, he was willing to sacrifice his son Isaac (Genesis 22:1–18). The sacrifice was kindly rejected for "the dead cannot praise Him," the living alone must respond to Him. This was Torah. The Land was promised to Abraham's seed and they never left it entirely. (As the archeologist William F. Albright points out, there were always Hebrews in Canaan, even while the majority dwelt in ancient Egypt.)

After two generations, Abraham's family migrated to Egypt to escape a severe famine. Jacob, a son of Isaac, had earned the name *Israel,* "He who strives with God"; his household became "the Children of Israel."

* The term *"Hebrew"* is explained by William F. Albright as meaning *donkey driver* and referring to the nomadic life of those to whom it was applied. According to Albright, the term is derived from "dusty," since these people with their donkeys raised a great deal of dust in passing over the roads. [*The Biblical Period from Abraham to Ezra,* New York and Evanston: Harper & Row Publishers, Inc. (Harper Torch Book), 1963.]

10

Soon they were enslaved as enemy aliens and forced to build mighty buildings for Pharaoh. After many years of servitude, they were freed, and under the leadership of Moses, they departed from Egypt (around 1280). Moses became their teacher; he gave them Torah; he taught them Mitzvot; he kept them in the desert for forty years to transform them from a group of slaves into a free people; he led them to the borders of their Promised Land.

The Land had to be reconquered and settled. Surrounded by enemy nations, the people were sorely beset; influenced by non-Hebrew neighbors with alien ideas, they frequently turned away from worship of the One God and embraced idolatry. Their unity dissolved, and they were repeatedly attacked and subjected by stronger neighbors. In moments of severe distress they united, selected an outstanding leader, and jointly took up arms against their enemies and overcame them. The leader then remained the people's guide for the rest of his life; he became a Judge, teaching Torah and deepening the spirit of unity among the people. His influence vanished with his death, and the whole chain of events was repeated with tragic monotony.

The people failed to realize that their strength lay in their spirit, and that, in recognizing God as their ruler, they would find unity and strength, which they could deepen through Torah and Mitzvot. Instead, they chose another expedient, a hereditary monarchy, which they hoped would guarantee perpetual leadership.

Around 1020 they chose *Saul* as their king; but Saul, more concerned with his royal prerogatives and the establishment of his dynasty, failed them utterly, leading them to crushing defeat at the hands of the Philistines. This warrior nation had settled at the coastline of Canaan and was able to subdue the Israelites by the strength of its better iron weapons against their bronze, and its unity against their disunity.

Saul's successor, *David,* around 1000 reversed the tide. He was both a general and a poet, a shrewd administrator, and tender-hearted lyricist. He had every human shortcoming but also the greatness to admit error, accept its consequences, and remedy his faults. He became Israel's ideal king; he conquered Jerusalem and made it his capital and led the nation to strength. He enlarged the Land and responded in psalm and in action to the command and rebuke of God. Thus he has set the image of the anointed, the Messiah, a man of his seed and of his wisdom, who would bring Israel and mankind to the age of abiding peace.

David's son *Solomon* (around 961) was inclined to see himself as an oriental monarch and politician. Building on the foundations of his father's work, he established the realm firmly and expanded trade. He built the splendid first Temple in Jerusalem and a magnificent palace for himself as well. He who liked to consider himself the wisest of men had insufficient psychological insight into the feelings of the common people whom he exploited by taxes and forced labor to carry out his grandiose schemes.

When the people approached his successor, *Rehoboam,* for a redress of grievances, they were scornfully rebuked. As a result, ten of the twelve tribes of Israel seceded to form the Kingdom of Israel in the North; only the tribe of the royal house, Judah, and the tribe of Benjamin remained with the family of David.

Both kingdoms had a checkered history, depending (in the Kingdom of Israel) on the ruling dynasty and the character of the king. The Kingdom of Judah possessed the national sanctuary of Jerusalem, and, in general, a greater awareness of its purpose under God. The northern kingdom was willing to exchange integrity for expediency. This period marks the ministry of the great literary prophets, beginning in the eighth century B.C.E., and stretching into the fourth century B.C.E.* The portions of their works which we still possess belong to the greatest documents of the human spirit; they preached, rebuked, called to task, but also comforted.

In 722 B.C.E. the Kingdom of Israel was destroyed by the Assyrians, its ten tribes lost. The Kingdom of Judah, submitting to Assyrian overlordship, survived. From now on there remained only the descendants of Judah.

In 621 a book was found in the Temple, bringing about a great religious revival. Modern Biblical scholars consider it to have been the Book of Deuteronomy, actually written at that time. Spiritual strength was being stored; it was badly needed.

Babylonian Exile

In 586, the Babylonians (now having supplanted the Assyrians as the great power of the East) conquered Judah and destroyed the Temple. A part of the Jewish community fled to Egypt, but the majority were taken to Babylonia into exile. Neither of these groups was lost. Having lost physical possession of the Land, they refined their faith in the crucible of exile.

Apart from feeling themselves exiles, the Jews found their lives pleasant: they governed themselves, enjoyed equal rights, and some of them even rose to high positions. Babylonia became a spiritual workshop. The Land and its redemption was transformed into a hope and aspiration. Torah was the center of life; its interpreter, the rabbi, came to occupy a key position. Worship took the place of sacrifices; Mitzvot

* Before the common era; used to designate dates preceding the Christian era. C.E. designates dates of the Christian era.

were both a response to God and the link which bound the House of Israel together. Synagogue and liturgy as we know them had their start.

The Effects and Meaning of Exile

In spite of their adaptation to life in Babylonia, the expulsion from their homeland to exile was a profoundly traumatic experience. Psalm 137 reflects their shock and a rather unworthy feeling of revenge, born out of hopelessness and impotence. As they emerged from the numbness of despair, two questions came to their minds: Why did it happen, and how long is it going to last? The immediate answer was: It happened because we have sinned by breaking the covenant. Was it going to be a short sojourn? The prophet Jeremiah made it clear to them that their sojourn among the nations might well be considered of long duration. He advises them to settle down and "multiply . . . and be not diminished." Dwelling among the nations, they must do more than simply come to terms with their fate: "seek the peace of the city . . . and pray to the Lord for it; for in the peace thereof shall ye have peace" (Jeremiah 29:4–7). Good citizenship thus becomes a religious duty. Jews are to look at the country of their homes and birth as a permanent dwelling place. The distrust of others—preached up to now to the unique people dwelling within a heathen world—was transformed, to be replaced by heartfelt concern for the welfare of the nation and its citizens, its inner and outward peace, expressed in prayer and in active participation. From this time on, we shall find Jews filled with earnest desire to promote the welfare of the countries of their dispersion. Thus it was in ancient Babylonia, Egypt, and Rome; thus it remained even in the countries where Jews were bitterly persecuted. With renewed vigor, they sought to make their contribution when they were permitted to live in lands of freedom.

Under these circumstances, the first question has to be taken up again: Was their life in dispersion exile and punishment or perhaps a task? A long exile as a result of sin would actually punish the children for the faults of their fathers. Both the prophets Jeremiah and Ezekiel addressed themselves to the problem:

'The fathers have eaten sour grapes and the children's teeth are set on edge.' Ye shall not have occasion any more to use this proverb in Israel. . . . If a man be just, he shall surely live. . . . If he begets a son that is a robber . . . he shall not live, having done all these abominations. . . . If he begets a son that sees all his father's sin . . . and considers and doeth not such like . . . he shall not die for the iniquity of his father; he shall surely live. (Jeremiah 31:29–30; Ezekiel 18:3–17.)

The impact and implication of this statement are fundamental and far-reaching.

The Babylonian Jewish community and all of their descendants were advised that they dwelt among people of other religious convictions because God had willed that they creatively participate in the upbuilding of a good society. Not sinfulness but a divine challenge had caused their dispersion. Thus Jews may identify fully with the lands in which they hold citizenship.

If they are persecuted in some lands, again it is not the result of their sins, but rather a divine test. The Jews, as a minority, are tested to show the strength of their faith. The majority is equally tested to show the spirit of godliness. They have an opportunity of graciously dealing with a minority; if the majority fails, then this failure points to *its own* shortcoming in thwarting the divine will. The contribution of the Jew under adverse circumstances consists in illuminating the world's failure in spiritual attainment, and in calling it to account before God.

The search for the meaning of their exile led to general discussion of suffering and sin in post-Exilic Jewish literature. The second Isaiah in his parable of the Suffering Servant (Chapter 53) demonstrates that the steadfast faith of the sufferer sets an example from which future generations may learn and profit. The legend of Job (also an inhabitant of a non-Jewish environment) dwells on it in great detail. Man must accept sufferings as a test of faith, and, in accepting, he will find insight and strength. Job, having lost his fortune, his children, his home, and his health, maintains against the strongest arguments of his friends his belief in two fundamental truths: he has not sinned, hence his suffering is not the wages of sin, and furthermore, there is a God who must have willed it: he rejects the suggestion that world and man might be subject to a purely accidental chain of events. God Himself justifies Job.

According to a rabbinic view (Makkot 24a), Ezekiel's statement boldly overrides a principle enshrined in the Ten Commandments themselves, namely, that God visits the iniquities of the fathers upon the children (Exodus 20:5). This reveals the deeper insight acquired by the Jews in the course of the generations: There is no inherited guilt, there is but personal responsibility of every person for himself and for those whom he may influence. This has remained the Jew's staunch conviction and stands in contrast to the Christian belief in original sin, which implicates all of mankind in the sin of Adam and Eve, their common ancestors. Jews do not believe in original sin.

Having understood the permanence of their position among other peoples, the Jews now had to put their religious life on new foundations. The Land could serve now only as spiritual inspiration. The Temple was no more; no sacrifices could henceforth be offered; the priestly caste (the family of Aaron) had lost its function. The adjustment, started in

Babylonia and continued even after the return of part of the people to their homeland, was so ingenious that it has served all of Western religion as pattern and example.

Torah and Mitzvot were strengthened to compensate for the physical loss of the Land. The word of Torah was to be read regularly to the people and explained, interpreted, and studied. This called for teachers, not priests; there emerged the rabbi. He could be a priest or a layman, rich or poor, of noble ancestry or a recent convert, but he had to be a teacher, upright in character, searching for knowledge, and dedicated to his task. All he needed was a group of students and a shelter against the elements. His work could be carried out anywhere and at any time. Thus came into existence with the rabbi the house of meeting, which also became the house of prayer. The national sanctuary at Jerusalem (like all the temples of antiquity) was not so much a place of popular assembly as a dwelling place of God. The people were primarily spectators at a set ritual. Now we have the meeting house, and the people are the participants. Here lies the origin of the form of the *House of God* in Western religions. Torah would now be the center of worship instead of sacrifices. The recital of Torah was surrounded by prayer and psalm and made meaningful by the rabbi's explanation. A pattern of worship was created which was again followed by many Western religions: Scripture reading, sermon, prayer, and hymn.

Return from Exile: Home-Born and Convert

In 538, Cyrus, conqueror of Babylonia, permitted the Jews to return. He was sure that in gratitude for this favor they would become a stable element in this outpost of his realm. Ezra and Nehemiah, who had been leading members of the remaining strong community of Babylonia and held high offices with the king, returned to Jerusalem eighty or ninety years later. Insisting on strictest family purity, they even compelled the settlers to divorce their non-Jewish wives; the Jewish kinship had to be deepened among all those who were committed to unyielding obedience to God and Torah. It was felt that only a family uncompromisingly committed to Torah and Mitzvot and brought up in them for generations could assure Jewish survival. The Samaritans, a people of Jewish and non-Jewish ancestry with a synthetic religion composed of many practices, were rejected.

The attitude of Judaism toward converts thereby underwent a change under the impact of external forces. During their early settlement, Jews had been hospitable to converts. They were the first and only people in antiquity to receive the stranger willing to cast his lot with them, while all the other nations excluded the "barbarian." The Book of Ruth, discussed later, is a charming testimony to this hospitality: the convert, lovingly accepted, became the ancestress of King David. Now, faced with the dangers of erosion, a barrier was put up. Since those days, the Jewish attitude toward conversion has remained ambivalent. At times (for instance, during the period of the Roman Principate) conversion activity was widespread. The feeling was: If men are looking for spiritual guidance and Judaism can give it, then we must offer it. Later, efforts at conversion became minimal, partly, of course, as a result of the prohibition of Christianity against it. At present, there seems to exist a more liberal outlook, at least among non-Orthodox Jews. The convert may become a full-fledged and beloved member of the Jewish people.

Restoration

After the return, the Torah was solemnly proclaimed to the people once again established in the Land, and a covenant of obedience to it was entered by all (444 B.C.E.). Although a second Temple had been built in 520–515, it was not enough for the leaders. Torah and Mitzvot in daily life and worship were placed in the central position, the rabbi's role increased, and the next centuries were devoted to consolidation and expansion of the knowledge and spirit of Torah. This has saved Judaism, for the Temple was destroyed a second time. Immediately, the center of Jewish life was shifted to the house of study.

The search for meaning in Torah went deeper and deeper, in debate, discussion, rabbinic decision, and commentaries. This growing body of interpretations was transmitted for centuries by word of mouth, Oral Torah evolved, and eventually, when the subject matter became too voluminous and persecution endangered the lives of the rabbis who held the knowledge, this "Oral Torah" was written down. This has come to be known as the *Mishnah* (Review), which then became the source for additional commentary, the *Gemara* (Addition), completed in Babylonia. Both Mishnah and Gemara form the *Talmud* (Compendium of Learning). It has remained the "encyclopedia of the Jew," and will be discussed later in detail.

When need arose, Torah was even translated to remain the guide for those Jews who had lost their facility in Hebrew. Translated into Greek, supposedly the work of seventy scholars, this early translation is known to us as the *Septuagint* from the Latin word for 70.

The arrival of Alexander the Great of Macedonia on the stage of history opened wide the gates to the influence of Greek culture (Hellenism). Conquering the world (336–323 B.C.E.), Alexander entered Jerusalem, and was so gracious to the Jews that they named their sons after him. Upon his early death, Judah first fell under the rule of the Ptolemies of Egypt (the first Ptolemy was one of the generals who had divided up Alexander's empire). So strong was the influence of Hellenism that many of the pious Jews of Egypt no longer understood Hebrew, hence the translation of the Septuagint, already mentioned.

Soon, however, Judah became attached to the kingdom of Syria, the House of the Seleucids. One of their kings, Antiochus IV Epiphanes, desirous of unifying his empire by means of Greek worship and thought, endeavored to suppress Jewish religion. In 167 B.C.E. this brought on a rebellion, led by Judah Maccabee (Judas Maccabaeus, The Hammerer) of the House of Hasmon, which eventually resulted in complete independence and is celebrated in the festival of Hanukkah. (See p. 173.) The Hasmoneans traced their descent to Aaron the high priest; they were, therefore, members of the priestly caste, the only one entitled to conduct the service in the Temple and to provide the high priest. The Hasmoneans now assumed the power of the royal purple as kings, adding to it the office of high priest. Their power was truly absolute and soon became corrupt.

Roman Domination

Locked in bitter struggle for the kingship, two brothers of the House of Hasmon, Hyrcanus and Aristobulus, called on Rome to be the arbiter of their claims. In 63 B.C.E. Pompey arrived on the scene, gave the power to the weaker of the two brothers, Hyrcanus, and assigned him an advisor—actually a supervisor—who would see to it that Rome retained the power that had fallen into her lap. The advisor was Antipater, an Idumaean, son of a people who had been forcibly annexed and converted to Judaism by the Hasmoneans without ever accepting the faith in sincere conviction. Antipater's son, for whom the father prepared the way to the throne, was Herod the Great (37–4 B.C.E.), who wiped out the Hasmonean family almost entirely, although he had married into the House, dealt cruelly with the people, and tried everything to please the Roman overlords. He also ordered the execution of John the Baptist.

After Herod's death, the Romans took over completely, governing through administrative agents called *Procurators*. These men were cruel and venal, having been sent to the province with the understanding that they might enrich themselves. One of their methods was to taunt the people by exhibiting the Roman Eagle, a graven image abhorrent to the Jews. Fanning the spirit of rebellion, they would then cruelly suppress it, condemning hundreds to death by crucifixion, and confiscating their belongings for their own pockets. Unrest grew, and the cry for freedom from intolerable oppression increased. Galilee in particular was seething with rebellion. Among these brutal men, Pontius Pilate stood out as one of the worst procurators. It is not surprising, therefore, that he saw in the activities and messianic pronouncements of Jesus an act of rebellion, and had him crucified as "King of the Jews," to show what would happen to anyone who wanted independence and to be "King" or Messiah. Crucifixion, the brutal Roman way of execution, was the lot of many Jews, who despised Pontius Pilate and resisted him, ready to die rather than give up their tradition.

Eventually Pontius Pilate was too much even for Rome, and he was recalled. In 64 C.E., Florus, the last procurator, took office. He provoked the Jews to such a degree that they finally rose in armed rebellion. Florus could not quash it; the Roman legions had to be called in under the command of the general Vespasian (later Roman emperor, 69–79 C.E.). After years of war, Titus, Vespasian's son, finally conquered Jerusalem (70 C.E.) and destroyed it. By that time, a religious center had already been established in a little city, Jabneh, in order that Torah could immediately take over as the central force, should the Temple fall.

The spirit of the Jews had not been destroyed. It led to several rebellions in an effort to reconquer the land in full Jewish sovereignty. The Bar Kokhba rebellion (132–135) was the last one. It failed, broken by the Roman Emperor Hadrian, who then realized that the Jews could not be overcome as long as they had Torah and Mitzvot; he prohibited both. The Jews became martyrs of faith. After Hadrian's death (138 C.E.), Jewish religion was again permitted. The province of Palestine— so-called to deny the Jews the right of name and ownership—remained the center of Jewish life throughout the world. Here, the Patriarch had his residence, serving as central authority for the Jewish Diaspora, which was widely spread, including Babylonia, Egypt, and Rome and its provinces as far as Germany.

Gradually gaining adherents, Christianity became the state religion of the Roman Empire (the Council of Nicaea in 325 was already a high point). Jews were now subjected to ever greater disabilities under Christian Rome; they had become the accursed race. In 425 the Jewish office of Patriarch was abolished, and the Christian bishop of Jerusalem took the title of Patriarch. By that time, the center of Jewish life had moved to Babylonia, a non-Christian country.

The Impact of Greek Thought

It must not be assumed that Judaism excluded foreign thought. Although it remains dedicated to Torah, Judaism has always been open to non-Jewish culture and thought. It has been hospitable to those ideas and practices which were considered valuable, embodying some of them even into the faith itself. It has rejected only those which it considered detrimental.

Greek thought was a particularly strong and lasting influence. The prophets had not been systematic thinkers. They were moved by the spirit of God and spoke with emotional fervor. Under Greek influence, systematic thinking was introduced, to become a permanent feature of Jewish study. Plato, Aristotle, and the Stoics were taken seriously. The Sanhedrin, the ancient Jewish supreme court, in its function of innovator in law reminds us of Greek legislative bodies.

A good example is the attitude of Judaism to universal study of Torah. Plato had called for a universal system of public education. Aristotle had shown that the pursuit of knowledge spells man's true and greatest happiness, admitting however, that this happiness would be denied to those who lacked the material means to afford leisure for study. Combining these two elements with the injunction of Torah to teach diligently (Deuteronomy 6) and applying them to the study of Torah, the Jews concluded that education must be universal, and that man must do with the absolutely barest minimum of existence—if need be, even depriving himself—in order to find the happiness of study. "Eat bread with salt, drink water in small measure, sleep on the ground, accept a life of deprivations, but toil in Torah. If thou wilt do thus, hail unto thee, good will be thine, hail unto thee in this world, good will be thine in the world to come." (Mishnah Abot 6:4.) The Talmud itself tries to follow Aristotelian patterns of logic wherever possible. On the other hand, Judaism turned down the philosophy of Epicurus, who denied the existence of God and the future of the soul after death. The worst epithet that can be hurled against a Jew who has fallen away completely is Epicurean. Under the impact of worldly wisdom, Jewish philosophy emerged.

The Jewish philosopher Philo, who lived in Egypt during the first pre-Christian century, spoke and wrote Greek, and conducted his own life in the spirit of the Stoics, yet remained a deeply religious and observant Jew. Influenced by the Greek thinkers of his time, who interpreted Homer allegorically and as a guide to ethics, Philo undertook the same task in interpreting Torah. The events related in it thus point to deeper meanings of ethical significance; the Mitzvot are visible means by which God tries to make manifest eternal truths of reason. In studying Torah and performing the Mitzvot, Jews therefore rehearse and reveal eternal and universal truths.

The Sects

The period from Ezra to about the end of the second century of the present era was one of great activity. Under the influence of Hellenism, there emerged a number of sects which remained in existence up to the destruction of the Temple.

Among them were the *Sadducees,* rich, well-born assimilationists, who reduced the Torah to the minimum contained in the written Word, and fawned on the Romans in an effort to gain favor with them. Caiphas, the high priest appointed by Pilate, was one of the Sadducees, for by this time the office of the high priest had become a political plum awarded by the Romans. The Sadducees, as described by the Jewish historian Josephus, were a selfish and power-hungry group.

The *Essenes,* in contrast, saw the end of the world around the corner, eschewed worldly possessions, and traveled about calling the people to repentance. Some groups withdrew into monasteries, wishing no contact and compromise with the world. They would be the remnant to be saved when the final day of reckoning came, the battle between "the sons of light and the sons of darkness." The *Dead Sea Scrolls* have given us a report of their lives, organization, and beliefs.

The *Zealots,* believing that the only good Roman was a dead Roman, walked about with daggers under their cloaks, calling for war.

The leading group was that of the *Pharisees.* Dedicated to Torah and scrupulous in the performance of Mitzvot, they knew that these were the pillars of Jewish survival. But perfunctory performance was abhorrent to them: the heart must be attuned to God. The emphasis on Mitzvot is clearly demonstrated in the lives of the Pharisees. There exists hardly any group in history that has been treated so unjustly by posterity. Condemned as hypocrites, they were just the opposite. They maintained that service of God calls for the human heart. Love for Him and fellow man must undergird our actions, for the intent matters, not the empty act. Humility and modesty are the virtues God demands. "Do not do unto others what would be hateful to you were it done to you," was the motto—indeed, the foundation of Judaism—to Hillel, a Pharisee. Judaism proudly acknowledges the Pharisees as its spiritual fathers.

The Pharisees were extremely careful in the observance of Mitzvot. Pharisees means "the Separated Ones," and they considered themselves as the "Elect" in the sense that they were to set an example. They desired to "build a fence (of Mitzvot) around the Torah" so that it might never be harmed under the impact of external influences. Love of God, love of man, Torah, and Mitzvot, seen as response to divine law in ethics and religious observance—that is their legacy. These are the bulwark against destruction.

One of the greatest of the Pharisee teachers was HILLEL (about 30–10 as leader of his school). Believing that love of neighbor was the basic element of Judaism and its starting point, leading to true study of Torah, Hillel opened an academy, trained many disciples, and, whenever possible, adjusted Torah to life, even as life must remain under Torah.

He had many controversies with his strict and unbending contemporary, Shammai, who was also the head of a school. Judaism has considered the teachings of both to be "the words of the living God," for Judaism permits divergence of thought. But the decision has remained according to Hillel. Hillel had faith in the people, hence his patience became proverbial: "If they are not prophets, then they are the sons of prophets." Here is one of the sources of modern conservative philosophy, maintaining that the unspoken will of the people evolves Torah with God's consent. By their graciousness and humility, the pharisaic teachers —who were not professional rabbis but small artisans or farmers— became the abiding leaders of the Jewish people. They are among the world's greatest ethical teachers.

When Jerusalem was besieged by Rome, the Pharisee rabbi, Johanan Ben Zaccai, obtained an audience with Vespasian and gained his permission to open the school at Jabneh. When Jerusalem fell, the other sects disappeared, and the Pharisees became *the* teachers, the rabbis. In the academies they studied Torah and tradition meticulously, word for word; debated, and decided issues in law on the basis of majority decision. Thus was evolved *Halakhah* (Jewish law). As preachers they conveyed ethical principles to the people, frequently using *Aggadah* (parables). Some of their maxims were collected for the guidance of generations as *Sayings of the Fathers* (Father being then a title of the rabbi). By word of mouth, this Oral Torah was transmitted from generation to generation. In this form of transmission lay a danger. Who could remember it all, as it constantly grew, and who dared to entrust the whole tradition of Judaism to a few men, who might take their knowledge prematurely with them?

RABBI AKIBA (50–135) had studied for twenty-four years to become the master of the people; he died a martyr of faith in the persecutions following Hadrian's edict prohibiting Judaism, which he had braved. Both he and Rabbi Meir, his successor (130–160), had already been compelled to prepare lecture notes.

Mishnah

In view of this situation, Rabbi Judah, Patriarch and friend of the Emperor Antoninus Pius (and perhaps also of his nephew, the emperor and philosopher Marcus Aurelius) decided that Oral Torah had to be edited and written down. The work, the *Mishnah,* of which we shall say more, was completed around the year 200, none too soon, as conditions became difficult. The masters who speak in it are called *Tannaim,* the Teachers.

Additional discussion based on the Mishnah was carried on, but this work, the Talmud of Jerusalem, remained incomplete. Time did not allow its completion. By that time, however, the Jewish center of Babylonia had begun to flourish.

Babylonian Jewry

When two of Rabbi Judah's disciples went to Babylonia during the early years of the third century to establish there the center of Jewish learning, they did not take any great risk. Babylonian Jewry had already behind it a proud history extending over 800 years. The prophet Jeremiah had written them at the beginning of their settlement in exile to consider their new dwelling place a permanent residence for many generations and to devote themselves faithfully to the tasks of good citizenship. As soon as Jerusalem had been resettled by their brethren, they considered it the spiritual and intellectual, as well as physical, core of Jewry, but did not neglect the development of their own institutions. Thus Hillel had received his early training in Babylonia and migrated to Judaea for completion of his studies and eventual leadership. Now Abba Areka (Abba the Tall), a giant of a man both physically and intellectually, and his colleague, Samuel, set out to establish in Babylonia the center of leadership.

Babylonian Jewry was happy, wealthy, and respected. The community was large, counting several million. The Jews had all the rights of citizens and actually formed their own autonomous state within the kingdom, comparable to one of the states within the United States. At the head of it stood the *Resh Galuta,* the Exilarch, who was a descendant of the House of David and governor in the real sense of the word. The Jews in Babylon were well-adjusted and deeply religious, and proud of their two leading academies in the cities of Sura and Nehardea (the academy in the latter city was later on transferred to Pumbedita), whose presidents were the spiritual heads and chief justices of the Jews. They bore the title *Gaon,* which means Excellency. Abba Areka and Samuel became the presidents of these two schools. So great was Abba Areka's prestige that he became known simply as *Rab,* the Master. Henceforth, all the leading rabbis of Babylonia—who speak to us from the pages of the Talmud—were given the title rab, in contrast to those of Palestine, who were known by the title rabbi.

The Talmud

In an effort to evolve the Mishnah both in theory and practice, an interesting system was evolved. Twice a year, in spring and fall, the scholars assembled for a whole month of discussion and debate; then they were given homework to study for the next assembly, or *Kallah,* while pursuing their regular ways of making a living. These debates closely followed the Mishnah, and were recorded verbatim. As we have seen, these formed the *Gemara,* "Completion" of Mishnah. *Gemara* is no dry code of laws. Through it breathes the living spirit of question and answer, legal analysis and homiletic exegesis, of bon mot and jest; often it is rambling, following a free association of thoughts.

Eventually, the material became so voluminous that it had to be edited, a task which was completed around the year 500 under the leadership of the Rab Ashee and Rabina. Thus were Mishnah and Gemara combined in the *Talmud.*

New Problems: Islam, the Karaites, Saadia

Study and research went on. Babylonia fell into the orbit of Islam (see p. 25) and the relationship between the two religions was excellent. By this time, however, a number of new spiritual problems arose: One Jewish sect, the Karaites, denied the validity of the Talmud, basing itself entirely on the written Torah; this would have perverted the inner meaning of Torah itself. More important was the challenge presented by the ever-increasing knowledge and study of the works of Aristotle, whose conclusions, so logically developed, clashed with the teachings of Torah. The claims of Islam to be the only true religion had to be logically refuted as well.

The GAON SAADIA (882–942) addressed himself to all these tasks. He stands out as the first Jewish "scholastic," making an effort to synthesize Aristotle and Jewish tradition whenever possible, and to refute him by logic when synthesis was impossible. In his work, *Book of Doctrines and Beliefs,* he was to claim Judaism as the religion of reason. To him, nothing in Torah is beyond reason. Even divinely revealed truth, whose meaning is yet hidden to us, will eventually be understood by human reason. These truths were revealed only in order that we might improve our lives while still searching for their meaning. To Saadia it is unthinkable that God might give us any instruction that does not square with reason. Writing in Arabic, the common language of that time, he could be understood by everyone.

He likewise attacked the views of the Karaites in tract after tract. For the use of his people he translated the Bible into Arabic, compiled a Hebrew grammar, and edited the prayer book. His life was stormy, but his intent is clear: the living Torah, growing and evolving, had to be preserved against the deadening outlook of Karaites and against any influences of alien philosophical thought. Whatever was good in

Aristotle—measured by the yardstick of Jewish tradition—had a right to be incorporated. By the Karaite interpretation, Mitzvot would assume a totally changed character, different from the form tradition had given them; this had to be avoided at all costs. Torah and Mitzvot were the mainstays of Diaspora Jewry.

Eventually Babylonian Jewry lost its key position as disturbances and wars swept over the Near East, although a Jewish community in Persia exists to this day. By that time, however, new centers had arisen in Spain and in Germany.

THE WORLD OF THE MIDDLE 3
AGES

For the Jews, the Middle Ages opened with the rise of Christianity in Europe and began to recede in Western Europe with the Emancipation of the eighteenth and nineteenth centuries, while in Eastern Europe, some of the conditions still bear a medieval character.

The medieval world was divided into two religiously oriented spheres of influence. As we have seen, the Roman Empire, extending through Western Europe as far as Britain, became Christianized in the fourth century. In the seventh century, Islamic influence spread from Arabia eastward to Babylonia, and westward across North Africa and into Spain. Migrating and settling within these two spheres, the Jews developed a number of varieties in customs and practices, including a different pronunciation of Hebrew. These differences still exist, but have not destroyed Jewish unity.

One group, following the road of the Roman Legions, settled in Italy, France, Germany, Britain, and eventually in Eastern Europe. They established great centers of learning, particularly in Germany, and eventually in Poland and Russia. They are called *Ashkenasim* because it was assumed that the term *Ashkenas* in the Bible meant Germany. Their descendants constitute the majority of present-day Jewry.

The other group followed the advance of Islam and established settlements in North Africa and eventually in Spain, making it a center of Jewish learning and of a flourishing Jewish culture. This group is called *Sefardim,* the word *Sefarad* in the Bible being interpreted as meaning Spain. Their pronunciation of Hebrew has been adopted as the official one in the State of Israel, and, as a result, will probably become universal in Jewry. We shall speak of them first, after a brief discussion of the relation between Judaism and Islam.

Judaism and Islam

In the seventh century, when Mohammed appeared on the scene of history, the Jews constituted a fully integrated community on the

25

Arabian penninsula. Their pattern of life was the same as that of their neighbors. They may have introduced the cultivation of the date palm into Arabia. Their only distinguishing feature was their religion. Known as "the people of the book," they were admired by their neighbors for their steadfastness in faith. Mohammed saw himself as a new prophet whose revelations would supersede those of earlier religions, especially Judaism and Christianity. He felt sure that the Jews would accept his teachings, especially as they were held by the Arabs as brothers—the belief had developed that the Jews, being so close to them, were the descendants of Abraham's son Isaac, while the Arabs were the descendants of Abraham's son Ishmael (Genesis, Chapters 16 and 21). To Mohammed's chagrin, the Jews steadfastly refused to give up their faith. Mohammed, who had incorporated many Jewish ideas in his teachings,' turned against them, feeling that it was imperative that Arabia be united under one faith. (He had first seen Jerusalem as center of the faith, now he changed it to Mecca.) He attacked the Jews and inflicted severe massacres upon them.

After Mohammed's death, his successors found a form of modus vivendi with the non-Islamic religions and their adherents. They were permitted to remain and to hold their possessions, but subjected to restrictions which varied according to the rulers, and had to pay heavy taxes.

The Koran, Islam's holy book, shows the influences of both Judaism and Christianity. Jesus, for instance, is regarded as a prophet next to Moses. With Judaism, Islam shares the belief in one unitary God, as against Christian trinitarianism. The Koran itself shows an ambivalent position in regard to both Jews and Christians, both praising them as religions of the one God, and rebuking them for their unwillingness to accept Islam as the final and highest divine revelation.

Sefardim

In the Islamic sphere, Jews were theoretically not considered equal to Mohammedans; in practice, they were free to participate in the fullness of the political, social, cultural, and economic life. Many of them rose to high office at the court of the califs, the Islamic rulers, and used their position to safeguard the position of their brethren. Some of the most outstanding Jews are described below:

HASDAI IBN SHAPRUT (912–961), royal physician and political advisor, was in contact with Jewish communities all over the world. He heard and then established that c. 740 the king and entire nation of the Chazars (a country on the eastern shores of the Black Sea) had accepted Judaism. (Eventually the Chazars intermarried with the rest of Jewry and disappeared as a distinct group.) Hasdai also was instrumental in placing the spiritual leadership of Spanish Jewry in the hands of one of the great masters from Babylonia who had become shipwrecked and landed in Spain. Spanish Jews supported this academy at Cordova abundantly, and, in turn, saw their community become a center of learning, with new schools emerging steadily.

SAMUEL (993–1069), whom his people called *ha-Nagid,* the Prince, was born at Cordova and started his life as a dealer in spices. He rose to become the vizir of the king of Granada. He served his master well, giving the state an exceptional administration, and headed the royal troops victoriously as a general in battle. Yet he was a Jewish scholar, who wrote an introduction to the Talmud, a compendium of law, and interpretations of Scripture: Torah and Mitzvot had to be established ever more firmly. Through correspondence with Jewry all over the world, the bond of kinship was maintained. Lavish gifts went to scholars who needed them, in Spain as well as abroad, that they might carry on their work undisturbed. It was indeed possible to hold highest office in dedicated citizenship and, at the same time, be a Jew devoted to God-Torah-Mitzvot—and people. As master of his own academy, Samuel himself trained a generation of leaders to carry on his work.

Among his friends he counted the poet and philosopher SOLOMON IBN GABIROL (1021–1069), who could both sing of wine and equally write majestic liturgical poems which have graced the worship of the synagogue. Gabirol was also versed in general philosophy, and wrote a philosophical work, *The Fountain of Life,* in which he sees all of the world emanating from God, similar to the neo-Platonic view. The work was translated into Latin, and so was the name of the author, from Gabirol to Avicebron. Up to the nineteenth century, the work was regarded as the writing of a non-Jewish scholar. Spanish Jewry had indeed effected a synthesis of general culture and Jewish tradition, of citizenship and deepest Jewish loyalty.

Through the Jews, Greek thought came to Europe, translated from Greek to Arabic, to Hebrew and to Latin.

JUDAH HALEVI (1080–1140) was a tender soul. Born in Toledo, he was attracted to medicine, as so many Jews have been drawn to this great profession which, in its entirety, is true Mitzvah, the healing of God's children. He was a man of great charm, a poet who sang of spring and beautiful women, but found his true subject when he expressed his undying love, and the love of his people, for the Land of Israel:

> Zion, wilt thou not ask if peace's wing
> shadows the captives that ensue thy peace . . . ?
> Lo, west and east and north and south—worldwide—
> all those from far and near, without surcease

salute thee: Peace and peace from every side.

To weep thy woe my cry is waxen strong,
but dreaming of thine own restored anew,
I am the harp to sound for thee thy song.
Thy God desired thee for a dwelling place
and happy is the man whom He shall choose,
and draw him nigh to rest within thy space.

Here is the call of the Land, with its force to form the fate of its people
—if not as a reality, then as hope and aspiration.

In old age, Halevi left the comforts of his home in Cordova, where he
had settled, to make his pilgrimage to the Holy Land. Legend will have it
that he sank into the dust in adoration at the sight of the city of
Jerusalem; an Arab galloping by crushed him under his horse's hoofs.

Judah was also a philosopher. Taking the story of the Chazars as a
framework for his discussion of Judaism, he relates that the King of the
Chazars was unhappy with his heathen religion. The King calls in three
sages, a Mohammedan, a Christian, and a Jew. The Jew convinces him
of the value of Judaism, which offers Judah the opportunity to expound
the ideas of Judaism. The Jews are indeed God's chosen people, but to
serve mankind. They are the heart of mankind, beating for it, suffering
for it, and indispensable for it. Torah and Mitzvot are explained in this
work, the *Chuzari,* and the kinship of the people is strongly emphasized.
To this sense of kinship, Judah—in poetry, life, and death—adds the
Land of Israel as the force, which, under God, has maintained the Jew
as a guiding light and suffering servant of all mankind.

The most famous of all Spanish Jews was MOSES MAIMONIDES
(1135–1204), a universal genius of whom it has been said that "from
Moses (the Master of Sinai) to Moses (Maimonides) there was no man
like Moses." In him we see clearly the interplay of internal and external
forces that have shaped Judaism and the Jews. When he was born at
Cordova, Jewry found itself oppressed by a fanatic Islamic sect, and
forced either to accept Islam or to emigrate. For ten years, Maimonides'
family had to move from country to country, which gave the boy a
chance to study under many masters. The Land of Israel drew him to
spend his years there, but finally, he settled in Fostat (Cairo), Egypt,
where Maimonides was to become court physician and head of the
Jewish community. In Cordova, city of his birth, a square bears his
name; in Acre (Acco), Israel, the gate through which he entered is
marked by a plaque; and at Tiberias, his grave, to which he supposedly
was transferred in death, is shown. This encompasses his spiritual
pilgrimage through the wisdom of Israel and the world to become the
master of Judaism and one of the world's great philosophers.

Maimonides' first concern was preservation of Torah. In its behalf, he
wrote a commentary to Mishnah, synthesizing Jewish thinking and

Aristotelian philosophy. His "Eight Chapters" in explanation of the Sayings of the Fathers are still widely studied in popular courses; they fuse Aristotle's ethics with Jewish tradition. Being a systematic thinker, he tried to condense basic Jewish beliefs in a form of creed, which—though attacked—is still followed by traditional Jewry, and later was rendered in the form of a poem, the *Yigdal,* widely used as a hymn in the service.

His creed is expressed in thirteen basic beliefs:

1. That God alone is the Creator.
2. That He is absolutely One.
3. That He has no body or bodily shape.
4. That He is the first and the last.
5. That only to Him may we pray and to no other.
6. That the words of the prophets are true.
7. That the prophecy of Moses is true, and that he is the father of all prophets.
8. That the Torah, now found in our hands, was given to Moses.
9. That this Torah is not subject to change, and that there will never be another Torah from the Creator.
10. That the Creator knows all the thoughts and deeds of man.
11. That He rewards and punishes according to the deed.
12. That the Messiah will come; though he tarry, I will expect him daily.
13. That the dead will be resurrected.

The power of his statement of principles is exemplified by the fact that the martyrs of the Warsaw Ghetto went to their death with a hymn on their lips, based on Maimonides' fundamentals of faith, "I believe."

The eternal validity of Torah was thus impressed once again on the people.

Maimonides' second concern was Mitzvot. He underscores their social significance in addition to their spiritual one. Feeling that the law of the Talmud needed clarification and codification, he wrote a compendium of the entire Oral Torah, called *Mishneh Torah,* which, he felt, would enable anyone—especially a rabbi—to find the authoritative answers quickly. It was a complete digest of Torah and Talmud, systematically arranged and rationally explained. There could be no doubt any more about the importance and the practice of Mitzvot.

His third work, *The Guide of the Perplexed,* shows the impact of his surroundings. A disciple had written the master that Aristotelian philosophy had confused many, who felt that they would either have to give up the teachings of Torah and be untrue to their heritage or surrender their intellectual integrity, rejecting the arguments of Aristotle to preserve their faith. In response, Maimonides wrote his philosophical work, explaining the absolute Oneness of God philosophically, showing that anthropomorphisms are actually only an expression of

God's effect on man, and not part of Himself. People receive His message, as if a mouth had spoken, which does not mean God has a mouth. Actually, God is incomprehensible to the human mind, we know not *what* He is, even though we know *that* He is. This has been called "negative theology." It is born out of deepest faith in God and an awareness of human limitations.

Maimonides subjects Aristotle's idea of the eternity of the world to rigorous philosophical scrutiny and criticism. The order in the universe as a whole to him testifies to a divine creator. It is furthermore a basic error to assume that the creation of the world *as a whole* follows the same laws and conditions as the creation of the things within it. Considering the things of the world, creation out of nothing is impossible; but this very principle and law that nothing can come out of nothing had to be created, too. In the beginning it did not exist either, hence cannot be applied to creation as a whole. Therefore it must have been created out of nothing by God who equally created the world out of nothing. According to Maimonides, Aristotle's mistake is in assuming that the very laws prevailing now must have prevailed in creation. The question why God created the world, and why He did so at a certain given time, is illegitimate, since we do not have an adequate knowledge of God. In view of this and several other arguments against Aristotle and his followers, Maimonides feels that Aristotle's position has become so weak that we must wisely follow the teachings of religion, which establish a free-willing creator God, who created the world in time.

In this manner, Maimonides is equally able to recognize the existence of miracles. But he makes several reservations. Not all the events reported as miraculous really were miracles; they can be explained as ordinary events, seen by the people as miracles, or as simply anchored in the vision of prophets and seers. Of miracles which he actually recognizes, he points out that these were not introduced in the events of the world as a divine afterthought, but planned in the original work of creation to happen at the given time and place.

Most significantly, Maimonides does not simply *permit* the study of philosophy; he considers it a *duty*. To him the rabbis were philosophers; the philosopher occupies an inner chamber in the divine palace whose entrance all men must seek. His is the highest rung on the ladder of perfection. The use of reason is legitimate; and Maimonides gives a striking example of how reason can be applied to evolve Torah. All the commandments have a reason. The sacrificial cult, for instance, can be explained psychologically. As long as all the other nations offered animal sacrifices, God felt he could not forbid it to His own people immediately. He directed them to make sacrifices in one place only, the Temple, and to offer the sacrifices to Him. But the true worship, to which He wished to lead them, was prayer; hence it can be offered anywhere.

Open to all influences, Maimonides thus builds the structure of Jewish life and learning on their synthesis. The inner forces, God-Torah-Mitzvot-Land, which he stressed, permit admission of external ones, if they can be assimilated. Maimonides was attacked for his ideas, but his influence on Jewish and Christian philosophy—including that of St. Thomas Aquinas—has been profound.

There were other great minds—exegetes, poets, world travelers, mystics—which reached out to the divine beyond. The few whom we have mentioned offer a picture of the greatness that was Spanish Jewry's.

Christian Conquest: the Inquisition

As the Christians pushed slowly forward, dislodging the Moors, the lot of Spanish Jewry deteriorated. At first they still served as royal counselors in the newly established Christian kingdoms, but their task of protecting their brethren became harder and harder. In 1233 the Inquisition was introduced in Aragon, directed by the newly created order of Dominicans.

In 1263, the leading rabbi of the time, Moses Nahmanides, was compelled to engage in a public disputation with the Dominican friar Pablo, a converted Jew, on the question "Has the Messiah come, or has he not yet come?" Nahmanides knew he could not be permitted to win the argument, which was conducted in the presence of king and court at Barcelona; the cards were stacked against him. He even pleaded with his opponents to stop the event, from which he foresaw only evil for his people, but this was not permitted him. A few years later, Nahmanides left Spain, which he had loved, and went to the Land of Israel.

Expulsion from Spain

Jews had to listen to Christian sermons even in their own synagogues. Popular opinion turned against them, and the rabble rose. In 1492, after expelling the last of the Moors and uniting the territory, Ferdinand and Isabella, King and Queen of Spain, decreed the expulsion of the last remnant of infidels, the Jews.

Only converts could remain, and many Jews accepted Christianity as a veneer, practicing their faith in secret. This was extremely dangerous, for once having known Christianity and turned from it was heresy. On the slightest suspicion, the Inquisition would swoop down upon them, extract confession through torture, and have them burned at the stake. The people in general distrusted the converts, and called them *marranos, dirty fellows.* Surviving in spite of it all, some of them re-emerged

professing openly as Jews only in the twentieth century. It has been
claimed that even Columbus may have been a marrano, though the
proofs are very inconclusive. But he speaks in his diaries with great
compassion of the departing Jews, whose rickety boats he passed on his
way toward a new world. This was the end of Spanish Jewry, but the
Spanish government of today favors the return of the Sefardim who
were once Spanish citizens, who may wish to resume their rights as
citizens.

The fugitives settled in Holland, Turkey, and other countries. These
countries profited from their ability. Some groups went to Palestine,
others to the colonies of the new world. Seeing the distress of a dispersed
and persecuted Jewish community, a leading rabbi in Palestine strove to
establish a central rabbinical body there, a *Sanhedrin*, to unite the people
around Torah and Land. He failed, but one of his disciples, JOSEPH
KARO (1488–1575), recognized the need for a unifying bond and found
it in Mitzvot. He wrote a code, the *Shulhan Arukh*, The Well-Prepared
Table, outlining in every detail the minutiae of Jewish law. With
additions, adjusting it to Ashkenasic usage (by Moses Isserles, 1530–
1572), it became and has remained *the* code of traditional Jewry.

Ashkenasim

In the destiny of Ashkenasic Jewry, we see reflected the struggles and
conflicts of kings and popes, of nationalism against the Universal
Church, of Renaissance, Reformation, and Enlightenment, of social
unrest and political revolution.

The Jews may well have come to Germany with the Roman Legions;
first documentary proof of an established Jewish community goes back to
321. By the time of Hitler's efforts to exterminate them, they had lived
in Germany longer than any other ethnic group, presenting to the
German people an opportunity to establish a true spirit of justice, for
these Jews demanded but one thing, to be permitted to live as human
beings in the full expression of their religious tradition. That Germany
failed to live up to this ethical challenge is one of its greatest tragedies.

In the beginning, the Jews were treated well. When Charlemagne
consolidated his empire (800–814) he treated them kindly, and we find a
Jew named Isaac among the delegation the emperor sent to Harun al-
Rashid, the Calif of Baghdad. Isaac, the only one to return, having
survived the rigors of the journey, brought back an elephant as a gift
from the Calif to Charlemagne; the animal, heretofore unknown in
Germany, created a sensation.

The Jews were welcome in Germany, where they served as merchants, providing the link between the farmer and the nobility, a position they also held in other countries. Permitted to own real estate, they established stately homes when their means permitted it.

The famous Calonymus family, from which great scholars, poets, mystics, and saints were to emerge, was called from Lucca (in Italy) to Mainz probably between 917 and 990. They were granted the right to exhibit the imperial eagle as a sign of the emperor's favor. We still have the pillar on which it was shown. It has a medallion with the emperor's portrait beneath which a humble man, unclad, offers his homage on bended knees. Thus did they acknowledge their debt to their imperial master, who was the source of their food, shelter, and clothing, and to whom they felt deeply obligated in love and heartfelt allegiance. These were, indeed, years of well-being for the Jews.

As the fervor and the worldly ambitions of the Church increased, the status of the Jews declined. The Cluniac reforms of the tenth century included a strong prohibition of money trade by Christians. Hence the Jews were pressed into it.

The Crusades, beginning in 1096, marked the turning point in their fate; thereafter they were oppressed. Many crusaders felt that before going to the Holy Land to free it from the infidels they might as well start with those who lived among them, the Jews. This also promised rich loot. The Jews in the Rhenish cities of Mainz, Speyer, and Worms, mother cities of Jewry, fought valiantly, but were overcome by the hordes, and preferred to die rather than give up their faith. Thousands perished.

Their lives became most precarious with the decrees of the Lateran Council of 1215. Pope Innocent III, who saw himself as supreme head and arbiter of all Christianity, determined to plunge the Jews into shame, degradation, and despondency. As an accursed race, they had to wear on their breast the yellow badge of outcasts, and on their heads a cone-shaped hat, the horn of the devil, whose brood they were. (See p. 137.) This made them easy prey for their tormentors. Seclusion and persecution were officially ordered.

Emperors and kings considered them their own, personal property, forcing them to engage in money lending, which was considered illegal for Christians by religious law of the time. This suited the Christian businessmen, who had by now acquired the skill to engage in all branches of trade, and insisted that Jews be pushed out of the trades. The craft guilds never accepted them, thus excluding them from pursuing the crafts. As money lenders, the Jews served the rulers as "sponges to be squeezed out." They might enrich themselves for a while; then their goods were expropriated. A ruler might give the Jews of a town as a "gift" to a vassal or a community, which meant that the Jews' belongings were surrendered to the "receiver." They might even be driven out, naturally leaving everything behind. Or the debts owed them by Christians might be cancelled by order of the ruler.

Being forced to borrow from the Jews, and at high rates, the population naturally developed a deep animosity against them, often attacking them in mob action. The Jews learned to know the precariousness of worldly possessions. Every child from earliest youth had to recite, therefore: "The Torah, and the Torah alone, is the [assured] heritage of the congregation of Jacob." Nothing else was secure. Such conditions knitted the Jews closely together. The wealthy Jew of today might be a homeless fugitive tomorrow; thus he would give hospitality to any brother who knocked at his door. When communities needed Jews again, they would invite those they had driven away only yesterday to come back and settle—for a while. It was a sad merry-go-round.

Eventually, Christian bankers in many lands began to ignore the prohibitions of the Church and set up money lending on a grand scale, taking even higher rates of interest. The Jews were pushed out, to be permitted money lending only on the lowest level, or trade in old clothes; this was all that was left to them. In other instances they were expelled from the country altogether when they were no longer needed economically as money lenders.

Vicious slanders were spread about the Jews. One of the worst was the accusation that they were using the blood of Christian children for the Passover service. A similar accusation had been leveled against the early Christians by those who did not understand the character of the Mass, the transubstantiation of the wine into the blood of Christ: Christians had been accused of killing heathens to obtain their blood for communion. Now Christians used the very slander from which they themselves had suffered so much against the Jews. The popes raised their voices in vain to proclaim the total falseness of this accusation, and to prohibit it; the mob would not listen. Jews were accused of desecrating the sacred host, thus attacking Christ. It did not matter that the Jews did not believe in transubstantiation and the sanctity of the host, and that such a desecration, which implied acknowledgement of this sanctity, would be meaningless to them and never occur to them. The slander persisted and claimed its victims.

England, France, and Germany

Among the places where the accusation of using Christian blood was used to incite the population was Lincoln, England (1255). The relationship of king and people to the Jews became so difficult that the

Jews were finally expelled from the country altogether, only a few years after the incident (1290).

It is not surprising that there were a few Jews who escaped by becoming Christians; it is remarkable that there were so few of them. Some of these converts—in order to justify their actions—now became rabid Jew-haters and ardent missionaries among Jews. Realizing that Torah was the source from which Jewish strength was renewed, they vented their hatred against it (not the Scriptures, which were shared by the Christians, but against Oral Torah, the Talmud). The Talmud was accused of containing anti-Christian statements. One such accusation led to the public burning of carloads of precious manuscripts in France (1242). Having been singled out by this public condemnation of their holiest treasures and branded as bearers of a hostile outlook based on subversive teachings, the Jews came to be regarded by the people not only as anti-Christian, but as enemies of the emerging nationalism.

As people in France rose against the burdens of taxation (induced, they felt, by the Jewish money lenders with their alien spirit), the king appeased them by expelling the Jews from French soil (1394). Only in the papal province of Avignon were they permitted to remain. The expelled Jews now sought homes in Germany and Poland. A few years before the events in France, a terrible fate had befallen Jews throughout Europe. In 1349 the Black Death swept over Europe, leaving death and destruction in its wake and stirring the downtrodden masses to rebellion against their fate. Again, the Jews became scapegoats. Due to their religious practices enjoining cleanliness, the death toll among them may have been less; now they were accused of having poisoned the wells and were massacred or expelled. Many of them left Germany forever to find a new haven in hospitable Poland which needed their skill. This was the beginning of large-scale settlement there. They did not know how short-lived their peace was to be.

A great many German Jews remained, however. This was possible because the Jews were considered personal property of the Emperor, who could squeeze them out whenever he pleased. In 1356, the "Golden Bull" established the election procedures for the imperial office. Seven "Electors" (the highest dignitaries of the Empire, both clerical and temporal lords) had the right to elect the emperor. In this bull the Jews residing in their territory were transferred to the Electors by the emperor as "milking cows"; the rest remained with him, to give to whomever he pleased.

After the Black Death, many states and cities were glad to accept the Jews back, a privilege for which the Jews had to pay heavy admission fees and annual fees for the renewal of their residence privileges. But now they had to dwell within a separate district, a few small streets, entered through gates that were closed at night, the *ghetto*. Since this ghetto could not be enlarged with the growing population, story had to be built upon story in crowded quarters, until the very light of the sun was practically excluded, even as the Jews' contact with nature had long been cut off.

Masters of the Ashkenasic Community

To speak of all the masters who emerged out of the Ashkenasic Jewish community, is not possible; only a few may be mentioned here.

The House of Calonymus, mentioned previously, used its wealth and prestige to develop academies of learning. Soon the cities of Mainz, Speyer, and Worms became centers of Jewry. The family itself produced sages, poets, and mystics. Its outstanding representative, RABBI CALONYMUS BEN MESHULLAM (11th century) is the author of one of the greatest liturgical poems of Jewish literature, expressing the holiness of the Days of Awe and acclaiming God as supreme Judge, who decrees man's destinies but is ever ready to accept repentance, prayer, and deeds of kindness in expiation of any sin. His son and grandson were given the right to settle in Speyer (1090), where they established a house of learning. Judah, another member of the family who arrived later from Italy, died at the height of the Crusades (1200). He lived both in Worms and Ratisbon, and moved in a somewhat different direction than the rest of his family. He immersed himself in prayer and mysticism, escaping into another world from the one that was so unhappy. He was called JUDAH HA-HASID, Judah the Saint (Mystic), and through him the mysticism of *Hasidism* (see pp. 42–43) found a foothold in Europe, to be transplanted and given new appeal by the Hasidim of later Poland.

During the years 960–1040, GERSHOM BEN JUDAH was head of the Academy of Mainz. So great was his prestige that he became known as the "Light of the Diaspora," and so great was the prestige of his school that its ordinances were accepted as binding by all of Western Jewry. He ruled that no one might read a letter not addressed to him; that no woman might be divorced against her will; he prohibited polygamy, which had long been discarded but not yet been legally outlawed; and he trained many disciples.

Out of his school and the academy of Worms emerged the most important of all scholars, RABBI SOLOMON BEN ISAAC, abbreviated RASHI (1040–1105), without whose commentary the Talmud would be for us a closed book. Born at Troyes, France, he spent his youth studying in the cities on the Rhine to return home to a small vineyard and wine business by which he made a living—and to the academy he headed without charge. Returning to France just in time to escape the massacre of the first Crusade, he died in the town of his birth. In the simplest of words and utter clarity of style, Rashi wrote a commentary to both the Bible and the Talmud, following them sentence by sentence, clarifying obscure passages, critically analyzing the text, elucidating its meaning. Sometimes he would even translate difficult words into the French spoken by the Jews, a sign of their adjustment to their surroundings.

We could not do without Rashi, and posterity has seen in his abbreviated name the contraction of another three words: *R*abban *s*hel *Y*israel, the Teacher of Israel. His commentary was to be influential in Christian circles as well. Nicholas de Lyra studied his work extensively, especially his Bible commentary; in turn, his work became Luther's guide in his translation of Scripture. Rashi's clear explanation may well have put doubt in many minds regarding the interpretation of the Roman Catholic Church, thus contributing to the spirit that led to the Reformation.

Based on Rashi, the masters of the French schools wrote additional commentaries, analyzing specific points in the Talmud; these are called *Tosafot,* additions. Every edition of the Talmud contains Rashi's commentary on the inside margin of every page and Tosafot on the outside margin.

In 1286, a great Rabbi, RABBI MEIR OF ROTHENBURG, who had cried out in bitter elegy at the burning of the Talmud, decided to migrate to Palestine; there alone could Torah be developed, for "the soil of the Land makes wise," while here there were only trials. Meir failed; he was recognized and captured during his journey and was imprisoned for ransom, by order of the Emperor Rudolph von Habsburg. Meir forbade his people to pay it lest a precedent be established and more rabbis be captured for ransom. He spent seven years in confinement, and then the ransom had to be paid anyway—for his body.

Meir's disciple, RABBI MORDECAI BEN HILLEL, decided that Mitzvot must be emphasized to provide stability among the physically rootless, and he proposed a code. He died a martyr's death at Nuremberg in 1289.

His colleague, RABBI ASHER BEN YEHIEL, succeeded in his escape to Spain, thus linking Ashkenasic tradition to the Sefardic. Synthesizing the work of the German and Spanish masters, he and his son Jacob, completed the proposed code, calling it *Turim,* "Rows," after the four *rows* of precious stones in the breastplate of the high priest. It was a four-volume work; Mitzvot are the precious stones. Joseph Karo based his *Shulhan Arukh* both on Maimonides and the Turim. Writing his work in Palestine, he thus symbolizes the unity of the Jewish people through Mitzvot and Land.

Customs and practices (*Minhagim*) do vary among Jews in various lands. They are based on the interaction of outward and inward forces, of environment and tradition. Hence a supplement had to be written to the *Shulhan Arukh* for Ashkenasic Jewry, which was done by Rabbi Moses Isserles.

Renaissance and Reformation

The Renaissance did not bring much change in the conditions of the Jews. A great and courageous humanist, Johannes Reuchlin, might save Jewish books out of his knowledge of Hebrew by defending their innocuousness against the attacks of a convert, Johannes Pfefferkorn (1510); Italian Jews from the distance of their ghetto might be able to share in the cultural revival of the time; but the general position of Jewry on the continent remained the same. Actually the ghetto in Italy was established at this time. This may be explained by the fear of the Catholic Church that the spirit of the Renaissance, which had led to the Reformation, might lead the people toward new heretical concepts out of their contacts with the Jews. The Jews had to be sequestered. Pope Leo X, the humanist, did, however, order the reprinting of the Talmud because he felt that ancient literature ought to be preserved.

Martin Luther at one time favored the Jews in the hope that they would join his movement, as Mohammed had done. When they refused, Luther (again like Mohammed) turned viciously against "The Jews and Their Lies" (1546). By doing so, Luther endowed his doctrines with a spirit of anti-Semitism. Luther's theology and thought contained two elements which were to bring the greatest suffering to the Jews: The first was the anti-Semitism of his later years, which influenced many of the adherents of his church. The second element was his insistence that faith and not works brings salvation, and that the Lutheran Church in all temporal matters had to obey the rulers. In Nazi times, the Church, therefore, spoke up only when its own faith was threatened by the government and the faith of the people was being attacked. It did not take a stand against the un-Christian, murderous actions of the rulers against the Jews, an action which might have had some effect. This may shed light on some facets of German anti-Semitism. To its honor, the Lutheran Church has publicly confessed this error, calling itself to repentance.

Only in England do we find a decided change as a result of the Reformation. Oliver Cromwell became convinced by his study of Scripture that Christ would not return until Jews were spread out over all parts of the world; hence they had to come to England again. Negotiation with a Dutch Rabbi, Manasseh ben Israel, eventually led to the formal declaration that there was nothing in English law preventing their settlement on English soil (1655). This marks the beginning of the modern Jewish community in Great Britain.

In spite of their trials, the Jews kept their faith, their mental balance, their sense of humor, and even their contact with the world. Never knowing how long a family might remain together, they deepened its spirit. Never certain if the precious manuscript they owned might not be burned tomorrow, they immersed themselves in its contents, the study of Torah. Never assured that their possessions might not be taken away at a moment's notice and they themselves be uprooted overnight, they gave help and hospitality to the fugitives from other zones. Through Torah and Mitzvot, in the fervent hope that the Messiah might come at any time to restore them to the freedom of their land, they retained their emotional equilibrium. This in itself is a proud evidence of the power stored in the Jewish heritage, environment and tradition.

By the fifteenth century, the customs of German Jewry had already diverged from those of Polish Jewry. The rabbis of the period collected these customs and ruled on their performance. RABBI JACOB LEVI MOELLN (abbreviated Maharil), who died in 1427, not only established these Minhagim as valid guides to practice, he was also an accomplished cantor (singer of liturgy), and ruled that the traditional tunes, which spoke of the yearnings of centuries, could not be changed, especially those of the high holy days, to which people had come to be accustomed. His own city of Mainz abided by this rule most faithfully, and modern cantors, trained in the standard tunes, had to undergo a special training to acquire the special melodies used in the community. Transmitted by ear, these songs are unhappily going to be lost with the destruction of German Jewry.

A distinct difference thus developed in customs as in Jewish music between Eastern and Western European Jewry, which increased the difficulties Eastern European Jews encountered when they began to settle in large numbers both in Western Europe and in America, and the conflicts between the two groups.

The Fate of Eastern European Jewry

The fate of Polish and Russian Jewry appears like a condensed version of Jewish destiny throughout history, ranging from well-being to abysmal suffering.

Migration to Poland and Russia began with the Crusades, as conditions in Germany became unbearable for many, and increased with subsequent peaks of persecution to reach high proportions at periods such as the Black Death, when escaping Jews in great masses streamed eastward. The rulers of Poland welcomed them, whereas the Catholic Church disliked them intensely.

The Polish kings saw the economic advantages which the Jews could bring to their undeveloped lands, badly in need of a middle class of merchants, and took them under their protection as their own "property," allowed them to settle throughout the land next to its Christian inhabitants, accorded them freedom of movement and of enterprise. Subsequent centuries saw the Jews as pawns in the struggle between kings and Church; if the Church found itself powerful enough to have its will prevail, the Jews suffered; if the kings prevailed, opposing the Church in their own effort to retain absolute power, the lot of the Jews was happier.

In general, deterioration proceeded at a fast pace. The native population had neither a fully developed language or culture; the Jews, therefore, retained their German language, transforming it into Yiddish, and their German garb, the *caftan*. Their culture was that of Torah. Recognized as aliens, and regarded, therefore, with suspicion, they formed the easy target for the preachments of clergymen against them, and, as their "error" of being Jews was constantly impressed upon the Poles, they could now serve as scapegoat in times of disaster or social unrest. When a fire broke out in Cracow (1494), they were baselessly accused of having caused it, and, on restoration of the city, were placed in a ghetto.

Afraid of the brutality and ignorance of the civil magistrates, the Jewish community early in its history in Poland had pleaded for and obtained the right to self-government. The chief rabbis of the communities were recognized by the kings as Jewry's justices and chief administrators. A council was organized, "The Council of the Four Lands" (of which Poland was composed), which met regularly, allocated taxes, and served as spokesman for Jewish interests, especially through those of its members who had access to the court as royal financiers. Thus, the power of the layman of status, the *Shtadlan,* became great; it was to be felt even in the eventual organization of American Jewry so largely composed of immigrants from Eastern Europe. District Councils carried out the ordinances of the superior ones, and each congregation (*Kahal*), formed an administrative unit, regulating every aspect of life, conduct, law, custom, and relations with the non-Jewish population. Indeed, the Jewish community formed a body within the body of the State, sternly controlled and disciplined. This eventually made it inevitable for Jews used to communal life to remain closely together in small congregations reflecting the customs and habits of their home towns when they settled in America.

The separation from the rest of the world and that world's lack of a comparable culture led to an immersion in the Talmud unequalled anywhere. Printing establishments provided early an abundance of books (Bible in 1530; Talmud begun to be printed in Lublin, Poland, in 1559).

RABBI SHALOM SHAKNA (1500–1599) developed a method of Talmud study that led to the most detailed analysis of every verse and word in an effort to bring about a basic "agreement" in the opinions of a variety of conflicting commentaries, written by numerous authors, in a variety of countries, and during different ages. This was possible only by hairsplitting logic and became a kind of mental gymnastic, which sharpened the mind but was actually meaningless. This method of *pilpul* has remained in some of the old-time religious academies and has removed them from the main stream of Jewish evolution.

Now commentaries were piled upon commentaries. Education was practically universal. At an early age, the child was taken to *cheder* (the school room), where he started to study Bible and Talmud from early morning until late at night, often under the guidance of a teacher who was far from being a pedagogue. Advanced students were sent to a *yeshivah* (academy) in the city, where the people provided them with their meals by taking turns, having a different student every day.

Now study became the young man's full vocation, deep into the night; the bloom of youth would fade from his cheeks. Many never emerged from this mode of life. When they married, their inlaws might provide for them; if this was impossible, the wife would eke out a living for the rest of her days to afford undisrupted study to her husband. The prestige of the learned was high; the great rabbis were revered; the brilliant students were sought by the wealthy as most suitable sons-in-law.

To finalize law and practice in accord with the tradition of Ashkenasic Jewry, Rabbi Moses Isserles (1530–1572) wrote his annotations to the *Shulhan Arukh,* calling his work *Mappah,* the "tablecloth" he was providing for Karo's Table.

The seventeenth century was to witness the first of the many truly frightful and large-scale persecutions of Jews, the Chmielnicky Massacres. This man was the head of a free-roaming band of warriors, the Cossacks. Professing the Greek Orthodox faith, they rebelled against the Roman Catholic Poles, and the Jews were in the middle in the ensuing civil war. The serfs, dissatisfied with their fate, joined the Cossacks. Jews were slaughtered by the tens of thousands, while the entire country was ravaged.

When it was all over, the search for redemption from these horrible sufferings moved in several directions: Immersion in the Talmud grew deeper and with it the withdrawal from the world. Mitzvot became ever more embracing. Injunctions, such as the prohibition of cutting the corners of the beard (Leviticus 19:27) were taken literally, resulting in long earlocks, never cut. Thus self-imposed seclusion was added to the enforced one. Mitzvah formed the wall of separation.

There was the re-awakening hope of a speedy return to Palestine. History conspired to make it seem a reality. A young and glamorous man from Smyrna (in Turkey), SABBATAI ZEVI (1626–1676) proclaimed himself the Messiah. Thousands in Germany as well as in Poland were captivated by the news, sold their belongings, packed their goods on wagons, and were ready to go. It turned out to be a cruel hoax; Sabbatai was an impostor without character. Captured by the Turks, he was given the choice of becoming a Mohammedan or of being executed; he chose the former. His followers for many years were unwilling to accept the blow: he would surely arise again. But their lives returned to the ancient pattern of suffering. Poverty deepened.

Hasidism

At this moment there arose RABBI ISRAEL BAAL SHEM (1700–1760), founder of Hasidism. Going about among the people with words of encouragement and inspiration, using the simple approach of parable and story, he gave them hope. He taught them that God Himself needed redemption, for He too was in exile with His people as a result of the world's sinfulness. In order that the world be restored to that unity which it had lost by man's sinfulness, God needed man's redemptive act. In that task the Jew has a major role to fulfill. Every human task, be it menial work or study or eating or drinking can be a response to God, if performed as Mitzvah in joyful service to Him. Every person, even the most unlearned—and perhaps he more than others—carries the messianic burden of preparing the world for the future. Every limb of our body can become a tool in this service.

The people flocked to the Baal Shem. They would rouse themselves into ecstasy, their bodies swinging and swaying in worship to express with every bone and muscle their allegiance to God, for prayer must pour forth out of man's innermost soul to reach God, and be expressed with the total personality of the worshipper. They would dance before Him in joyful abandon. They had found new hope.

The leaders of the movement were believed by the people to have a deeper insight into the hidden meanings of Scripture. They were Masters of the Divine Name (*Baal Shem* in Hebrew), that creative Word by which the world had once been shaped and by which it could be influenced again. Thus the people came to their leaders to get help in their individual needs and hung on their lips for mysterious words of revelation. Each leader was called *Zaddik,* the Righteous; he did not have to be learned, for he would inherit the divine gifts from his father.

Here lay the roots of Hasidism's eventual decay. The Zaddikim held court in princely fashion, rival groups sprang up, each clinging to its Zaddik. Eventually the movement lost its spirit. Yet it shows the power of Mitzvah. It underscores the deep feeling of the Jew that he is related to all mankind and responsible for mankind's ultimate salvation.

The ideas of Hasidism have made themselves felt in our own time. The enthusiasm which fired the pioneers in Israel to undertake the most backbreaking tasks in redemption of the Land of Israel stems from it. Every act promoting this redemption was Mitzvah; it was Hasidism translated into secular terms, applied to the physical redemption of Land and people. The dances of the pioneers have one of their sources in Hasidic abandon.

The modern philosopher MARTIN BUBER, a deep student of Hasidism, has made the stories of the Hasidic masters available to the common reader. He fashioned his philosophy of "I and Thou" on Hasidic foundations, as we will discuss. Buber, and through him Hasidism, has deeply influenced the thinking not only of many Jewish but also of many Christian thinkers. Although it has been transformed in many ways, Hasidism has been a significant force in our world.

ELIJAH BEN SOLOMON (1720–1779), affectionately called by his people the Gaon of Vilna, had an answer based on reason and vision. He felt that Judaism, in spite of it all, had to be pulled back onto the highway of reason to study in meaningful ways; even some secular knowledge was advisable as it improved the understanding of Talmud and Codes. Worship was to be made more meaningful and more "modern" in a modest way. Yet this advice of great wisdom was not generally accepted; it had limited immediate appeal, looked too far into the future. Worshipped by thousands for his great personality, he did not succeed in weaning away the millions from the method of *pilpul*. Had he succeeded, the transition to modern life, especially in America, might not have been so abrupt, and a good deal of alienation between children and parents and their religious practices would have been avoided among the immigrants to the new world.

Life under the Russian Czars

During the eighteenth century, Poland was three times divided among Prussia, Austria, and Russia. A large segment of Jewry now came under Russian rule. The Russian government felt that they must be made to give up their faith, or, at least their strange ways. As they refused, they must be kept out of Russia proper. A special district, the *Pale,* was created, and Jews from all over Russia were dumped into it (1804). Thousands thus lost their livelihood, contact with the world was cut off, the Jews became desperately poor, and sitting ducks for pogroms. The *Kahal* of each town had to see to it that the taxes came in on time and in full; eventually, the Council of the Four Lands became just a tax-gathering arm of the government. Jews were to open state-supervised schools for secular learning. The ultimate purpose of this was to draw the youth away from their tradition.

Then came the Napoleonic invasion of Russia, and with it a glimpse of the spirit of the Enlightenment in the West. There were Jews who delighted in it, but the community—fearing for its survival—strictly forbade study of non-Jewish subjects; these had to be studied in secret without guidance. Thus emerged the small Enlightenment movement, *Haskalah,* of dilettantes and amateurs, who were placed in opposition to religion. This, too, was to have severe consequences, as the intellectual became estranged from his faith. Had the Gaon of Vilna prevailed, an orderly transition might have taken place.

With the defeat of Napoleon, reaction set in all over Europe, and the pressure on the Jews increased. Under Nicholas I (1825–1855), the Pale was narrowed and the Jews squeezed closer together. To enforce conversion, Nicholas ordered the conscription of Jews (1827). They were to serve for 25 years without any opportunity of promotion unless they became Christians. In "preparation" for this service, which was to start at the age of 18, children of the age of 12 could be (and were) conscripted, dragged away from their homes, mistreated, and tortured to make them give up their faith. Many perished in heroic "stubborn-ness."

The Russian system of elementary education was to be enlarged; a German rabbi, Max Lilienthal (1815–1882) was called to direct it; but when he found that, in essence, he was to create an organization for the conversion of Jewish children, he fled in terror. Eventually he had a distinguished career as one of the early rabbis in the United States.

While the most severe restrictions were removed with the death of Nicholas I (1855), new pressures were applied later under Alexander III and Nicholas II. The masses of Russia were dissatisfied and groaning under their yoke. To deflect their fury, pogroms were arranged against the Jews, beginning in 1881, which shook the world by their extent and brutality, and were denounced by Christians throughout the West. Migration to the United States now became a torrent.

At the same time, Leo Pinsker (1821–1891) published his appeal for auto-Emancipation, and migration to Palestine got under way, led by young Jews who called themselves *BILU* (an abbreviation of the Hebrew sentence: O House of Jacob, come, and let us go!). Another group, "The Lovers of Zion" emerged, dedicated to the same purpose. Zionism was on the march; Theodor Herzl was to give it its name and organization.

The routine never varied, discrimination—even against Jewish soldiers in World War I—pogroms. The Czar fell, Jewry thought it was free, only to suffer again under persecution. There were pogroms in the Ukraine; Jews, as members of the "middle class," were to be wiped out by the Bolsheviks (1917), the war against religion hit them. Their persecution in Russia has not ended today.

On the Blending of Cultures

The history of the Jews during the Middle Ages was one of adversity. It is so much more remarkable, therefore, to note how deeply they cast their roots in their new homelands. They learned to live in two civilizations, a demonstration to the world—even today—that mankind can live together, and that cultures can preserve their individualities while sharing with each other the best that each has to offer. Yiddish, the language spoken by Ashkenasic Jews, and Ladino, the language of the Sefardim throughout the Middle Ages, are based on German and Spanish respectively. These languages are frequently used even today as a second tongue by many Jews. Similarly, the caftan, once the dress of the medieval burgher, became the "Jewish dress" in Eastern Europe. As frequent Church edicts calling for stricter separation of Jews from Christians reveal, contacts with friends were retained. They were able to help their Christian neighbors, for, among other skills, they were almost universally literate, which the rest of the population was not. They equally received help from Christians. But they would not give up their faith, although the door of the Church stood always open, and baptism would wipe out all disabilities.

They never lost their zest for life. This may be a source of that peculiar kind of Jewish humor, whimsical and tender, skeptical and optimistic, born of faith and love, critical of both God and man, and yet encompassing all human foibles with amused compassion. This humor emerged from the reflection on their fate. God's beloved, yet they could barely subsist; His chosen people, yet they were totally insecure on earth. This was indeed "divine comedy." But who could doubt Him? Their optimism, and their faith in God and man's ultimate goodness—evidenced even in Anne Frank's deeply moving diary—carried them through.

Yet scars remained. Their socio-economic situation was completely abnormal. They were excluded from the soil they had so deeply loved. Early known in history for the kind of inventive craftsmanship which allowed for mass production, they were excluded from the guilds. Some of the scars are still visible in modern Jews, who are so recently removed from persecution that most of them have received eyewitness reports of it, if they were not its direct victims. In this manner we must understand certain socio-economic imbalances, still existing and perpetuated by present-day forms of job discrimination. We may also understand the "exclusiveness" born of long inbred apprehension regarding their acceptance by the world at large, and their ambition for success and acceptance —a truly ambivalent position. Perhaps we may find in these conditions one explanation for the temptation felt by a number of Jews to escape from the dominance of religion into a general humanitarianism; this is the first time that such an escape is possible without involving abandonment of Jewishness.

Indications are—specifically in the United States—that conditions are changing, and with them the reactions of the Jews. Out of this change new problems may arise concerning the retention of Jewish identity in a civilization which is a great leveler. This new trend of events was slowly set in motion by the Emancipation to which we shall now turn.

EMANCIPATION AND THE   4
MODERN AGE

THE RENAISSANCE of Europe in the sixteenth century, characterized by man's faith in himself, resulted in the breakup of the unity of faith and life. It led to the Enlightenment of the eighteenth century, whose motto was "Reason and Progress." For the Jew of the Western World, the Renaissance did not arrive until the Enlightenment had made its impact, and in Eastern Europe it never came at all. It spelled dissolution of the once-unified fabric of God-Land-Torah-Mitzvot, the elements that had fashioned the spirit of Jewish peoplehood. Using reason, individual leaders endeavored to fashion a Judaism in tune with the times and in step with science. This led to the Emancipation.

Emancipation means the attainment of freedom by those who have been without it. In connection with the Jews it had a twofold meaning. The Jews were to be given equal rights as citizens, their civic disabilities were to be removed. In return, the Jews were to cast off their isolation, relinquish their internal jurisdiction, and immerse themselves wholeheartedly in the society and culture of the countries in which they lived. This was an experiment, undertaken by governments and the progressives. While the Jews in Western Europe greeted the Emancipation as the dawn of a new day and wholeheartedly plunged into their task to adjust to their environment in assuming its culture and the obligations of citizenship (sometimes, perhaps, too eagerly in their search for acceptance), governments and society were slow, moving haltingly, frequently undoing what they themselves had granted, retaining their distance and many of their biases.

Gaining Citizenship Rights

The French Revolution brought the Jews equality in France, and Napoleon carried its ideas to the lands he conquered. To have them truly obedient to himself, he organized their congregations and even called a group of leading rabbis to Paris to form a Sanhedrin, which had the difficult task of adjusting Jewish laws to Napoleon's desire without harming Jewish tradition. The Sanhedrin could well proclaim that the Jews recognized no country but the one in which they held citizenship, but the sanctioning of interfaith marriage, for example, was another story. They compromised by saying that a person who had entered such a marriage in a justice court would remain a Jew, but that rabbis could not officiate at them.

Following Napoleon's example, the European states organized the Jewish communities as religious bodies, eliminating such rights as their internal self-government and the judicial powers of rabbis over family relations. Judaism was religion. Given their citizenship rights, the Jews were willing to fight for their countries. In Prussia, hundreds volunteered in the war against Napoleon (1815), but when Napoleon had been beaten, the rights of the Jews were once again rescinded.

A new uphill struggle began. So harsh were the laws (for instance, in Bavaria, where marriages were restricted), that many migrated to the United States. Efforts to unite Germany on a democratic basis led to revolutions in 1830 and 1848, both of which failed and forced many liberals and Jews to find a life of freedom in America.

Slowly the Jews obtained citizenship rights, but never in Germany were they granted full and unchallenged equality, in fact, until 1918. Until then, with few exceptions, they could not be judges, or civil servants, or army officers while maintaining their faith.

It was their hope that by exhibiting their patriotism they might show the world that they were deserving of full equality. Insecurity turned many into super patriots, holding aloof from their Eastern European brethren, whom they supported, but from whom they kept apart. Yet the developments of the time did give hope that equality would emerge, and German Jews saw in Germany their home. After all, they had lived in it for at least 1500 years, and had taken their place in the cultural life of the country, benefiting it economically as well by their industry. They were a good, substantial middle class with all its virtues and faults. About half a million strong, they left 15,000 of their youth on the battlefields fighting for Germany in World War I.

Moses Mendelssohn

In Moses Mendelssohn (1729–1786) German Jewry found its great leader. A small, hunchbacked man, his early growth stunted by hunger and deprivation, he was of brilliant intellect, immersing himself early in Jewish and non-Jewish philosophy. Liberal of thought, progressive in his ideas, he was deeply religious, and faithful in the performance of Mitzvot. As a young man he won a prize for a work submitted to the

Prussian Academy, his competitor being none other than Immanuel Kant. Admired by the literary world, a friend of Kant and of Lessing (who patterned the personality of Nathan in his play *Nathan the Wise* after him), known to Frederick the Great, who granted him a residence permit in Berlin (though most reluctantly), Mendelssohn became a leading representative of the Enlightenment. But he was a truly faithful Jew, defending his faith courageously against Lavater, a Swiss clergyman, who challenged him to either explain Judaism in the light of reason, or to become a Christian: "My examination . . . has strengthened me in the faith of my fathers," Mendelssohn boldly affirmed, "I hereby witness before the God of truth . . . that I shall abide by these my convictions as long as my soul shall not change its nature."

Mendelssohn made it clear that, in the light of the Enlightenment, all of mankind must be assumed to have equal access to the truth that brings salvation. The ideals of religion could be found only through reason, which was granted to all men. The Jews at Sinai were given not ideals but a law.

Judaism was revealed law; its core was Mitzvot. The mind is free to search wherever it may. Thus Mendelssohn wished to educate his Jewish brethren to be a group fully adjusted and fully contributing to the culture and thought of their environment. To guide them, he translated the Pentateuch into modern German, writing a Hebrew commentary as well. Thus Jewry could acquire the language, gateway to communication and participation, out of its own most sacred treasure. In modern German they would be called to the performance of Mitzvot as found in Torah, and the Hebrew language would elucidate, so that they might remain staunch adherents to divine commandments throughout life. Mendelssohn expected the Christian world to grant full recognition to the Jewish citizens in their midst and to respect their faith, even as Judaism respects all faiths. This was a step toward Judaism as religion, pure and simple, even though Mendelssohn was unaware of it.

Religion Adapts to a New Age

But what about the Mitzvot and the spirit of common destiny that kept alive the sense of Jewish peoplehood? The leaders of the French Revolution had an answer to that. Should the Jews have equal rights as citizens? "To Jews as individuals we shall give everything, to Jews as a nation, nothing." The impact of this principle went deep. To be in accord with modern life and able to enjoy the blessings of citizenship, Jews had to remold their own thinking. Some of Judaism's age-old supports were thus weakened, others might have to be strengthened.

A first task was the scholarly and scientific investigation of Judaism, its origin and the development of its doctrines and institutions, all to be undertaken with reason as the guide and by the use of modern scientific methods as tools. The "Science of Judaism," founded by Leopold Zunz (1794–1886), came into being. The modernization of Judaism began.

Worship and practice had to be brought into line with the culture of their surroundings and with its forms, which they were quick to accept. This led to conferences and resulted in the emergence of leaders who became the founders of Reform (Abraham Geiger, 1810–1874), Conservatism (Zacharias Frankel, 1801–1875), and neo-Orthodoxy (Samson Raphael Hirsch, 1808–1888). Rabbis had to be trained academically in universities and in modern seminaries [Reform in Berlin: *Hochschule füer die Wissenschaft des Judentums* (University for the Science of Judaism), Geiger was one of its teachers; Conservatism in Breslau: *Jüdisch Theologisches Seminar* (Jewish Theological Seminary), founded by Zacharias Frankel; Orthodoxy in Berlin: *Rabbiner Seminar,* founded by Israel Hildesheimer].

Reform Judaism

Inevitably, the Mitzvot, which for Mendelssohn had still been untouchable, came under scrutiny. Did dogmas and principles relating to the Land and to Jewish peoplehood still have a place in the religion of the modern Jew as a citizen of a Western European country? What about the Mitzvot expressing these ideas, or those setting Jews apart from the rest of the population? A number of conferences were called (notably in Braunschweig in 1844 and Frankfurt in 1845) to examine Torah and Mitzvot scientifically. Characteristically for this Jewish Renaissance movement, individuals provided the driving force, forcefully implanting their ideas upon the rest.

In these conferences ABRAHAM GEIGER (1810–1874) stands out as the towering genius of Reform Judaism, and is essentially its founder. To him the scientific man cannot accept revelation, for science offers no proof of any revelation. Mendelssohn had seen Judaism as *revealed* law; Geiger rejected this idea, as he equally rejected any revealed doctrines. He refuted the hope for a return to the Land, for the land of citizenship is the land of the Jew. This was an attack on the validity of Torah, of Mitzvot, and of the Land. What remained, then, was the deep-seated sense of kinship with the Jewish *people* (a feeling of which Geiger himself may have been unaware, but which kept him from suggesting the dissolution of Judaism in favor of a general religion of ethical conduct). Thus Torah to him becomes a source of ethics, performance of Mitzvot becomes a matter of individual decision, but not binding, the Talmud and *Shulhan Arukh* have no power of commitment, and the messianic hope has been fulfilled in Jewish Emancipation. However, the genius of the Jewish people as teacher of ethics was strongly emphasized. The Hebrew language of prayer was to be retained in part, at least, for its emotional appeal. Education, sermon, and worship now were to form Torah in this new interpretation, and Mitzvot were to be understood as the missionary ideal of spreading ethics throughout the world. For these the Jew must live. The effect of Geiger's Reform Judaism was to be strongly felt, especially in America.

Conservative Judaism

Among the participants of the first rabbinical conference was ZACHARIAS FRANKEL (1801–1875), but he left it, convinced that this radical approach was a negative Judaism. He, too, was a man of science, who knew Jewish history as a process of evolution. Judaism had never stood still, hence its future development could be promoted on the basis of a *"positive historical Judaism."* The Torah, heritage of the congregation of Jacob, belongs to the people. Between its instructions and the changing conditions of life there exists a constant creative tension. The people in their inherent wisdom slowly and gradually adjust Torah to life, the Talmud being a prime example of such an adjustment. The Torah is thus anchored not in an unchanging word of God, but in the *people,* who, as His co-workers, by common, unspoken consensus, develop it. This is a slow process, but it retains Torah, Mitzvot (unless changed by the people), and the principles of Jewish peoplehood and of the Land and its redemption. The link with past and future is never broken. Thus study and education are essential, and as in every living organism, cells will die and new ones will be fashioned. This is Conservative Judaism, strong in Germany; we shall note its rise in America as well.

Neo-Orthodoxy

A third rabbi, SAMSON RAPHAEL HIRSCH (1808–1888), never attended the conferences. Strictly Orthodox, he was imbued with the ideas of Moses Mendelssohn, and even influenced by Geiger, in whom he saw his great adversary. To Hirsch, Torah was literal divine revelation both in law and in doctrines, hence it could never be changed. Yet the missionary ideal of which Geiger had spoken was also to be pursued. This could be done if the Jew both studied Torah and lived by the Mitzvot in every detail. By setting an example of exemplary obedience to God in his religious conduct and in all of his human relationships, the Jew could thus set a standard of human being, showing the way back to

God to a world that had become estranged from Him. He could be
"Man-Israel." The performance of Mitzvot would set him apart;
beyond that he was to seek the friendship of his Christian neighbors and
was to immerse himself fully in the culture and civilization of the
Western world. This was a duty, even as the esthetic values of the West
were to be fully utilized in the construction of religious worship and life,
provided they did not disagree with Torah. The Land—whose redemption was not denied—had to take a secondary place. It would be redeemed in God's own good time; to restore it through man's own doing
would be against His will.

This was Neo-Orthodoxy, strictly separating itself from all other
religious groups, and requiring a highly educated Jewish community for
its implementation. Organizationally it has therefore remained compara-
tively small in America, but its increasing influence is felt in a number of
Orthodox groups, for better (in the acceptance of Western cultural
values) or for worse (in the denial to other Jewish religious groups the
right to be considered authentic forms of Judaism).

Zionism

In the meantime, Russian Jewry was suffering agonies. The thought
stirred (in line with the emerging nationalism of the nineteenth century)
that only a return to the Land could provide freedom. *Auto-Emanzipa-
tion* (Self-Emancipation) was the slogan of a Jewish physician and
leader, LEO PINSKER (1821–1891), who saw in anti-Semitism an
incurable affliction of the world. Only national independence could
cure it.

AHAD HA-AM (1856–1927) (pen name of Asher Ginzberg, meaning
"One of the People") was, like Pinsker, a product of the Enlightenment
movement (Haskalah) that had taken hold within some Eastern Jewish
circles. He also believed in Jews as a people. But no people can be
creative, he felt, unless it has a spiritual and cultural center in a land of
its own. Let Palestine be restored as center of Jewish life, and Judaism
will be reborn. Sovereignty over the land would be desirable, but is not
necessary. Thus *Cultural Zionism* was born.

The yearning for freedom from intolerable pressure and a hopeless
fate in Russia expressed itself in a number of efforts to resettle on the
Land. Organizations were founded, such as the "Lovers of Zion"
(*Hovave Zion*), student groups exchanged classrooms for the wilderness
of Palestine and its backbreaking work. For the new immigrants, the
French Baron Rothschild established colonies there. Migration was
difficult, however, since the Turkish government, in whose domain
Palestine lay, placed great obstacles in the way of a large scale *Aliyah*

(the "going up" to the Land). There was great need for a true leader who would provide the program, organization, and spirit to direct and solidify the movement. Such a leader was found in Theodor Herzl.

Theodor Herzl (1860–1904)

Born in Budapest, which was then Austrian, Herzl was the son of a family strongly assimilated to Western surroundings and life. Handsome, charming, and brilliant, he nevertheless had to cope with anti-Semitism in his student years. He eventually chose the career of a newspaper correspondent; he also was a successful playwright and novelist. His paper, *Die Neue Freie Presse* of Vienna, sent him to Paris to cover one of the most sensational trials of the century, the Dreyfus trial. Dreyfus, a Jewish captain and only Jewish member of the French general staff, was accused of having submitted secret documents to the Germans. His accusers knew that he was innocent, the German emperor knew the identity of the traitor who had surrendered the documents, but Dreyfus, the Jew, was made the scapegoat. Witnesses were forced by threats to perjure themselves; Dreyfus was convicted and sent to Devil's Island. He was rehabilitated several years later, thanks largely to the efforts of dedicated and courageous men, including the French novelist Emile Zola and the statesman Clemenceau. The trial led to anti-Semitic agitation and outbursts in France.

To Herzl it was an eye opener. If this could happen in France, mother of democracy in Europe, then Jews were nowhere secure. The only answer was a free and internationally recognized homeland. In his brochure, *Der Judenstaat* (The Jewish State, 1896), Herzl proposed its creation. He then organized a Jewish Congress, which met in Basel, Switzerland, in 1897, and set as its goal "the creation of a Jewish, internationally recognized homeland in Palestine." The Congress outlined the steps to be taken toward the achievement of its goal. This was *Political Zionism*.

The burden of implementation fell upon Herzl. His job was twofold; he had to convince his fellow Jews in Western Europe that his plan was not only feasible but desirable. Here he met with a great deal of opposition among those who felt secure in their surroundings and had constructed their thoughts and lives on the assumption that they were to be and always remain full-fledged citizens in the countries to which they had given their full emotional and physical allegiance. At the same time, Herzl had to meet and plead with princes, potentates and governments to get a hearing and gain support for his project. The immensity of his task can hardly be imagined. Here was an individual, backed up by no power, representing a mass of powerless, oppressed people, venturing into the arena of power politics, where might alone spoke. In the pursuit of his mission, Herzl wore himself out completely and died prematurely at the age of 44 years, and exactly 44 years before his hope was to become a reality. His work was taken up by his disciples, including Chaim Weizmann (1874–1952), a brilliant chemist who placed the high reputation his scientific work had given him in the service of his people and was to end his life as the first president of the State of Israel.

Nineteenth Century Jewry

During the Emancipation period, the various branches of the House of Israel showed wide divergencies. We can discern roughly four major groupings. They were to become united again by the tragic events of the post-Emancipation period. First there was the Western European Jewish community, centered in Germany, where the neo-Orthodox and Conservative outlook was typical; next, Eastern Jewry, Orthodox in its views; third, the Jews in Palestine, soon to become the State of Israel, to whom the upbuilding of the Land was part of their living religion; and finally, American Jewry (discussed in Chapter 5), as yet amorphous but tending to be pragmatic in its approach.

In Western Europe, where Jews enjoyed citizenship rights in varying degrees, Germany, as fountainhead of ideology, formed the center. In religious philosophy, English Jewry followed the general principles of Samson Raphael Hirsch, although it was hierarchically organized in the pattern of organization of some of the German States. French and Italian, and to a degree, Austrian, Jews were more inclined to follow the general outlook of Conservatism, the school of Frankel. In all of these countries, Judaism was seen by its own adherents and by the population in general as a *religion*.

Eastern European Jewry was primarily Orthodox in the pre-Mendelssohnian sense. It lived by itself in deep piety. There were some stirrings of "Enlightenment" among the intellectuals, but there was no understanding of the philosophies of Judaism and its practices which were advanced in Germany. Emancipation in the full political sense never truly occurred.

Anti-Semitism

Anti-Semitism was far from dead. There was an anti-Semitic party in the German Parliament. Anti-Jewish sentiment was found among Christian teachings. Frequently, it had been so deeply instilled by the events of history that, for many, it had become second nature.

As we have seen, it broke out violently in France in connection with the Dreyfus case.

In Germany, the state, assuming supervision of all religions, organized the Jewish community along the pattern of the Protestant Church. Judaism became a religion and no more. This was basically not in disagreement with the ideas of Mendelssohn, Geiger, or Hirsch, hence the German Jews could see themselves primarily as a religious group. Full civil equality in fact was given Jews only during the short years of the German Republic (1918–1933). Prejudice among the Christian Germans was widespread. The German Jews felt, however, that if "they demeaned themselves good citizens, giving their country at all times their effective support," the Germans would recognize them in their true character and prejudice would disappear. German Jews became fervently patriotic and rejected Zionism which would have directed their concerns to another land (and which, according to Hirsch, was against Jewish law as well, for only in God's own time and with the coming of the Messiah was the Land to be redeemed; no premature action was permissible). Insecure themselves, they set themselves apart from their Eastern European brethren, assisting them without associating with them. At the same time, a considerable number of German Jews were well-educated Jewishly and faithful in observance of Mitzvot, although some groups became outright assimilationists.

However, the years after World War I were troublesome. The German economy broke down. Ill-equipped to understand democracy and live by it, Germans degraded their new government. The heavy war reparations did not help. It was a fertile period for demagogues. Hitler gained popular support by promising the Germans greatness, power, and wealth in exchange for freedom. The immediate tangible goal for Germans to pursue was the expropriation of the Jews. Useful as scapegoats, they also could be held out as a source of wealth for the have-nots, for, supposedly, they were very rich.

With the Germans, the Jews shared a belief in law and order, love of education, thrift, ambition. Through Torah, they had internalized their aversion to violence (as had Russian Jewry as well). By the teachings of their leaders they had come to accept the idea that society was improving (moving toward a Messianic age). All of this conspired against them when Hitler came to power in 1933. They had frequently been made scapegoats in the years since the Emancipation, but they considered these incidents hold-overs from a tragic past, which education and time would eventually help to overcome. It was inconceivable to them that the constitution, the basic law of the land, could be overthrown. They had become acculturated, hence could not fathom the possibility of a whole nation turning against them at the behest of a few maniacs. They abhorred violence, hence did not take up arms (as their forebears had done in Germany when Jews were attacked during the Crusades, and as the heroes of the Warsaw Ghetto were to do, after long hesitation when their cup of misery was finally running over). Dwelling in all sections of the German cities, they therefore had no emotional preparation, physical training, or even opportunity for united action.

From 1933 on, their lot deteriorated rapidly. Racial laws were promulgated in 1935, completely excluding Jews from the cultural, economic, and social life of the country; in 1938 the synagogues were burned down and Jewish property looted. The Jews were taken to concentration camps, which had been well prepared. As World War II progressed, the Jews were forced to live in ghettos and wear the yellow star and were systematically exterminated wherever Hitler's armies conquered. Six million Jews perished.

Why did Germany become the focal point of modern anti-Semitism? (Russian anti-Semitism was of the medieval type.) Because Jews had lived in Germany without interruption for close to 2000 years, there was a chance in Germany for the various forms of anti-Semitism to be piled on one another as history progressed. (They had been expelled from England and France for many centuries, and gradually been accepted later.) Prejudice against Jews became ingrained, and the Jews, as a prosperous but small minority, could therefore be used as scapegoats.

As we briefly trace the various forms of anti-Semitism which culminated in Hitler's extermination of six million Jews, we find the following:

In Roman Days, they were looked at with antipathy. They would not accept the Roman gods, frowned at the libertinism of Roman society, would not eat in Roman homes on account of their dietary laws, were considered lazy as they observed the Sabbath, and engaged in widespread missionary activities, making converts among leading citizens who were looking for spiritual guidance which Roman religion could not give. In short, the Jews were a nuisance, their ideas rather subversive of the Roman way of life, and they were gaining adherents. Christianity would build on these foundations of Jewish missionary work.

Medieval Christianity held the Jews responsible for the death of Christ and thus rejected by God. It explained their survival simply as a divine decree, that by their misery they might be the witnesses of the triumph of the Church. This was theological anti-Semitism, based on a doctrine which was declared false by the Ecumenical Council in 1965. Yet it was taught for centuries and built into German consciousness by Luther's anti-Semitism. The hatred of the Jews as unbelievers and deicides led to their exclusion from agriculture and all trades except the money-lender's, which was forbidden Christians by the Church. Through it, however, the Jews earned the additional accusation of being usurers, sharp and dishonest business manipulators. Since the Church saw them as *one* condemned people, they were an international, accursed enemy of humanity.

The Enlightenment saw no reason for theological anti-Semitism, and in its spirit Jews were emancipated. Then followed the age of science, which weaned many from adherence to theological dogma, thus further weakening anti-Semitism. But the Enlightenment was followed by Romanticism, the age of emotion, of looking backward to a past considered better than the present. With it came the strong outburst of nationalism. Looking back on the supposed glories of the past, the Germans found that the Jews then had been excluded from the life of the nation when Germany was supposedly strong. Now, Germany was weak while the Jews were equals. Contaminated by anti-Jewish teachings, the Germans became prey to demagogues: Why not make the Jews the scapegoats for all that had gone wrong? They were the enemies of the national state, and, it was claimed, were actually an international conspiracy. This accusation was based on their international status as an accursed race, given them by the Catholic Church in a different age. A forgery, "The Protocols of the Wise Men of Zion," supposedly the plan of Jewry's international leaders to destroy the nations and assume world power, was put into circulation. It has served its purpose of fanning hate all too well, right up to the present.

As science became the ultimate authority, replacing faith and dogma, a new science, or pseudo-science, was put to work *by the already prejudiced* to prove that the Jews were, scientifically speaking, a rotten, destructive race. There is no vestige of scientific truth to the fact that Jews are even a race, but the "science-minded" anti-Semites took up the idea, planting the seed which was to produce a harvest of terror.

A Jewish Renaissance

During the years preceding and during the Nazi regime, German Jewry had strengthened itself spiritually. Philosophers like Hermann Cohen (1842–1918), Franz Rosenzweig (1886–1929), and Martin Buber (1878–1965) were joined by great rabbis such as Leo Baeck (1873–1956). A Renaissance of Judaism took place. Jewish learning increased; books in Hebrew and German were published in increasing numbers, and adult academies of Jewish learning were organized in every community. Men like Rabbi Leo Baeck, who voluntarily shared the concentration camp with his brethren, continued to teach, inspire, and give meaning to Jewish life and suffering to those in the camps, though this instruction had to be offered without books and in secret, as it was forbidden by the Nazis. In adversity, German Jewry had one of its finest moments of greatness.

As if in preparation for this hour of need, German Jewry produced Jewish thinkers, schooled on German philosophy, but filled with a profound love and knowledge of their heritage. That some of them were *Baale Teshuvah* (Men of Return) from the fringes to the core of Judaism, makes their work even more significant for modern Jews. Interestingly enough, they grappled with the problem of Torah-Mitzvot-Land, and each of them saw the essence of Jewish survival in a different one of these elements, without eliminating the others.

HERMANN COHEN was a Kantian, founder of the Neo-Kantian School in Marburg. In the beginning, he was so imbued with the culture of Germany that he felt that even the Sabbath could be shifted to Sunday, in line with general practice. Later he freely confessed that he had repented this early aberration. His greatest work is *Religion of Reason from the Sources of Judaism.* Reason (Torah in the widest sense) is the cornerstone of his system. God—inconceivable to man—is an eternal challenge; every new insight leads us closer to Him. Applying Kantian terms, he makes God Thing-in-itself. But the Thing-in-itself is *not* forever hidden from us, as Kant would have it. If we throw a stone into a pond, the water forms circles, each wider than the other. So does every partial knowledge of God lead us on to ever new knowledge, endlessly. And with knowledge of God's world comes our moral duty. Nature and morality belong together, for they have one source, God. The Oneness of God is proven by the fact that the realm of nature and the realm of morality are fully keyed to each other; hence they must have had one Creator. To strive for a world where perfect moral action is universal is our task; this is symbolized in the idea of the Messiah, in the future. Perfect love extended to all is the Jewish command; there must be *justice,* based on ethical principle, but it must grow into *compassion,* which is the element of religion.

Living and suffering for these ideals, the Jews are indispensable to mankind. Thus did Judaism give to the world the idea of the One God who is Spirit, placed before it the Messianic Idea for which to strive (though not a personal Messiah), and revealed God to humanity as the loving Father, embracing all, and freely pardoning the sinner in the fullness of His compassion.

Thus Jews must remain a people, obeying the Mitzvot which educate them to their task and help preserve them as the representatives of pure monotheism in the world, although the laws do evolve. All this is done in behalf of mankind.

If we see in these ideas the reflection of Frankel's teachings, we are correct, for indeed Cohen had been Frankel's disciple in his early years when he had intended to become a rabbi. This spirit of peoplehood, which Frankel emphasized, was demonstrated by the fact that Cohen went to Poland in the hope of bringing its Jewry the means of adjustment, through Judaism *plus* culture. World War I shattered this hope. To Cohen, peoplehood took the place of Land. *Torah*—Reason—provided the rationale of survival.

Here was a synthesis of German thought and Jewish tradition, so typical of the German Jews, even as it was a synthesis of German citizenship and Jewish belongingness. But here was also an answer for trials: Jews are tried while showing mankind the way.

FRANZ ROSENZWEIG, disciple of Cohen, was a Hegelian. Mitzvot as the response to God through action is the capstone of his thinking. Rosenzweig had almost accepted Christianity, seeing in the Judaism of his family merely a form of ethical humanism. A last effort to know what he was giving up before he took the step convinced him to remain a Jew. Rosenzweig had learned from Hegel that history is in a constant process of becoming; it is the unfolding of the Absolute. He accepted this idea as true for all the peoples of the world and for all religions except Jews and Judaism. All are coming to the Father, and Christianity is one way to come to Him, and a good one. The Jew, however, *is* with the Father. No longer do the Jews move forward toward a goal; they have reached it. They live in God's presence, and express this through their inner evolution in Mitzvot and thought through life. Thus the world can realize that all mankind equally can come to Him. To demonstrate this fact eternally, the Jewish people must survive.

We may see the universe in the form of a triangle of God-world-man. God is the apex, man and world face each other at the base in fulfilling His purpose. The dynamic elements resulting in evolution in the world may be schematized in the form of an opposing triangle. Its points are: creation (cause of the world), revelation (giving man his task), and redemption (the unity of man and creation). The world is trying to combine these two triangles; that is its history. The Jew, having passed through history, has already reached this synthesis of redemption. The two triangles thus form the six-pointed star, symbol of Judaism, the *Star of Redemption* (title of Rosenzweig's major work). The core of the system is life.

In the prime of life, Rosenzweig was felled by a paralyzing disease, which, for nine years, made him increasingly incapable of even moving a limb, yet he kept on working. This was Mitzvah, responding to God. He who is with God requires only the spirit. In this fashion his people could see Rosenzweig's life itself as a symbol of their own being and their worthiness before God, even when the enemy paralyzed and extinguished their physical existence.

Again, we have a synthesis of German Hegelian and Jewish thought. We have God, Torah (Revelation), and Mitzvot; and Mitzvot, subject to evolution, are the key. The Land is neglected in Rosenzweig's thinking; with the rebuilding of the Land Israel, the Jews would once again move onto the stage of becoming, of historical evolution, trial and error in search for the road to the Father. Unaware of the tremendous change about to take place, rejecting the early efforts to rebuild Israel, Rosenzweig found himself in error. Yet the recognition of Jewish *peoplehood,* the people with the Father, is strong and central.

MARTIN BUBER is the third thinker of this period. Land and people were the focal point of his thought. A student of Hasidism, about which he wrote extensively, he saw the relationship between man and man, and man and God in existential terms. I can relate to my fellowman by using him as my tool; this is a bad relationship, for he becomes an object for me, an *It.* I must rather relate to him as *Thou.* Even as in a dialogue of equal partners both of them find themselves and each other in the process of talking to each other, so in life. There must be the dialogue of action between I and Thou. (*I and Thou* is Buber's fundamental work.) The same dialogue goes on between man and God. I must listen to Him, must know what He wants me to do. Whatever it is, He reveals it only at the moment of action, and then only to me, who am the only one to do it. God guides my action-dialogue with my fellow man, telling me what to do, and as I do it, I remain in dialogue with God. God-Man-Fellow man are inextricably linked together; the most direct way to God is through humanity. This is a universal philosophy, and Buber has left a deep impact on Christian thinkers.

Does it not lead out of Judaism (if I should find, for instance, that all of the Mitzvot of Torah no longer speak to me as a living word of God)? Where is the rationale for Jewish existence? It lies in the fact that the Jews are a *people.* There is a *special* dialogue between Israel and God; it expresses itself in Jewish social living. In this special Jewish experience of life, we see the influence of Hasidism. But Buber goes further. Judaism finds fulfilment only in a Jewish society on its own land; in Israel, a society can be created which sets the example for mankind. Having partaken of the spirit of the East as well as of the fruits of the West, Israel can become the bridge between cultures and peoples. Israel works for the vision of the future, the messianic age; it acts, and in acting finds God. It reads the Torah ever afresh in the light of its function (and Buber, with Rosenzweig, has translated the Torah into magnificent German). Land and peoplehood make both Torah and Mitzvot Jewishly meaningful in the dialogue with God.

Emergence of the State of Israel

During World War I, when the disposition of the Turkish Empire was arranged by the Allied Powers, the Jews were promised Palestine as

Jewish Homeland for all those who might wish to go there (Balfour Declaration of 1917). Unfortunately, conflicting promises regarding disposition of the land had been made to the Arabs. They turned hostile when confronted with a Jewish settlement dedicated to social progress and a modern way of life, and destructive of the old, feudalistic rule of the big landholding magnates, who literally held their people in slavedom. Britain, as the Mandate Power, severely restricted Jewish immigration in an appeasement move toward the Arabs, and many fugitives of Hitler's extermination camps had eventually to be smuggled in as "illegal immigrants." Britain also promoted the partition of the territory originally promised the Jews; that they got anything at all is due, not in the least, to the strong representations of Winston Churchill, who considered himself a lifelong Zionist.

In 1948, after many struggles, independence of a small territory (half its original size) became a reality. Israel emerged, hopeful that it might be a useful partner of the Near Eastern states in the development of the territory. It was not to be.

Immediately Israel was attacked by the Arabs and Egypt, but it won this, its "war of liberation." In another war in 1956 (the Suez Crisis) it had to curb the marauder raids against its borders which had been going on in increased intensity for quite some time. Joining England and France in an attack against Egypt, which had just expropriated these countries who had held ownership over the Suez Canal and wished to regain it, Israel was equally concerned with her future rights to use the Canal, now in Egyptian hands. President Eisenhower insisted on a cessation of the war, and pledged his resources to provide and guarantee free access to the Canal for any nation. However, the Suez Canal since then has remained closed to Israeli shipping.

Israel is still faced by hostile neighbors. It is plagued by the "refugee problem," those Arabs who left Israel in 1948 at the request of the advancing Egyptian and Arab armies, and who have not been permitted to return in view of their hostile outlook. These people have not been resettled elsewhere, either, which could have been done, for instance, in "exchange" for the Egyptian Jews who were expelled and had to leave their property behind.

Smallness and threats against survival have not prevented the building of a great civilization and the best scientific and cultural institutions on continental Asia. Israel and Japan thus form the two truly modern countries on the continent, and have been cooperating in various economic enterprises. But the same elements have given the people an exaggerated nationalism and a somewhat overbearing attitude which hides the awareness of their physical smallness and exposed position. This is understandable and should vanish when peace finally comes to the Middle East. The legitimate pride in their attainments will then serve as a further incentive for development of this truly dynamic society. Were peace established, common enterprise could make this region into a Garden of Eden, as once, in antiquity, it was the fertile crescent and mother of civilization.

To the existence of Israel, millions of Jews owe their very lives. When World War II was over, the remnant of Jewry, deeply wounded by the loss of six million of its people, converged once more, and the leadership fell to the children, the Jews of the United States and of Israel.

Israel Today

As we have seen, settlement began in earnest in the nineteenth century, although Jews had always lived there without being builders of the Land. They lived on charitable gifts of world Jewry. Israel, with a population of two and three-quarters million at this writing, is a nation with a mission. Fervently nationalistic, the Israelis are imbued with the ethical ideals of the Bible and are trying to build their land in the form of a model society of progress and social justice. They are even rendering assistance to underdeveloped nations in Asia and Africa. There is a messianic idealism in the people, a spirit of dedication which draws its strength from Biblical and Hasidic thought. But they are not religious, with the exception of some small groups, among them fanatic defenders of Eastern European ways, including dress, practices, and habits. In the majority, Land and nation are the rationales of survival. With great love they have received the uprooted Jews from many lands, taught them Hebrew, helped them adjust, and transformed them into proud and productive citizens. With unequalled tenacity, they have wrested rich harvests from once barren soil, developed industry, and established institutes of culture and higher learning. This is their faith.

Yet religion might have a more significant impact had the religious leadership been attuned to the times. The Chief Rabbinate in Israel, as a state institution, is entrusted with many state functions, such as cases of family law when Jews are involved. The rabbinate has been strictly and fundamentally Orthodox. It will not grant non-Orthodox rabbis the right to officiate, has refused to honor religious acts performed by those rabbis abroad, and will fight with every weapon, including political pressures, against the establishment of non-Orthodox Jewish congregations in Israel. Non-Jewish religions are fully protected and generously endowed by the State; non-Orthodox Jewish groups face severe disabilities. Unable to accept this form of Judaism and incapable of developing others, Israeli Jews in their majority have no religion. Against severe odds, American Jews (discussed in the next chapter) have sponsored some Conservative and Liberal synagogues in Israel and have established research institutes there. The movement is in its infancy and suffers from the fact that it has to address itself to Jews who have developed negative attitudes toward both religion and "imports" from abroad, since they look down on the institutions of Diaspora as the makeshift answers of those who do not come to Israel. Yet the results so far have been encouraging.

The Chief Rabbinate of Israel likes to consider itself the central religious authority for all of world Jewry, a kind of Jewish "Vatican." American Orthodoxy accepts that, hence has to fall in line with its decisions, including the relationship to the other branches of Judaism, who will not accept this authority. The great rabbis of Eastern Europe never made a bid for this power. Like the Israeli rabbinate, they lived in a totally Jewish environment, but they preferred to let their wisdom establish their position in world Jewry, and they succeeded. With the fall of Eastern Europe, Israel has the most uniform Jewish society in the world. Yet the Chief Rabbinate has not elicited a voluntary response by Jewry. Non-Orthodox Jewry has not been able to incorporate the philosophy of the Chief Rabbinate. A separation of church and state in Israel might actually be in the interest of religion itself. Not only would it give full freedom of development to all Jewish religious groups in Israel, but it might also lead the rabbinate into the creative contest of ideas, thereby revitalizing it to the benefit of all.

Jews Outside Israel and America

The impact of time and events has been felt in many countries, especially those where Jewry is slowly emerging from the severe losses of the war.

In *Holland* and *South Africa,* Orthodox rabbis have been known to decline appearances on public platforms with non-Orthodox rabbis.

England has a Jewish population of approximately 500,000 Jews. The United Synagogue is the official religious body although there exist both Liberal synagogues and a rabbinical school, the Leo Baeck College, and ultra-Orthodox synagogues. Orthodox in its character, the United Synagogue used to be hospitable to a fairly wide spectrum of ideas and practices, ranging from very Orthodox to mildly Conservative. Today, the United Synagogue no longer permits any deviations from absolute Orthodox *doctrine,* even when Orthodox *practices* are in no way challenged or changed. The reason for this change may lie in the growth of the Eastern European element due to recent immigration, but perhaps also in a complete disenchantment with the culture of the West and efforts to adjust to it, as a result of the total failure of Western Civilization to prevent the terror of the Hitler years. New efforts to come to grips with the theological problems posed by the twentieth century are being made. The most brilliant theologian in the Orthodox group is Louis Jacobs, yet his authorization to hold rabbinical office within the United Synagogue was revoked as a result of some doctrinal differences, and he had to organize his own congregation.

France has recently become the third largest Jewish community in the world. With a Jewish population of over half a million, it is surpassed only by United States' Jewry (close to six million), Russian Jewry (approximately three million), and Israel. Due to the events of the war and post-war years, the composition and character of French Jewry have changed radically. The largely Ashkenasic Jewish community of the pre-war years was mostly exterminated by the Nazis. Fully acculturated to French patterns of life, these Jews followed a rather complacent Conservatism in their religious attitudes. Upon this decimated population was grafted a large Sephardic element of deeply Orthodox Jews, the immigrants from the former French possessions in North Africa, particularly Algeria. These Jews, who held French citizenship, fled to France when Algeria became independent, being in fear of Arab hostility. Resettled with the help of the French Government, they established Jewish communities all over France, revived moribund ones, and brought about a widespread Jewish population distribution throughout France, both geographically and occupationally. The leadership of French Jewry has become aware of the fact that Judaism has to be explained to the French people as a whole, and its contribution to mankind has to be shown. At the same time, a new synthesis of Jewish religion and worldly wisdom, of old-time citizens and new settler, has to be achieved. Due to the size of its community, French Jewry has become a leading spokesman of European Jewry as a whole. The French Jews have responded to this challenge and opportunity. Since 1955, some universities, notably Strasbourg and Paris, have had chairs of Judaism, thus placing it in the main stream of academic thought. Professors have thus become the representatives. They consider it their task to present the authentic teachings of Judaism to the world in a genuine dialogue, and are motivated by the conviction that a Judaism basing its development on its *own* resources and life forces holds a vital function for mankind as a whole. Thus they have followed the lead of Franz Rosenzweig. The works of men like Emmanuel Levinas (*Difficile Liberté*), André Neher (*L'Existence Juive,* 1962), and *La Conscience Juive* (by the two mentioned authors, 1963), are exerting their influence upon the French-speaking thinker by presenting a full picture of Judaism, its traditions, values, life, and its contribution out of its own resources to mankind in search of spiritual guidance. The outlook of these men is traditional.

There exists also a Liberal rabbinical seminary in Paris. Established with American help, it can provide Liberal spiritual leaders for congregations who may require them.

German Jewry, numbering roughly 30,000, has no future. Those living there at present are either people who were spared by the Nazis due to the fact they were married to "Aryan" women, or they are refugees from the East who got stranded; with them we find a small number of old men and women who returned, being unable to adjust abroad. The government aided these Jews in the building of a number of new synagogues, some of which are architectural gems. A few rabbis have returned. Worship is neo-Orthodox in character and is not too well attended. There seems to be little hope for the young people born since the Second World War. Strenuous efforts are being made by government and enlightened citizens to curb any instances of any emerging form of anti-Semitism. In Austria it has shown itself in some ugly ways.

Russian Jewry is subjected to a form of spiritual genocide by the Russian government. Stalin was a brutal anti-Semite; Khrushchev had no love for Jews. The old tradition of harassment has continued. Synagogues are being closed, rabbinic leadership is lacking due to lack of institutions training them. Neither prayer books nor religious articles may be imported. Christians as well as Jews throughout the world have strenuously protested against this new form of extermination, which the Russians—counter to all eyewitness reports—claim does not exist!

The conditions in the satellite states are better, but the future is insecure. The number of Jews in most of them is small due to Nazi extermination and emigration. The treatment of the Jews rests on the will of the rulers, their dependence or independence from Russian pressure, and the changing whim of the Russian rulers, as well. In some countries, such as Czechoslovakia, Poland, Rumania, and Yugoslavia, Jews are, therefore, faring better, but the outlook for a creative Jewish future is none too hopeful.

South American Jewry holds a potential which is as yet unrealized, due to lack of trained rabbinical leadership. Where such leadership exists, as in Buenos Aires, progress has been made. This offers a challenge to United States Jewry, which has to train a leadership prepared to work within the framework of local conditions and character. The same problem exists in the Caribbean. In contrast to Argentina, which has problems of anti-Semitism, Jews in places like Curaçao actually are the leaders of society, but there are few fully trained modern rabbis in the area, and religious neglect and apathy are widely evident. The total Jewish population in South America is now almost three-fourths' million.

The leadership, as we have seen, has devolved upon American Jewry, which has the resources, both spiritual and material, the numbers, and the freedom. The challenge to *spiritual* leadership, in addition to material assistance, is inescapable, and requires the cooperation of every Jew.

5 THE AMERICAN DESTINY

WHEN Frederick Jackson Turner read his epoch-making paper on "The Significance of the Frontier in American History" before the American Historical Society in 1893, he did not think of the Jews, yet he could have cited their destiny as a prime proof for his hypothesis. Challenged by the frontier, immigrants from many European lands created a new society of Americans in a distinct American spirit, a "democracy born of free land, strong in selfishness and individualism, intolerant of administrative experience and education, and pressing individual liberty beyond its proper bounds." This society had its dangers as well as its great advantages.

Early Struggles

This American spirit was immediately apparent among the 23 poverty-stricken refugees from persecution who arrived at New Amsterdam in 1654. Without a moment's delay, they fought not only for their right to establish themselves, but also for the citizen's privilege to bear arms in defense of the colony, and succeeded in having Governor Stuyvesant's anti-Jewish decisions overruled. Yet these immigrants had only yesterday been the victims of persecution. Self-reliant, they pledged themselves to take care of their own indigent brethren without resorting to public assistance. Their tenacious insistence brought them permission to establish a synagogue.

Only 2500 in number by the time of the American Revolution, the Jews fought patriotically; although some of them felt conscience-bound (like many other Americans) to support the British crown, the majority was prepared to give their all, life and property, to the cause of the United States.

In contrast to their European brethren, they could count on the support of the Founding Fathers of America. Benjamin Franklin, first on the list of subscribers to the synagogue building in Philadelphia;

Thomas Jefferson, in whom some could find a sympathetic listener regarding endeavors to modernize religious worship; John Adams, who expressed the hope that all prejudice against them would vanish from the earth through the example of the United States. In Maryland, a Scotch Presbyterian, Thomas Kennedy, powerfully spoke out for their rights; though he knew no Jews, he felt justice demanded it. Their greatest support, however, came from George Washington himself, who (in a letter to the Jewish congregation of Newport, Rhode Island) made it clear that "happily the government of the United States, which gives to bigotry no sanction, to persecution no assistance, requires only that they who live under its protection shall demean themselves as good citizens in giving it at all occasions their effectual support." This was assurance and challenge.

Jews became patriots without giving up their faith. Only in America could personalities develop like JUDAH TOURO (1775–1854). Wounded in the battle of New Orleans, successful in business, he became a peerless philanthropist, aiding churches in the spirit of interfaith cooperation, and providing one-fifth of the total cost of Bunker Hill Monument.

Only in America could a Jew like URIAH P. LEVY (1792–1862) aspire toward a career in the Navy and reach the highest rank, that of Commodore. He did indeed have to combat anti-Semitism, but nowhere in Europe would the thought have occurred to a Jew that he could make the military his life's work. There he would be scornfully chased away.

Only in America could a MORDECAI MANUEL NOAH (1785–1851) emerge and devise a scheme of setting up a Jewish State in the United States, to gather in his persecuted people from abroad. Like other efforts to build states on ethnical grouping, it (fortunately) failed. But Noah, undaunted, then advocated the project of rebuilding Palestine, if this was the place the Jews preferred. This public affirmation of his dedication to Jewish peoplehood did not in the least interfere with his position as a public servant, as a United States representative abroad (consul at Tunis), and as a society leader.

These men were individualists, their schemes and lives were adventurous, they were men of the frontier, that place where the old pushes forward toward the new.

New Society

In this new environment, in a society built on the spirit of the Enlightenment, the European form of the synagogue, its worship, and its customs eventually came to appear as an anachronism. There were no ordained rabbis until the middle of the nineteenth century, so some immigrant a bit versed in Judaism would be appointed to lead the service, teach the children, and perform religious functions. The lay leader (already a power in medieval Jewish life) now became all-powerful in individualistic America. As a man of success in life, he assumed dictatorial powers in his congregation, which he directed as president. Frequently religiously nonobservant in their own lives, the majority of these leaders insisted on a strict (pre-Mendelssohnian) pattern of religion in the synagogue. They were supported by the new arrivals, who found shelter from the new world in the synagogue of old-time religion.

Yet the second and third generations could not abide it; they saw no link to life in this form of faith. Those who were attracted by the lure of the West might be swallowed up by its vastness and be lost to their faith. Those who remained in the East and South, where organized Jewish life existed, found themselves confronted with "bossism," an outmoded form of worship, and a community divided between newcomers and old-timers.

Reforms were to come, but the clash of individuals, the power of leaders prominent in the world without necessarily being religious, the independence of congregations, each going its own way—these elements can still be found in American Judaism. Under the impact of the frontier, a community had emerged to whom Torah and Mitzvot frequently were at best psychological defenses against the overpowering experiences of the new environment during the period of adjustment to it. At worst, they became a mechanical performance. The universal affirmation by these Jews of their belonging to the House of Israel therefore stands out as a positive element. They wanted to be full-fledged Americans, but as Jews. It was an affirmation of their individualism and approved by the spirit of America.

The Old Faith and the New World

The growing Jewish community reached a total of 250,000 by 1875. The majority came from Germany to escape civil repression and found a ready haven in the Midwest, where Christian Germans had settled, among them many liberals, who had left Germany after the failure of the revolution of 1848, which was to have brought democracy. The Jews who arrived were poor but brought with them their skills, the typically German talent for organization, and, in many cases, a liberal outlook schooled on the principles of the Enlightenment. They were capable of speedy acculturation and were economically successful in the frontier region where they had settled. Adjustment of religious patterns became imperative.

The first one to undertake the task was ISAAC LEESER (1806–1868), who was not a rabbi. A recent immigrant from Germany, he showed so profound a Jewish knowledge that he was appointed spiritual leader of the congregation in Philadelphia. He used his position as a base from which to affect all of American Jewry. Leeser was strictly Orthodox and deeply influenced by Mendelssohn. The Mitzvot must be upheld; at the same time, people must be educated to understand Torah. Leeser translated the Bible and the prayer book into English, published a periodical, traveled widely. His hope was to equip strictly Orthodox Jews for living in two civilizations, as Mendelssohn had done. He was not a theoretical theologian as the German rabbis were (the American leaders were not primarily concerned with philosophical considerations), but was pragmatic in his approach, for the spirit of America is pragmatic. Later religious leaders were to follow him.

A few rabbis arrived on the scene; some of them, like the brilliant David Einhorn, radical in their reform ideology. Then came Isaac Meyer Wise, imbued with a fervent love of liberty, which had made him leave Europe.

American Reform

ISAAC MEYER WISE (1819–1900) became the founder of American Reform. His basic idea was to create a united and integrated American Judaism. He started out, therefore, as a Conservative, choosing a middle road which he hoped would rally American Jewry. Immediately he found himself in trouble with the Orthodox leadership. Still striving to find a common ground for all American Jews, he organized The Union of American Hebrew Congregations as a roof organization for all types of congregations but which would not interfere in their internal affairs. The Orthodox group refused to join. He then developed a rabbinical seminary, the first in the Western World, The Hebrew Union College in Cincinnati. It was to train rabbis for all religious groups, but again he was rebuffed by the Orthodox group. His final hope for unity was pinned on the organization of a rabbinical body in which rabbis of all persuasions could hold membership. It led him to found The Central Conference of American Rabbis. The Orthodox rabbis refused to join; they wanted none of his spirit even of moderate reform. In his middle position, Wise suited neither the radical reformers nor the Orthodox traditionalists. If he wanted any kind of organization without surrendering his hopes for some kind of unification, he had to shift to the liberal wing. Thus he turned to Reform.

Eventually, his organization was to grow into one of the powerful wings of American religious Jewry, Reform Judaism. Yet Wise's dream was to be fulfilled in a fashion. American Jewry became organized, not in one, but in three groups, and each group followed Wise's organizational plan.

During its early stages of exuberant reform, the movement became radical. Geiger's most extreme ideas were translated into reality. Beyond that, many innovations were approved, the elimination of the hat in worship being one of them. Torah was no longer binding except in its ethical pronouncements; Mitzvot were equated with ethical conduct. The Land of Israel was regarded as of no concern; the messianic hope was considered meaningless.

Fortunately, Reform Judaism saw and sees itself not as *reformed* in one completed act, but rather as *given to Reform*. Thus Reform was to move back into the main stream of Jewish living. Today, the Torah is recognized as the treasury of sanctions and norms, its spiritual ideals as the source of life. While the individual still has the right to adjust Torah to the dictates of his conscience, the general outlook is quite close to that of positive historical Judaism. Judaism is the soul and the Jewish people are the body, hence the link with the branches of Jewry may not be broken. Religious observance and study are duties, the support of the Land of Israel an obligation. In this new spirit, Reform Judaism officially has restored Torah-Mitzvot-Land under God, affirming Jewish peoplehood while leaving the decisions regarding religious beliefs and practices to the individual. This may possibly be too big a task for the individual, and many Jews, instead of being Reform Jews, may simply be looking for a permissive form of Judaism. It must be remembered, however, that some of the most ardent fighters for the restoration of the Land of Israel and some of the most intrepid champions of human rights have come from the ranks of the Reform rabbinate.

Cultural Jews

We clearly see the impact of the American environment in these developments, the influence of individuals, the spirit of the frontier which beckons to endless experiment, and then the closing of the frontier in settled compromise.

The German Jews, now grown affluent, were happy. They had their niche, socially and religiously. Were they to ask whether they were not going too far in their religious experimentation, they might well find comfort in the thought that America was after all "the child" of Jewry and permitted a bit of latitude. The reservoirs of Jewish life were in Russia and Poland, whence new immigrants would come to restore Jewish life and Jewish strength. Beginning in the 1880's, they did indeed arrive, came by the millions, and created new problems, in turn affecting the character of American Jewry.

For the newcomers, life in the United States spelled the transition from the Old World to the New, from a homogeneous Jewish society to a heterogeneous one composed of many groups, and from life as small farmers and traders in a rural environment to urban sweatshops. True to the pledge of the first settlers, the established Jewish community gave aid to the newcomers, hoping to assimilate them quickly to American ways and the American pattern of Jewish religion, which was Reform. What they failed to see was that the immigrant needs the shelter of his ethnic surroundings as a psychological defense against the overpowering influences of the new, and, later on, as a transitional stage toward his assimilation. The newcomers thus refused to adjust in line with the hopes of the settled Jewish community; they maintained their little Orthodox congregations (each group having its own congregation), continued to speak Yiddish among themselves, and preserved their old traditions.

This resulted in a number of significant developments: An antagonism developed between the German Jews and the Eastern European Jews, which only time has begun to heal.

When a new generation came along, ready to move into the main stream of American life yet unwilling to accept Reform Judaism as being too formal and too cold for their taste, the leaders of Reform were the first ones to provide the means (both physical and intellectual) for the establishment of a religious movement which would synthesize American ways of life and Jewish thinking based on the way of thought of tradition-bound Eastern European Jewry. Living up to the American ideal of unity in diversity, the Reform (lay) leaders organized the Jewish Theological Seminary, fountainhead of Conservative Judaism.

The initial efforts to assimilate the new arrivals to existing life by means of a crash program had another, negative effect: the immigrant generation held on to its traditions with even greater tenacity. As a result, their children (brought up in America and in many cases educated in college by the severe sacrifice of their parents) became alienated from the culture and religion of their parents, which was frowned on by Americanized Jews and appeared alien on American soil. Many of them did not join Conservative congregations. They saw in America an example of ethnic communities living side by side and retaining their identity by folkways. Identity thus did not have to be based on religion.

These Jews became "Cultural Jews." They did not accept religious practices and beliefs, as they were in conflict with scientific thought and American ways of expression, yet they remained Jews, feeling strongly that survival was assured by maintaining Jewish peoplehood and culture. They had an additional example in the development of the Land of Israel, where a nonreligious Judaism was emerging. Religion thus was not regarded as essential. Zionism, folkways, culture (ethnical identification) were sufficient. Eliminating God, they identified Torah with education in general. Mitzvot meant working for social justice similar to the manner in which the Social Gospel movement interpreted the message of Christianity. The Land of Israel (still but a hope) added another strong force making for Jewish survival.

An example of such an outlook (without Zionist aspects) is found in the personality of Samuel Gompers, founder of the American Federation of Labor. A cigar maker, he studied while pursuing his work. Out of the Jewish spirit of social justice he came to build a great labor organization.

American Jewry thus came to consider itself either a religious group, as is more and more the case, or simply an ethnic group. Many an intellectual eventually would consider himself an ethnic Jew, but free to enter into relationships with any ethnic group he wished. This included interfaith marriage.

It must be considered fortunate that the concept of American Judaism as *religion* is acquiring ever greater hold, since there seems to be very little hope that ethnic groups will survive. The future of American Jewry as an ethnic group would be dim; as a religious group, it will endure. As a result of the traditional respect for learning, it is not a stigma among Jews to be considered an "intellectual." Intellectuals have come to form a subgroup in American society, cutting across ethnic lines. Its members are naturally attracted to each other, and—furthermore—feel free to follow the conclusions of their own individualistic reasoning. Unfettered by tradition, they make their choice in marriage across the lines of religion and ethnicity. As interfaith marriage may increase in this group, many brilliant people may be lost to Judaism.

We might almost say that this "cultural" movement anticipated, in a fashion, the outlook of modern "God-is-dead" theology, which has made inroads in some Christian circles. Both believe in the primacy of basic human values to be established without reference to God. Though the foundations of the two movements are different, the latter might learn from the Jewish experience that the potential of meaningful survival is most questionable for a spiritual society that yet eliminates God.

Conservative Judaism

Conservative Judaism has been based strongly on Frankel's principles. SOLOMON SCHECHTER (1850–1915), the guiding spirit of the Jewish Theological Seminary, maintained that the development of Torah and Mitzvot is squarely placed by God in the hands of the Jewish people, who by unspoken consent adjust and develop it.

Following the example of Wise, Schechter developed similar institutions for Conservative Judaism but reversed the process of their creation. First came the Jewish Theological Seminary, based on a philosophy of "positive historical Judaism," then came the Rabbinical Assembly, and finally the United Synagogue, the congregational organization. The Seminary thus remains the fountainhead, and, organizationally at least, holds the key position. According to Conservative doctrine, the decisions of Torah and Talmud must be followed, Zionism is a key principle, and Mitzvot must be practiced, except as the people change them. Due to the autonomy of individual congregations, even in the evolution of Jewish practices, the changes vary. Some congregations, for instance, have an organ; others reject it. The rabbinical leaders and the Seminary can authorize only those changes, which have been universally adopted. The approach is pragmatic and as such, typically American. It failed, however, to provide strong support to individual rabbis and communities while changes were being debated by their own membership. Reform may have been too categorical. Conservatism, placing the decisions in the hands of the people with a rabbi but a guide, followed very much the thinking of American democracy, but proved indecisive when firmness might have helped.

Conservatism has grown into a very strong movement; both its strength and its weaknesses are still with us.

Orthodoxy

Orthodoxy, finding itself weakened by the onslaught of the American environment, took two widely divergent directions: Communities led by rabbis without academic training retreated into a pre-Mendelssohnian Judaism of strictest performances of Torah and Mitzvot as divinely ordained and eternal. These communities would see in separation from the world the answer to its danger. On the other hand, communities were also led by academically trained American rabbis. To educate them, the Yeshivah (the Orthodox rabbinical seminary) was expanded into a university. These men tried to adopt a philosophy akin to that of Samson Raphael Hirsch as far as the education of their membership permitted. Orthodoxy in all its ranks is Zionist, thus adding love of Land to all the other elements, but is very slow in evolution.

As the generations became more Americanized and frequently less Orthodox with the passing of time, Orthodoxy has raised a wall of separation, hopeful that this might preserve it. The antagonism to non-Orthodox Jewry has grown rather than diminished. This attitude has been strengthened by the fact that the state-supported Chief Rabbinate of Israel would like to be regarded as Chief Rabbinate of the world. The Chief Rabbinate in Israel has no understanding for non-Orthodox

Judaism and by this attitude has actually alienated large segments, even of Israeli Jewry, from religion altogether. Hoping to strengthen the cause of Orthodoxy in America, the Orthodox leadership in America has endorsed the claim and outlook of the Chief Rabbinate of Israel, which is unacceptable to the rest of Jewry. This had led to a deepening split of Jewry along denominational lines, something which is contrary to the spirit of Judaism. It is equally contrary to the spirit of America, which has always recognized unity in diversity and has followed the spirit of cooperation.

American Orthodox Jewry might well fulfill a great function, both in setting the example of life and in developing thought. This can come to pass if it comes to grips intellectually and realistically with the problems of our time, and if it maintains contact with other branches of Jewry, as equals.

Orthodox Jewry *can* provide thinkers. From the rabbis of the Talmud through Maimonides, Mendelssohn, and Samson Raphael Hirsch, it produced such leaders, who advanced the frontiers of traditional thought because they were equally aware of the world around them. Yet they were uncompromisingly observant of the Law. In the vision of Rabbi Abraham Isaac Kook, late Chief Rabbi (1865–1935) of what is now Israel, we find similar wisdom. He was a mystic who built the secular Zionist enterprise into his own, entirely religious system of God's plan. Thus even the most secular activity in building the Land was given religious meaning and value. Such leaders may yet emerge.

It would be unfortunate for Orthodoxy in America to lose touch with the rest of American Jewry. The three branches of American Jewry can sustain each other if they come to recognize each other. Solomon Schechter, head of the Conservative Jewish Theological Seminary, once speaking at a convocation of the reform Hebrew Union College, spoke of the disagreements as "loyal opposition." Opposition and disagreement may remain, but the dialogue may never cease.

Reconstructionism

Reconstructionism is a philosophy of American Jewry that takes into account all these elements and bases itself on the American experience, the unity of Judaism, the impact of science, the significance of Israel, and the centrality of the people. Reconstructionism as a school of thought and movement was founded by MORDECAI KAPLAN (born 1881). Mordecai Kaplan sees the Jews as a people not in any way chosen, but simply imbued with the will to live and to contribute to the welfare of humanity. Judaism is not simply a religion, but an "evolving religious civilization." This civilization enhances the lives of its followers, making their lives more meaningful. It is religious, for it is impossible to remove religion from it, as religion is expressed in every one of its facets; it is civilization for it expresses itself in a totality of forms, in language, literature, art, music, even cuisine. It never stands still but evolves. God is seen in naturalistic terms. He is the Power which makes me follow ever higher ideals; I must feel Him. Inspired by Him, I must make a contribution for man's and society's salvation, not in a world to come, but here and now.

Since Judaism is not seen as the religion of a chosen people, nor God seen in anthropomorphic terms, what becomes of the Mitzvot? Kaplan answers, they are *sancta,* holy symbols. To us Americans, the flag is a sanctum, a symbol representing our history and our ideals. Thus, for Jews, the Sabbath (which removes the burden of work) became a symbol of freedom and a challenge to work for universal human freedom. If a Jew can no longer see any meaning in a Mitzvah, if it is no longer a sanctum for him, he is free to discard it. What matters is that a Jew be committed to the survival of the Jewish people and its civilization. The nonreligious Jew is valued as much as is the religious one. The value of Judaism lies not in its doctrines, but in what it does to the Jew. It must be able to give him inner strength, pride, peace of mind, and creative ability in following ideals.

The value of Judaism is thus seen pragmatically. The ideal of the good society is attained in a true democracy, and since America is the workshop of such a democracy, it has reached a higher state of perfection than have other countries and systems. The Jew, as an American, must therefore attach himself proudly to America as his country; he has the privilege of living in two congenial civilizations, the American and the Jewish. To Kaplan, the great documents of our American history are equally "scriptures" with the books of the Bible. Both of them call their adherents to build an ever-improved and never-finished society.

As can be seen, Mordecai Kaplan is strongly and consciously influenced by the philosophy of John Dewey. His is a system of thought developed on the soil of American thought. Like Dewey, Kaplan is a pragmatist, naturalistic thinker, and fervently patriotic as an American, which compels him to criticize our flaws. At the same time, he is utterly dedicated to the ideal of the Land of Israel and the Jewish *people.*

Here is a true synthesis of American and Jewish thought. We recognize the call of the prophets in conjunction with the ideals of the Founding Fathers. God-Torah-Mitzvot-Land have all been woven into a seamless garment, and yet this philosophy can appeal to the scientifically schooled modern Jew. Here lies its strength, but also a reason for its limited acceptance by the masses. God seen in naturalistic terms may be too abstract for them and the whole system may be too philosophical.

Kaplan's philosophy has remained a guide to leaders and rabbis and has fused a number of Conservative and Reform rabbis, opening the door of dialogue between the groups. In this manner it has had an indirect but strong influence on American Jewry. It is an evidence that Judaism is capable of reconstruction, and its name, "Reconstructionism," is well suited to it. At this time, it is a fully developed answer to the spiritual needs of modern Jews. As a movement it has begun to branch out, organizing fellowships and congregations under its ideology, and providing its own prayer books and literature.

Other men of distinction and champions of Jewish rights and of social justice in general were to emerge: Louis Marshall (1856–1929), lawyer and advocate of Jewish equality; Louis Brandeis (1856–1941), Supreme Court Justice, defender of the people, and ardent Zionist; Rabbi Stephen Wise (1874–1944), champion of universal justice and founder of a rabbinical school (Jewish Institute of Religion) to serve all branches, but later merged with Hebrew Union College; Henrietta Szold (1860–1941), who became instrumental in bringing thousands of Jewish children to Israel, rescuing them from Hitler's clutches; and Samuel Gompers (1850–1924), founder of the American Federation of Labor (1886).

Jewish Organizations

Defense was also required. As early as 1843, when Christian fraternal orders refused to take Jews, the Jewish order B'nai B'rith was founded; it spread all over the world, and has strengthened the internal fiber of Jews through education while organizing their defense against discrimination as well. The American Jewish Committee (1906) and American and World Jewish Congress (1933 and 1936) serve similar defense purposes. In the twenties, when the fraudulent pamphlet, "Protocols of the Elders of Zion" (originally directed against Napoleon III, it was adapted to make it seem that the Jews had a plan for world domination) was given wide publicity by Jew-haters, a great deal of defense work had to be done; in some ways, it has had to be continued.

The Jews in the Armed Services have been served by the Jewish Welfare Board, which is also the sponsor of Jewish Community Centers, similar to YMCA's (1917). Finally, as a true sign of full acculturation, Jews have organized a university open to students of all races and creeds, Brandeis University in Waltham, Mass. (1948). There are many other organizations such as the Zionist Organization with its very active women's branch, *Hadassah,* fraternal orders, and book clubs.

There is a great deal of proliferation among Jewish organizations, a sign of the diversity of interests, perhaps also of the power drives of individuals, and a resulting lack of unity. We have seen that every congregation is fully independent.

The one unifying element is philanthropy. The work of the United Jewish Appeal has been unexcelled by its scope and the number of people saved and rehabilitated. Here, American Jewry has responded with true sacrificial nobility to the demands of the hour.

In contrast, the Synagogue Council of America, supposedly the spokesman of all religious organizations, has remained weak and impotent due to the rivalries of its constituent groups. Laymen and lay organizations, thus, are the spokesmen of religious Jewry. But this is historically conditioned, and the result of a great deal of factionalism. A true dialogue between the various branches of religious Jewry has yet to come.

Post-War Challenges

The devastation of Jewish life throughout the world resulting from Hitler's extermination program provided American Jewry with a twofold challenge: First, it had to provide homes and a new start for the multitude of refugees not only in the United States, but in other parts of the world. They were all destitute, and only American Jewry had the resources to restore them. Secondly, it had to give help on the widest scale to the impoverished Jewish communities in many lands, assistance to young settlements that sprang up as a result of migration, and aid to the upbuilding of Israel. These challenges were fully accepted in a response of outstanding generosity. Israel, the communities in Europe, and the fast-growing Jewish communities of South America owe their emergence and development to American Jewish aid. The Land of Israel could not have been redeemed, nor could its institutions have been developed in such unique fashion, without the unstinting support of American Jews. The South American Jewish community, which has begun to come to life through the leadership of German Jews and rabbis, has been aided spiritually by the establishment of religious training centers, including a rabbinical seminary organized and staffed by Americans. The kinship of the Jewish people was thus affirmed, the Mitzvah of providing life was exemplified, the love of the Land was abundantly reaffirmed, and Torah was planted abroad.

Yet, American Jewry, having come of age so suddenly, finds itself faced with a second challenge, to provide spiritual guidance and leadership, to develop a pattern of Jewish theology and life keyed to our time, and by living a truly Jewish life, to provide the model for the others. This has not been achieved. American Jews, in their overwhelming majority native born, have become fully acculturated and assimilated, belonging generally to the middle class of society. Anti-Semitism, though far from extinct, seems to be receding. Jewish "defense organizations" such as the Anti-Defamation League, are dealing with anti-Semitism in conjunction with their general purpose of combatting prejudice wherever it may be found, against whomever it may be directed. While ethnical distinctions among Americans are disappearing and ethnical subcultures vanishing, the religious division of Americans is regarded as permanent, legitimate, and valuable. This includes Judaism. The American Jewish community thus is seeing itself primarily as a religious group, an outlook which is destined to fashion its character increasingly as time goes on. This will leave less and less of a Jewish rationale for ethnically motivated Jews and for intellectuals who are opposed to religion because it contradicts science.

We also find a certain amount of conversion *to* Judaism, a result of the fluidity in religious movement among Americans combined with the recognition of Judaism as simply a religion. The emergence of American Jewry as a religion (and this concept exists generally, notwithstanding a sense of kinship to the rest of Jewry) holds the danger of leading to an alienation from Israel. Israelis see all of Jewry as a nationality, hopefully expecting that the majority of Jews will settle in Israel eventually. American Jews will support Israel, but have no intention of being anything but Americans. The Land is simply seen as a spiritual force.

The general religious outlook of American Jews thus resembles that of the average American. They affirm their belongingness to Judaism and the majority is affiliated with a congregation (though a sizable minority is not), but there is no great religious fervor as might be expressed in regular attendance at worship, home observance of Mitzvot, and extensive study of Torah. Although children are sent to religious schools and made *Bar Mitzvah,* and their parents hope they will find Jewish mates, in daily practice there is little Jewish content. Yet, there exists a feeling that one must work for Judaism. Numerous beautiful synagogues have been built, but most of them are empty much of the year. The urge to *do* something (in typically American pragmatic style) has led to a proliferation of charitable, social, and service organizations that are sharply competing with each other for membership and recognition.

Are we to see in these developments the symptoms of spiritual strain, a weariness perhaps consequent to the trials of the age?

To a certain degree, perhaps we are justified in so interpreting them. There are strong indications, however, that Judaism may actually be going through a period of an internal reassessment preliminary to the emergence of new forces and orientations in a revival of its eternal heritage, and in an effort to give this heritage its full relevance for our time. In the meanwhile, action fills the need for expression.

B'nai B'rith has embarked on an all-encompassing program of education, including student foundations (Hillel House), youth camps, and an adult study program. A day-school (parochial school) movement is growing. With slowly increasing emphasis, congregations have been expanding their adult educational work in response to the demand of the people, a demand that is felt rather than forcibly expressed. While American Jewry has not yet risen to its function as a spiritual guide to world Jewry, it has begun to bring its spiritual resources to bear in South America and even in Israel.

Reform rabbis are struggling earnestly to develop a liberal theology acceptable to the modern Jew. They are equally striving to evolve a set of guidelines for the restoration of religious practices in the lives of individuals, and, above all, in Jewish homes. Solomon Freehof, a great Reform rabbi and Talmudic scholar, has actually been issuing Responsa (decisions on Jewish law and practice) in reply to inquiries addressed to him by Reform Jews and congregations who are seeking once again the guidance of religious law.

So far, only Mordecai Kaplan's "Reconstructionism" provides a comprehensive system of theology and action, fusing the ideas and traditions of Judaism with those of American democracy and building them into the structure of modern American life. But ABRAHAM HESCHEL has met with widespread response as well. Heschel's ideas stand in contrast to Kaplan's. Where Kaplan is linking his thought to American pragmatism and bases it on naturalistic reasoning, Heschel goes back to his own experiences in the (unhappily lost) environment of the Jewish communities of Eastern Europe. Life in Mitzvot and Torah filled the Jew of Eastern Europe with an awareness of God. His heart and emotions provided the answers to his quest for God, a response to God's call to him. He knew that even as he needed God, God needed him. In living before Him, he found the reason for doing so. Out of their experiences through taking hold of Torah, the Jews of the large Eastern European community became aware of their chosenness. Judaism unfolded out of its inner life forces. We may call Heschel's approach existential and, perhaps, romantic. In moving language, Heschel wishes to awaken Jewry to this outlook, to the leap to God in performance of Mitzvah, to a response to God who calls them. In a way, he resembles Buber, who also drew his strength from the life of Eastern European Jewry and from Hasidism with its mystical bent. Like Buber he takes into account the thoughts of the non-Jewish world, and like him again, he has been widely read by non-Jewish thinkers. Unlike Buber, however —somewhat reminding us of Rosenzweig—he demands faithful obedience to the traditional laws of Torah. To Heschel the function of Judaism is to build *time,* that of the world to build *space.* The Jewish function can be fulfilled by a leap into Mitzvah.

To the anxiety ridden of our time, both Jew and Christian, the magic of Heschel's words alone conjures a deep emotional response. To a generation of Jews that once knew (though dimly, perhaps) the emotional shelter of Eastern European life and piety, he offers a glimpse of a world lost forever, that offered spiritual peace. But will Jews be willing to follow him, all the way or part way? Dedicated to reason, immersed in the life of the total community, they may find themselves not quite prepared to do so. Yet Heschel holds out a challenge similar to the one Franz Rosenzweig presented to German Jewry during the years of turmoil after World War I. While fully remaining in touch with the total of Western civilization, Jews are to evolve their way of life not so much out of the dialogue with the world, but out of their own inner forces, which may be felt, experienced through life, and yet not capable of being put in words.

Historical Summary and Conclusions

This rapid and admittedly sketchy outline of Jewish history raises the question of a purpose in the history. Some fundamentalistic Christian theologians might have said that Jewish dispersion is the divine punishment for their rejection of Christ. (See next chapter.) Jews reject this outlook categorically. First of all, it does not account for the migrations of Jews from the days of Abraham to Jacob, nor for the Babylonian Exile. Furthermore, is it a punishment? The rulers of the world often invited the Jews into their countries for the sake of hoped-for economic benefits. When these had been attained, the same rulers and countries—incapable of seeing the spiritual benefits—eliminated the Jews. How greatly they could have increased their stability by fashioning with inclusion of the Jews a society in which all groups might live in peace with each other! Jewish settlements offered the opportunity to the majority for "Christian living," for recognition of other people's convictions and practices, as these did not interfere with the life of society. Only America understood this; it may be a reason for its greatness.

Jews, feeling a true spirit of patriotism, and yet linked to each other in kinship, seem to have acquired a balance which the world badly needs: that of full patriotism, yet eschewing the excesses of chauvinism, through which so much unhappiness has come to mankind; all of humanity will gain by acquiring this balance. These are but a few elements, not including the cultural values given by the Jews to society as a whole. They have been fighters for social justice in the spirit of the prophets. They have, indeed, an ethical mission—as the Reform leader Abraham Geiger would have it—and they have been carrying it out, not as individuals, who are woefully weak and frail, but as a group, throughout history. They are, as Halevi claimed, the heart of mankind beating for all; and they can fulfill their task best if they are permitted to be themselves and to evolve their ideas out of a fruitful dialogue with their environment.

Like many persons impelled by ideals, they have suffered for them. This is not punishment but the concomitant of the commitment. Every pioneer, especially those pioneering in ideas, has known such suffering. This is the story of the Suffering Servant (of whom Isaiah speaks). It speaks for the power of their ideals that the world has never been able to overlook them. Numerically, so insignificant (c. 14 million), they can be praised or reviled, but never forgotten, for ideas do not depend on numbers.

To convert them, as Czarist Russia tried, would be a sin against the order of the world, against God himself. The Jews are a historical people. The elements of history are seared into their consciousness and conscience, that out of them they may help fashion a better tomorrow for all of humanity, even though the individual Jew may not be aware of it at all.

Unlike some other peoples of the world, Jews have had no capacity for bearing hate. We have seen colonial people rise up in brutality against the white man, remembering in hate their former state of servitude. Jews have borne no hate, nor do they bear it. Even as God forgives, so must they, and it has become part of their being. Working with the oppressor of yesterday, they hope only that in joint effort the vision of the future may be made more real with the years, and that vision is Eternal Peace.

6 THE IMPACT OF CHRISTIANITY

THE following brief discussion of Christianity's impact on Jewish history should be recognized by the non-Jewish reader as an analysis of the manner in which Christianity has *appeared* to Jews. It may surprise and at times even disturb the Christian reader, as he may find concepts and ideas questioned which to him are self-evident, as he has been brought up on them since childhood. It is my belief, however, that he will want to know and understand in order that a fruitful dialogue may become a durable reality.

The emergence of a genuine dialogue between the faiths may be considered one of the positive developments of our own time. It holds great promise of true human fellowship and brotherly concern among the faithful of these two religions, as among all men. In spirit and in character it is totally different from the religious "disputations" convened by the Catholic Church during the Middle Ages, whose outcome was a foregone conclusion, and whose purpose was simply to prove to the rulers, the world, and the Jews the "error" of the Synagogue and the triumphant truth of the Church. The spirit of these disputations can still be noticed in the sculptures on great cathedrals, such as at Strasbourg: the Synagogue in collapse, her eyes blind, her staff broken; the Church holding her banner aloft, with crowned head and proud eyes confidently viewing both time and eternity. Seen in this manner, and treated harshly on account of their "blindness," the Jews were naturally afraid of the Church.

The fortunate change that has come into being within our own time can be ascribed to a number of causes, among them the scientific temper of the twentieth century, the deepening of the democratic outlook which called for freedom of religion, and the secularization of life in general. The spread of atheism and communism actually called for a spirit of cooperation among the religious forces in the struggle against God-denying ideologies and forces. The holocaust of World War II, claiming six million Jews as victims of the accumulated impact of centuries of anti-Semitism, weighed heavily upon the conscience of humanity and aroused Christianity to a new spirit and attitude.

82

The Roman Catholic Statement

On the Jewish side, Martin Buber, among others, became a strong
spokesman in favor of a meaningful dialogue between the two faiths. On
the Christian side, Pope John XXIII became its strong advocate, placing
his authority and the great power of his office in the service of the task.
When he convoked the Ecumenical Council (Vatican II), for the
purpose of updating the teachings of the Church to meet present-day
requirements in the spirit of the Church's evolving tradition, he
specifically included in its agenda a statement on the Jews. It was to be
designed to eradicate long-established misconceptions about them, and to
eliminate opinions, beliefs, and practices which had done them harm.
Pope John died while the Council was in progress, before a statement on
the Jews could be promulgated. His successor, Paul VI, officially issued
the decree in the fall of 1965.

This statement on the Jews has many excellent points, offering and
inviting the dialogue between Catholics and Jews in discussion and life.
However, the statement, as a result of extended debate, bears the marks
of the conflict of ideas within the Council itself. Liberals were arraigned
against conservatives; bishops from Arab lands transmitted the heavy
pressure in their countries against any statement which would place Jews
and Judaism in a new light and erase ancient prejudices held by the
population. The concessions made to opposing views within the council
have been deplored by many progressive Catholic leaders, as well as
Jews.

The decree itself consists of five sections, of which only the fourth
deals specifically with the Jews. The first section outlines the purpose
and underlying philosophy of the decree. The next two deal with the
contributions of various religions, such as Hinduism, Buddhism, and
Islam, stating in straightforward language the insights of these faiths
which the Catholic Church considers valuable for itself and for all
mankind, followed by an exhortation to the Catholic faithful to engage
in prudent dialogue and collaboration with adherents of these religions.
The final section is a call to universal love; it reproves all discrimination
on account of race, color, condition in life, or religion. The fourth
section on the Jews is the longest and most involved. The most salient
points are condensed here:

> The Church acknowledges the spiritual ties binding it to the Jews through
> Abraham, the Patriarchs, Moses, and the prophets; it holds them to be
> the beginning of her own (the Church's).

> The exodus from Egypt foreshadows the salvation of the Church; the re-
> conciliation of Jew and Gentile is in the cross of Christ. Recalling the words
> of St. Paul (Romans 9:4–5) that "theirs is the sonship and the glory and

the covenants and the law and the worship and the promises, the fathers and Christ according to the flesh," recalling also that disciples and Apostles sprang from the Jewish people, the relationship is acknowledged. . . .

Jerusalem did not recognize the time of its visitation; the Jews did not accept the Gospel in large numbers, many even opposing its spreading; yet God holds the Jews most dear for the sake of their fathers, for God does not repent His gifts or the calls He issues.

In company with the Apostle (Paul), the Church awaits the day when all people will address the Lord in a single voice.

On the basis of the common patrimony, the Council recommends and wishes to foster understanding and respect resulting from Biblical and theological studies and from a fraternal dialogue.

The document points out that:

what happened in Christ's passion cannot be charged against all Jews then alive without distinction, nor against the Jews of today.

It also states that the Jewish authorities and those who followed their lead pressed for the death of Christ. It affirms that:

Although the Church is the new people of God, the Jews should not be presented as rejected and accursed of God, as if this followed from the Holy Scriptures. All should see to it that in catechetical work or in preaching nothing be taught that does not conform to the truth of the Gospel and the spirit of Christ.

Rejecting persecution against any man, mindful of the patrimony shared with the Jews, moved, not by political reasons but by the Gospel's spiritual love, the Church decries [*deplorare* in Latin, to cry out, lament] hatred, persecution, and displays of anti-Semitism directed against Jews at any time and by anyone.

The final paragraph asserts the abiding belief of the Church that Christ underwent His passion and death freely, because of the sins of men and out of infinite love, in order that all might reach salvation, and that it is, therefore, the burden of the Church's preaching to proclaim the cross of Christ as the sign of God's all-embracing love and as the fountain from which every grace flows.

An evaluation by *Life* magazine (December 17, 1965, p. 74, © 1965 Time Inc.) discloses the lack of decisiveness of the decree as seen by a non-Jewish publication. At the same time, it invokes the memory of Pope XXIII, which hovers over the achievement. *Life* states:

The declaration exonerates the Jewish people of corporate guilt for the crucifixion, and thus removes an old root of anti-Semitism. But however necessary and just, the exoneration is superficial and, as Hans Morgenthau has pointed out, does scant justice either to the unique source of Jewish durability through history or to the Catholic Church's affiliation to that uniqueness in the undoubtedly Jewish person of Jesus and his Apostles. The council would have done better simply to repeat Pius XI's statement—"Spiritually we are Semites"—or that of John XXIII in welcoming a Jewish delegation—"I am Joseph, your brother!"

Some Jewish Reactions

Jewish reaction to the decree was divided. A number of Jews were indifferent to it. Claiming that the Catholic Church cannot "absolve" the Jews of a crime they had not committed in the first place (which the decree actually does not intend to do; it goes further in stating that the Jews cannot be *charged* with it, which means they should not have been *accused* of it in the course of history), they maintain that in the twentieth century anti-Semitism is less affected by theological considerations than by social, political, and economic factors. To these Jews, the decree was of no basic import.

There is good reason to regard this criticism as based on the wrong assumptions. Results of a long-term study on anti-Semitism, undertaken by the Survey Research Center of the University of California and released in 1966, indicate that the majority of Christians who are anti-Jewish base their attitude on religious teachings of their churches learned in childhood. It was found that this attitude, once instilled at an early age, is retained permanently and cannot be eradicated. One of the primary sources of anti-Jewish attitudes is the teaching that the Jews were guilty of the death of Christ. The declaration of the Vatican Council must therefore be considered as being of the greatest importance as a weapon against anti-Semitism.

Another group of Jews resented it. They felt that what was needed after the slaughter of six million Jews was a gracious and generous affirmation of the Church, pointing out its affinity with the Jews, and the value of a faith that had fully claimed the allegiance of millions even unto death. This should have been combined with an outright affirmation that the Jews were not guilty in the death of Jesus and that they were not rejected. It should have culminated in an unequivocal *condemnation* of anti-Semitism and a call to love, dialogue, and cooperation on equal terms. Instead, they considered the document to be ambiguous in many of its pronouncements, with overtones of condescension toward Jewish religion and its worth in the modern world.

To those most deeply concerned with a dialogue, the document offers a great deal of hope. The statement on anti-Semitism, though not as decisive as it might have been, will be helpful. If even one soul is kept from harm by it, it is worth it. The affirmation of Jewish corporate innocence in the death of Jesus is an act of long overdue justice, proclaiming what the Jews had maintained throughout. This goes also for the rebuke of any belief that the Jews were accursed and rejected by God. The spirit, calling for friendship and brotherhood, is recognized as genuine, and sincerely welcomed.

Yet the document as a whole was something of a letdown. Ideally, so it was felt, recognition of religious plurality as a permanent part of the divine order of things might have created a perfect background for a dialogue. This might have been difficult for the Church at the time. However, it was not necessary or relevant to dwell constantly on the position and hopes of the Church in the context of this document, designed as an immediate and practical guide in mutual contact. Both the Jew and the Catholic (reading, for instance, the statement of the Church's hope that all will address the Lord in one single voice, reinforced by the profession that the Church must always preach the cross of Christ) may feel their dialogue to be hedged in by assumptions and conditions: the Catholic, that he is to be a missionary, the Jew, that his tradition may not be regarded as equal in worth, and that he has to be on guard against missionary intents.

Statements that the Church considers herself God's elect, that patriarchs, prophets, and the Exodus forecast its salvation, are elements of Catholic and Christian beliefs. Woven into the fabric of a document designed as guidelines in a dialogue, they may create the impression that they are to be understood as "*the* terms" by which the dialogue is to be conducted.

Jews feel that God holds them dear not only on account of the fathers. He holds them dear, first of all, because, like all of humanity, they are His children, and, like all of humanity, equally beloved by Him. He holds them dear for the ideals they represent, the lives they sanctify by their steadfastness in witnessing, the faith they humbly offer to Him. They see in Judaism not a forerunner of Christianity, but a faith and a way of life which has great truths to offer to modern man, and which, out of its fruits, can offer him help and guidance.

The insertion of the statement about the pressure of the Jewish authorities and their followers in connection with the death of Jesus is combined with the criticism that not a few opposed the gospel. Who the authorities were is not specified, nor how they came to hold their power. Yet this is a material element in judgment, since at the time of Jesus' death so many of the authorities, placed in power by the Romans, were utterly repugnant to the Jews. Caiphas is the best example. The Jewish leaders are blamed for dissuading their people from joining a new faith; this, actually, was their duty. The Church (and, in the political field, every political party) has always claimed and exercised the same right.

Traditional Christianity regards Jesus' ministry, and particularly the crucifixion, as cosmic events of such powerful universal witness that no one of good sense could remain unaffected by them. Judaism does not share this view. Whereas it may appear incomprehensible to a Christian why the rabbis should oppose the spread of the gospel when faced with such evidence, to the Jews there was no such evidence.

Jews might ask, does the statement cast a shadow on their revered masters? For a dialogue to be real, each party has to make a great effort to consider the thoughts, feelings, philosophy, and inner workings of the other while at the same time retaining its own perspective. The former element does not fully emerge from the document, hence the unease it creates. This, of course, is the result of compromise. Some of the statements found their way into the document in an effort to satisfy the divergent opinions of the Council fathers. Their impact on the dialogue may not be as powerful as it may appear in dissecting the statement. Time will make this evident.

Many Jews felt that the exoneration of Jewry in "what happened in His passion" and the statement that Jews should not be considered rejected and accursed of God "as if this followed from Holy Scripture" shows a certain weakness, lack of clarity, and might even permit blaming of the Jews, if not on authority of Scriptures, then on that of Church Fathers, who so often thundered against them as killers of Christ. Many had anticipated that, after all that happened under Hitler, the Church would pronounce as an act of justice an outright *condemnation* of anti-Semitism; "decrying" it might be too weak, especially as the term "condemn" was found in an earlier draft. In addition, the positive element of giving thanks to the Jews (also to be found in an earlier draft of the statement) is no longer included.

It should be remembered, however, that the Decree was promulgated as an internal document guiding the Catholic faithful. It had to take into account the total theology of the Catholic Church. To the Jews, the gospels are not holy, to the Catholic they are holy "gospel truth," allowing reinterpretation but not a challenge of the veracity of the account itself. The survival of Jewry does indeed pose a serious theological problem to Catholics, whereas Christianity presents no such problem to Jews. Jews can hold that the emergence of Christianity operates under God's plan, but Catholics are confronted with theological principles holding that theirs is an exclusive revelation, and the question of the continuation of Judaism as a living faith must be thought through again by them since it has been held that a new dispensation had superseded, and thereby made unnecessary, the older—Jewish—one, and largely deprived its adherents of their continuing function under the divine plan.

These are indeed problems with which a dialogue may be concerned. It should equally be remembered that the Decree on the Jews is meaningful in the context of other decrees, particularly the "Declaration on Religious Freedom, on the Right of the Person and of Communities to Social and Civic Freedom in Matters Religious." In it, the Council declares that the right to religious freedom has its foundation in the very dignity of the human person, as this dignity is known through the revealed word of God and by reason itself. It is also stated that "Religious communities have the right not to be hindered in their public teaching and witness to their faith, whether by the spoken or by the written word." The significance of this proclamation in connection with the declaration of the Jews is great, particularly in those countries where in the past the free profession of faith in open affirmation was hedged about by problems, laws, suspicions, and misunderstandings, especially Spain.

Jews may have wished to have a clearer statement because for so many centuries they were subject to the whims of rulers and potentates that they have become afraid of any ambiguities leaving the door open to interpretations adverse to them, should times change. A clear-cut declaration would make this impossible.

Yet it should not be forgotten that, with this document, walls which had become higher and ever more forbidding with the centuries have crumbled. A new spirit and a new direction are in evidence, and it is this direction that matters. For the first time Catholics will be able to learn what Jews really believe and hold dear; Jews will be able and should make the effort to find out the basic principles, beliefs, and practices of Catholics. In this atmosphere of the dialogue, misunderstandings and apprehensions may disappear, to be replaced by mutual respect and affection.

Shortly after the end of the Council, Cardinal Cushing of Boston was quoted as stating, "We have to get all this ecumenical spirit out of the hands of the scholars and get it down to the grass roots." In practice, interpretations of the decree may all look different. The tremendous spirit of good will is certainly evident on all levels of Catholicism. It emerged from the soul of Pope John, speaks out of the work of Cardinal Bea (who prepared the draft of the statement on the Jews), was made manifest by the almost unanimous push of the American bishops for a truly far-reaching document. On a personal level, I found it when I wrote to the Vatican for information; the help of the local bishop, Leo T. Maher and his chancery staff have been extremely valuable. In this spirit the various reactions within Jewry have been mentioned. A true dialogue calls for openness; then misunderstandings can be cleared up and confusion avoided. A fraternal dialogue not only permits, it *asks* for a critical position. Some Jews asked, "Is it going to last?" referring to the spirit of good will. By its motivation, transcending whatever its shortcomings, the decree invokes the spirit of the human soul among those who will carry it out. What it actually is will become evident from the use to which it is put under the leadership of the bishops and in its enactment by the parish clergy. The spirit guiding the pronouncements redressing the past and calling for a new attitude in the future may prove to be much stronger than the terms that seem to restrict, and "as it lasts," may lead to a revision of the letter itself at some time in the future.

In the light of this spirit, the leading Protestant Churches have passed similar resolutions. A stumbling block in Jewish–Christian relationships has thus been removed. In addition, the anti-Semite will be deprived of a source of agitation. Having based their allegations against the Jews on a foundation of "theological anti-Semitism," they found support in it for their various additional "reasons." We would be too optimistic in assuming that anti-Semitism will automatically be eliminated by this spirit, but a mighty support for it will have been removed, and Christians will find themselves challenged by religious duty and obligation to do battle against this terrible evil, which has caused so much suffering throughout the ages to millions of innocents, culminating in the martyrdom of the Jews in our own century.

The statement of the Christian churches simply expresses what Jews have maintained throughout: they are not guilty in the death of Jesus, and God has never rejected them. Deeply convinced that theirs is a God-pleasing, living faith, the Jews strive to keep their own within the fold, and will oppose any efforts toward their conversion.

As Reinhold Niebuhr, among leading Christians, has pointed out in *Pious and Secular America* (New York: Charles Scribner's Sons, 1958, pp. 107f. and 111ff.):

> If we measure the two faiths by their moral fruits the Jewish faith does not fall short . . . [Missionary] activities among Jews . . . are wrong . . . not only because they are futile and have little fruit to boast for their exertions. They are wrong because . . . the two faiths, despite differences, are sufficiently alike for the Jew to find God more easily in terms of his own religious heritage than by subjecting himself to the hazards of guilt feelings involved in a conversion to a faith, which, whatever its excellencies, must appear to him as a symbol of an oppressive majority culture.

Niebuhr's position does not, however, seem to represent the majority view of Christian theologians and people. The idea that Jews must be "saved" by being converted is still widespread. Connected with this outlook is the tendency on the part of some theologians to depict pre-Christian Jewry as endowed with serious faults of character and conduct. Some, for instance, see the message of the prophets as addressed to a stubborn, morally deficient people, rather than to a people for whom the prophets had set such high standards that any deviation from them appeared to the prophets as great sinfulness and wickedness. The former view ignores the fact that the rest of the peoples of antiquity had not even attained the ethical standard of the Jewish people to whom the prophets spoke. It also overlooks that the Torah is to be understood in Jewish terms, as a product of the Jewish experience. Any attempt to interpret the Torah in Christian terms is not acceptable to Jews.

Naturally, the right of any religion to make converts may not be challenged by any other religion, but neither should the right to resist it, and the stern efforts by the leaders to prevent it. This applies to Christianity, Judaism, and all others. The most fruitful dialogue will be based on the conviction that every religion has "the truth" for its own faithful, accompanied by a frank recognition of differences. It will require love and respect for the other's faith as being acceptable, pleasing, and worthy to God, and will embrace ideas such as those of Niebuhr, whom we have quoted, and men of like mind. It is to be hoped that their views may not only become more prevalent among theologians, but truly effective among Christians as a whole.

Jesus and the Jews

In this spirit we shall try to view briefly some of the impact of Christianity upon Judaism as seen by a Jew.

The effects of Exile were immediate and powerful, calling for direct action. The impact of Christianity was slow in emerging, gradual, and calling for endurance. Jesus himself may have passed through his lifetime without being known either personally or by his teachings to the overwhelming majority of his Jewish contemporaries in Judaea or to the millions in the Diaspora. Neither Josephus, the meticulous chronicler of Jewish history during this period, nor the Jewish philosopher Philo make mention of him. (A statement in Josephus is generally considered a later addition by an unknown, possibly Christian, writer.)

In the Gospels themselves we find contradictions regarding the year of his birth and crucifixion. The basic elements of his trial and conviction, as related in the Gospels, do not square with Jewish law and practice; fictional elements must have crept into the story. All this indicates that Jesus lived so simple a life that actual records were not available even as early as the Gospels. The circle of those who knew him well was small, and the word-of-mouth tradition transmitted by his disciples was subject to both embroidery and error, as in any oral tradition. The disciples were Jews; those who wrote about him later were not Jews in many cases. All of them had to whitewash the Roman government if Christianity was to be tolerated at all. Even Pilate, one of the most cruel and venal of procurators, is exonerated. As we have seen, he was so cruel that Rome had enough of him and recalled him. But he is shown washing his hands, thus performing a Jewish ceremony symbolically pleading for remission of sin in connection with the death of an innocent man. The ceremony has been misunderstood, however. (See Deuteronomy 21:1–9, dealing with an unknown murder victim found at a crossroads in the country-side; the elders of the closest city wash their hands, symbolically expressing their innocence of this crime due to lack of protection and help extended within their territory; then they ask divine forgiveness for the crime *having been* committed by unknown hands, not one they *are about* to sanction by consciously approving it.) We cannot assume Pilate suddenly adopted a Jewish practice, considering how deeply he hated the Jews and how determined he was to antagonize them by offending their religious beliefs. (Unless, of course, he had heard about the practice and repeated it in mockery, which throws an entirely different light on his action: it then becomes a blasphemous provocation of Jewish tradition.) It is equally hard to assume that the Jews would suddenly adopt a new religious principle, namely in accepting guilt for their children and for future generations. This would run counter to the fundamental conviction of the Jews, so firmly instilled in them by the prophets, that there is no such thing as an inherited guilt (as discussed in connection with Jeremiah and Ezekiel, pp. 13–14). We may consider Caiphas a tool of Rome; he was appointed by Pilate and was dismissed upon the procurator's recall. Otherwise the Jews had no jurisdiction.

The trial of Jesus by a Jewish court is so difficult to explain that Samuel Sandmel writes after close study, "The entire trial business is legendary and tendentious" (Samuel Sandmel, *A Jewish Understanding of the New Testament;* Cincinnati: Hebrew Union College, 1957, p. 128). The proceedings run counter to all the existing laws of trial procedures, evidence, and so on; in short, they flouted the entire body of legislation, which was strictly binding and permitted of no exceptions.

Solomon Zeitlin has advanced a different theory, which has the advantage of cutting through many of the inconsistencies, especially those of the discrepancies between the trial of Jesus as reported and the basic provisions of Jewish criminal law. In his book *Who Crucified Jesus?* (Ed. 4. New York: Bloch Publishing Company, 1964), he arrives at the conclusion, backed up by his researches, that there actually existed two Sanhedrins (supreme courts), one for religious matters, the other for political matters. The Sanhedrin for religious matters was composed of scholars, met at appointed times, was bound by Jewish law, and therefore never sat at night, never handed down a conviction in criminal matters on the day of the trial, hence never held any trial sessions on the day before the Sabbath or any holiday. The other Sanhedrin was government appointed, composed of partisans of the Romans who were willing to give the semblance of legal sanction to acts of the Roman overlord. It could be called into session at any time. After

Jesus had been arrested by the Roman soldiers, the governor, assuming that Jesus was a rebel desiring to make himself "King of the Jews," concluded that he had to be executed, and requested Caiphas, his henchman, to call the political Sanhedrin. Caiphas called the Sanhedrin to meet in his home, where Jesus was hastily convicted to please the Romans. The trumped up charge was blasphemy, although according to *Jewish* law, Jesus had not committed blasphemy at all. With the conviction handed down, the Romans took over again, treating Jesus as a *political* criminal, affixing notification of his "crime" on the cross, and confiscating his clothes as a political offender. (The property of a religious offender was not subject to confiscation.) We may then assume that a crowd of Caiphas' followers might well have been gathered before Pilate and at the crucifixion to provide "popular" support for the actions Pilate was about to take, the cruel execution on the cross. There is abundant evidence in history of dictators acting in this fashion, by so-called popular demand representing the dictator's own will.

After Jesus had died, we find a Jew approaching Pilate: Joseph of Arimathea pleads with Pilate to release the body of Jesus, which was in Roman custody, in order that he might be given burial as Jewish tradition prescribes (Matthew 27:58ff.). There may have been Jews present at the execution, perhaps at the sentencing, too; but who but a rabble or a collaborator would enter the palace of the *gauleiter* Pilate? If some Jews were there, too much has been made of it. No one has connected the Roman legionaries with the entire Roman people. Why then see in those Jews—who had nothing better to do on the eve of Passover than to watch the morbid spectacle of a Roman crucifixion—a representative body of the Jewish people? As for the rest, why should the Jews have thought harshly of Jesus? His teachings were in agreement with the principles of the Pharisees. His disagreements (such as his messianic claims) fell within the framework of permissible divergence of opinion.

Theological Differences

In the Apostle Paul's emphasis on faith as opposed to Mitzvot, we find the beginning of the dissent between the two faiths. But Paul himself was full of pride in his Jewish background and full of love for his Jewish brethren.

In Paul's missionary work, the strong foundations of Christianity's growth were laid; it became widespread, powerful, eventually the official religion of the Roman Empire. Non-Jews quickly outnumbered the Jews in it. They saw in Judaism a rival faith, also engaged in widespread missionary activity. Antagonism developed. As a result of Paul's doctrines, Judaism and Christianity had to go their own ways.

An understanding of some basic differences between the two faiths may help us in the dialogue between Christianity and Judaism. Both religions rest on the same foundation of monotheism. However, Christianity sees God in triune form whereas Judaism conceives of God in the most rigorous unitarian manner. Maimonides points out that God's oneness is so absolute that it goes beyond our human logical conception. (When we speak of one, such as one apple, we still find it composed of parts and qualities; God's oneness is absolute.) He states it in one of his thirteen principles of faith: "I believe in perfect faith that the Creator, blessed be His Name, is One, and that there is no Oneness in any way like His; and He alone is our God, who was, is and will be."

Judaism does not ascribe any bodily form to God. As Maimonides expresses it: "I believe in perfect faith that the Creator, blessed be His Name, is in no way body, and that the concepts of body in no way apply to Him, and that there exists no bodily likeness for Him whatsoever."

Judaism thus does not ascribe any divinity to any human being that ever walked on the earth, as this would be contrary to its concept of God.

Judaism does not accept the idea that the Torah has ever been replaced by a new dispensation. (Concepts held by Reform Jews that parts of Torah are no longer binding do not contradict this principle. To Reform Jews, the Torah is inspired but not literally dictated. It has to be examined on the basis of Biblical scholarship. The basic concept of a *divine* new dispensation therefore does not come into the picture at all and would in any event be rejected by them.)

Jesus himself spoke out against the thought that he had come to abolish the Torah: "Think not that I have come to abolish the law (Torah) and the prophets; I have come not to abolish them but to fulfill them" (Matthew 5:17). To this day the Torah is *not* "*Old* Testament" to the Jew. He does not consider Torah and prophets as forerunners and advent preachers of a new dispensation.

Paul, calling for obedience to God, disagreed with Judaism as to how this obedience would be expressed. The Mitzvah, indispensable to Jews, to him was superseded by faith.

The differences between Christianity and Judaism thus affect basic Jewish concepts of God, Torah, and Mitzvot, which explains the disagreement within the monotheistic principle held by both. Judaism does not have the concept of sacraments as means of divine grace. (In Christianity there is a divergence of views both in regard to sacraments, as such, and in the number of sacraments.)

In Judaism, man can approach God directly and immediately. Every human being is His child, and has direct access to the Father to receive His assured grace, compassion, and love. There is no need for any intermediary; the doctrine therefore is excluded from Jewish belief.

As we have seen, there is no inherited sin according to Judaism. There cannot be an original sin. Thus Judaism disagrees on the need for atonement for original sin. Christ's vicarious atonement for man's original sin is one of the central pillars of Christianity.

Paul maintained that Christ was the fulfilment of Judaism. To the Jews, the reasons we have tried to outline in brief constituted a strong counterindication. Acceptance of the new theology with its implications to them meant extinction of Judaism. They were and are opposed to that. This was not simply a will to live. The Jews have felt that the messianic age has not yet come. The day has not yet arrived "when they will beat their swords into plowshares and their spears into pruning hooks, (when) nation will not lift up sword against nation, neither will they learn war any more" (Micah 4:3).

Judaism does recognize the tremendous work done by Christianity in leading toward this aim. Maimonides points this out among others. Christianity is indeed needed if mankind is to reach its goal. At the same time, Jews feel that their approach is also vitally needed. They are so deeply convinced that their existence is essential to God's gracious will and mankind's need that they have literally staked their individual lives on it.

This pluralistic outlook springs from Jewish doctrine and conviction that the road to salvation does not lead exclusively through its own or any individual faith. "The righteous of all the world's nations have a share in the world to come" is Jewish teaching. Only obedience to basic moral principles is required of all men. These are known as Noahide laws, since they were supposedly imposed as early as Noah. They include: respect for human life, for family and property, for animals as God's creatures, and the existence of law administered justly by just courts. All who abide by these are assured of salvation.

Common Values

The fruitfulness of the dialogue will be enhanced by the ideals which Christians and Jews share, above all the idea of One God, Who is the God of love and mercy. "Have we not all one Father? Has not one God created us? Why then are we faithless to one another, profaning the covenant of our fathers?" the prophet Malachi cries out (Malachi 2:10). From the oneness of God as the Universal Father emerges the covenant of human brotherhood. We may well regard it as significant that the two basic commandments of Torah regulating our relationship to God and fellowman are literally repeated in the New Testament, thus strengthening the bond of common obligation. These commandments are: "Thou shalt love the Lord thy God with all thy heart and all thy soul and all thy might" (Deuteronomy 6:5—Matthew 23:37), and "Thou shalt love thy neighbor as thyself" (Leviticus 19:18—Matthew 23:39).

Out of these and others which will be discussed, there springs the common challenge to establish God in this world, to do battle against injustice, to fight for human equality, as all men are created in the image of God and therefore are brethren. It should not be forgotten that Jews and Christians equally draw their spiritual sustenance from the books of the Bible, the so-called Old Testament.

Both religions have experienced persecution and have produced saints and martyrs by whose example mankind can learn steadfastness in faith. Judaism does not have saints in the manner of the Catholic Church, but it accords this title to those who laid down their lives "for the sanctification of God's Name."

Finding themselves ostracized and defamed for so many centuries, the Jews may also serve as witnesses to the world, proving that faith in God has the power to sustain human strength under the most adverse circumstances, that it can purify human hearts to overcome hate even against persecutors, and that it can safeguard emotional balance and equilibrium. Jews have stood the test of unrelieved adversity for longer periods than any other faith. By this experience, they can support the faithful of all religions in times of testing, whenever they may come.

WELLSPRINGS OF THE
JEWISH SPIRIT II

7 TENAKH: HOLY SCRIPTURES

In the first part we have discussed the internal forces that have shaped Judaism and in the second part sketched in bare outline the basic currents of Jewish history. History and the various environments in which Jews have lived became the stage for the dramatic unfolding of Jewish ideas interacting with those of the surrounding world.

In the following chapters we shall discuss Judaism's own spiritual and literary creations, emerging out of the genius of the people and its heritage, above all Torah, both written and oral. This will enable us to understand the creative tensions and the blending of internal ideas and external forces, and the emergence of new forms and theological concepts held by all or some of the Jews in the contemporary world.

Of all the contributions made by the Jews, they are best known for having given to the world the Holy Scriptures of the Bible. Christians call it *The Old Testament;* Jews, who do not use the New Testament, simply call it The Holy Scriptures, or look at it as the Bible. A Hebrew abbreviation for the Jewish Bible is *Tenakh.* Tenakh is an abbreviation of three words: *Torah, Nevee-im, Ketubim.* These are the three sections making up Holy Scriptures. Torah (in this specific connotation) stands for the Five Books of Moses, the Pentateuch; *Nevee-im* (Prophets) contains the messages of the great prophets of Israel, but also the history leading up to their ministry. *Ketubim* (Collected Writings) is an anthology of a variety of works, including Psalms, Job, and the "Five Scrolls" of Song of Songs, Ruth, Lamentations, Ecclesiastes, and Esther.

Torah

The *Torah* or *Five Books of Moses* is the central source of Jewish law and ethics, guidepost for thought and conduct and for the relationships between man and God and man and man. Hence it is read to the people regularly during the cycle of the year, on Sabbath days, holy days, and every Monday and Thursday, once market days when the farmers came to town and thus could receive instruction in conjunction with their business. It is recited from a handwritten parchment scroll, which is stored in the Ark and removed for recital of its message while the congregation stands in reverence.

We shall not be concerned here with the conclusions of Biblical scholarship, the so-called Biblical criticism, but wish to present an outline of Torah, as its ancient editors understood it, and as they arranged its content and sequence.

1. *Bereshit* (Genesis) is the first book, dealing with creation and the lives of the patriarchs. The story of creation emphasizes the divine origin of the universe, and man's stewardship in it. Rashi, in his commentary to the first verse, points in an equally important, different direction: God tells Israel and the world that He is the Creator, and therefore, the owner of His creation, entitled to distribute it as He pleases. Should the world therefore say you are robbers, having conquered the Land of Israel from the peoples that dwelt in it, then you may tell them: the Land, like all the world, belongs to God who made it, and He has assigned it to us. Thus, in the consciousness of the Jewish people, the Land of Israel is woven into the very first utterance of Torah. Thus Bereshit sets up an historical awareness. The God of creation is God of history.

The very first chapters equally establish the principle of human equality: all mankind is equal before God, and all men must be so treated. "God created one man only," says the Talmud (Mishnah Sanhedrin 4:5), "to teach you that he who destroys one single soul is deemed as having destroyed a whole world, and he who has sustained one single soul is deemed as having sustained a whole world." Furthermore, the rabbis say, "God created only one person to promote peace in the world, that no one may say to his neighbor, my ancestors were more distinguished than thine." In this spirit, history must be fashioned.

The patriarchs appear on the scene; Abraham, confessing the one God, is translated to the land which is promised to his children. Knowing the place where his seed was to grow into an organic society, Abraham and his successors may actually spend large portions of their lives abroad. The Land can exert its influence even as an idea, once its spiritual significance is recognized. Jacob and Joseph, dying abroad and aware of the symbolism of their own lives for their descendants, request to be buried "with their fathers." These men and women are individualists; they have to be in order to stand their ground against the society in which they dwell; they hear God's call, and, in individual response, act upon it; with individualism inevitably goes human error, and these people show themselves all too human on many occasions. This makes them examples; were they perfect we could not follow them. They have

the strength to grow and transcend the shortcomings of their own past.
Thus, in the words of the Talmud, "the deeds of the fathers are the
guideposts for the children."

2. *Shemot* (Exodus) presents the transposition of the life of their
ancestors into the collective experience of the emerging people. They are
molded within a hostile environment in Egypt where they have been
made slaves; they are tested in their perseverance. They are to be a
collective individual, composed of individualists. They are shown the
differences between God-centered individualism which leads to salvation,
and man-centered, selfish individualism, which leads to destruction:
Moses and Pharaoh are the two great protagonists. Then they are
redeemed to find their way back to the Land of Promise.

No people can live without law; as a God-centered people they are to
receive a God-given law. Ten Commandments form the core of this law,
encompassing the relationship of man to both God and his fellow:

1. I am the Lord thy God who brought you out of the Land of Egypt,
   the house of bondage. [God is to be worshipped as God of history,
   creative, dynamic; hence:]
2. You shall have no other Gods before Me; you shall make yourselves
   no graven image. [Recognition of other gods denies divine omnipotence; graven images render Him as static.]
3. You shall not take the name of God in vain. [It denies His all-know-
   ingness and desecrates His majesty.]
4. Remember the Sabbath Day to keep it holy. . . . you shall not do
   any work; you, your son, your daughter, your male or female servant,
   or your cattle, or the stranger . . . . [God's creatorship is thus affirmed; He owns the universe and may enjoin us from work on it. But
   the equality of mankind is equally established; no one under your influence may work; all are entitled to rest from toil.]
5. Honor thy father and thy mother. . . . [Having brought thee into
   the world, they are next to God.]

As we turn to the second half of these commandments, we note that
they apply to human relations in terms parallel to those of the first five
relating man to God.

6. Thou shalt not murder. [Even as God is unique and His living presence inviolate, so is every human person unique, and his life is inviolate and holy.]
7. Thou shalt not commit adultery. [As God may not be compromised
   by worship of other Gods, even so is the creative unity of humans
   holy and may not be diluted.]
8. Thou shalt not steal. [It would mean considering other people's possessions to be expendable; the name attached to their possessions may
   not be taken away in vain, even as the name of God, owner of the
   world, may not be taken in vain.]

9. Thou shalt not be a false witness against thy neighbor. [As Sabbath
   rest makes you a true witness of God's omnipotence as creator, so
   must evidence against fellow man be true.]
10. Thou shalt not covet. . . . [Both the fifth and tenth commandment
   go beyond visible actions and appeal to thought, intent, and ethical
   principles. Honor of parents may express itself in outward forms but
   ultimately it is a matter of the soul's commitment. The prohibition of
   envy appeals exclusively to man's thoughts.]

Encompassing God and man, action and thought, law and ethical
motivations, the Ten Commandments are indeed the core of Torah.

Immediately, Exodus goes into case law, leading up to ethical
conduct: you must assist your enemy, you may not discriminate against
the stranger. As eternal reminders of your relationship to God and man,
you shall observe specific festivals throughout the year.

Individualism, doubt, and uncertainty lead the people astray to make
themselves a golden calf, turning their back on Him. Yet God forgives,
and in forgiving reveals unto Moses the attributes of His Being:
merciful and gracious, long-suffering and forgiving (Exodus 34:6ff.),
and He bids Moses to make a sanctuary, a visible sign that He dwells
within the people. Centered around the sanctuary, the people's life has
meaning. In connection with the revelation of the Ten Commandments,
a covenant is made with the people, making them God's treasured
possession among all peoples, and constituting them a kingdom of priests
and a holy people (Exodus 19:5–6). It is worth noting that this
covenant was not made in connection with a special dispensation of grace
or of obligations, but in conjunction with commandments that were
universal. Israel's position then was established as the priestly servant of
all mankind, all of which are God's possession. The rabbis actually told
the legend that God offered the Ten Commandments to the peoples of
the world first, entrusting them into the care of Israel only after all the
others had rejected them for reasons of expediency. The revelation took
place in no-man's land (Mount Sinai), the rabbis explain, to show that
it belongs to all, and is not connected with any country or nation. The
Jew has thus seen himself as missionary, not of a religion, but of the Ten
Commandments. That he failed all too often is already shown in the
making of the golden calf immediately following the theophany of Sinai.
In conjunction with the idea of being a "kingdom of priests," the "royal
court," God's sanctuary, is established.

3. *Vayikra* (Leviticus), the third book of Torah, sets up the sacrificial
service which is entrusted to the priests, the descendants of Aaron, who
are assisted in secondary functions by the Levites. The ceremonies at the
consecration of both the sanctuary and the priests are described. A
terrible accident happens: Nadab and Abihu, Aaron's elder sons, present
an offering that is not prescribed and are felled by a devouring fire.

Having been elevated, they had seen in their office a stepping stone to power and a means to unbridled individualism; it destroyed them. Priests and people must learn that their distinction lies only in service, in carrying out the divine command, in sanctifying God publicly by their obedience. Dietary laws are then handed to the people, who partake of the "royal table," and the priests are specially entrusted with the service of healing and of isolating communicable diseases and their bearers. Sexual purity is enjoined.

Now the book of Leviticus turns to the second command: Ye shall be a holy people. How can they become holy? By careful attendance to universal commands, by attuning their hearts as well as their actions to the will of God: revere mother and father; keep the Sabbath, provide for the poor; consider your neighbor by dealing with him in absolute honesty. Even though he may never be aware of any deceitful act, you will have sinned. He may be deaf or dumb or blind regarding all of these, but God knows it. "You may not hate thy brother in thy heart," nor take vengeance, nor bear a grudge, but must guide him. "Thou shalt love thy neighbor as thyself" (Lev. 19:18). This observance of God's unchanging law makes man holy; it is a universal commandment. Through absolute honesty in weight and measure and in compassionate concern for the equal treatment of the stranger, the spirit of holiness is universally revealed and individually implemented. Holy days, once more, are explained; and finally, the law of the jubilee is proclaimed. Individual enterprise is approved but its exploitation curbed. The wealthy may acquire the land of a needy seller, but only for 50 years; he may even hold him as bondsman, but only for a limited time. Then the land returns to its owner, the servant to his freedom under God. "Ye shall proclaim liberty throughout the land for all its inhabitants" (Lev. 25:10). Obedience to these laws and principles spells prosperity, the people are finally warned, disobedience can but lead to disaster. These are the details of the covenant.

4. *Bamidbar* (Numbers) starts with the assumption that the people are now ready for their march into the Promised Land. Their multitudes are numbered, the marching orders are given. The solemn blessing which the priests are to pronounce in God's name is exactly formulated. They may not bless on their own terms, nor "adjust" their blessings to their individual preferences, but must invoke God's name upon the people, that God—and not the priest—may bless them. This blessing has become universal:

The Lord bless thee and keep thee;
The Lord make His face to shine upon thee and be
gracious unto thee;
The Lord lift up His face upon thee, and give thee
peace. (Numbers 6:24–27.)

The princes of the twelve tribes are now permitted to present their gifts to the sanctuary; but they must all be identical so that there may be no envy and distinction, and—as a symbol of their equality, and the equality of the tribes they represent—all the gifts are recorded in detail, though they are all alike.

Spies are sent out to scout out the land. They are men of distinction but of small faith. One man is chosen from each tribe, twelve in all; but ten are convinced that even God cannot sufficiently sustain the people in battle against the fortified cities of the mighty enemy. In endorsing their views, the people prove that theirs is still the spirit of fainthearted slaves, hence they are not yet ready to enter the land. A whole generation must remain in the desert for a total of 40 years, until all the fainthearted have died. A new generation, under the leadership of the two men of faith, one of whom was Joshua, may enter the land.

The people become restive under their enforced leisure and homelessness. Rebellion breaks out against Moses. Korah, a member of the tribe of Levy like Moses, joined by friends, accuses Moses of self-centered love of power. Moses has to be vindicated or else his whole ministry as God's servant will remain misunderstood by the people, and egotism will assume the place of God-centered individualism in leadership.

Slowly the years pass. The people begin to move again. The conquest begins. Then, Balak, King of Moab, fearing them, devises a plan. He invites Balaam, a seer and diviner, to hurl a curse against the people and destroy them. Yet Balaam's curse turns to a blessing in his mouth as he looks down from the mountain heights upon the people in the valley. He cannot curse where God has blessed, and the people, by the purity of their lives, have deserved God's blessing. Thus did the Jew learn that God is indeed the mighty fortress, and obedience to Him the bulwark against the forces of destruction from without. They saw it even more clearly after they had fallen for another ruse; they had yielded to heathen orgies, weakening themselves in sexual license by joining the rites of those whom they had beaten. Their inner decay led many to defeat and death, and weakened the very fabric of the nation. It was Phineas who redeemed them by his passion for God. There was no leadership; thus, in true individualism, he went ahead, and stabbed the licentious couple who had set the pattern.

In preparation for entry into the land, the festive offerings are once more explained. All seems to be ready; Moses views the land from the distance, apportions it. A census of the new generation is taken. Aaron and Miriam (Moses' sister) have already been called to their rest; Moses knows he too must soon die and abandon his people. On God's behest he ordains Joshua as his successor. A new era is about to begin.

5. *Debarim* (Deuteronomy) has been adjudged by Biblical criticism to be of later date, but Jewish tradition has seen it as Moses' great

farewell speech to his people. He relates to them their whole past, not glossing over his own shortcomings. He impresses upon them that they must not let the past fade from their minds and never make graven images or worship idols. Once more, he reviews the Ten Commandments for them. His great affirmation, which has remained central in Jewish life and worship, is significant in every word:

> Hear, O Israel, the Lord our God, the Lord is One.
> Thou shalt love the Lord thy God with all thy heart, and all thy soul, and all thy might.
> And these words which I command thee this day shall be upon thy heart.
> Thou shalt teach them diligently unto thy children, and shalt speak of them when thou sittest in thy house, and when thou walkest by the way, and when thou liest down, and when thou risest up.
> And thou shalt bind them for a sign upon thy hand, and they shall be as frontlets between thine eyes.
> And thou shalt write them upon the doorposts of thy house, and upon thy gates (Deuteronomy 6:4–9).

This divine plea for love calls for an emotional response (all thy heart), a total commitment even of life (all thy soul), and a consecration of every act and human possession (all thy might). Thus in every performance of Mitzvah there must be found not merely the action in itself, but the attunement of the heart. "God the All-merciful wants the heart," is the conclusion the rabbis draw. (See also pp. 20–21.) Love cannot be commanded, it can only be a plea of one who, in turn, is full of responding love. It is made clear to the people that God loves them dearly and tenderly and unconditionally; this love did not result from their strength and numbers, but is truly God's freely extended gift. Out of this love we can understand God's "jealousness." He does not want His love to be diluted. Out of this love we understand the blessing He will give the people, if they will but respond, the penalties He imposes in an effort to lead them back if they have gone astray, and His readiness to pardon graciously and fully when they return. In this love is enshrined the variety of forces which have fashioned Israel, and Moses makes it clear in Deuteronomy 11:13–21:

> Thus shall it be: if you will listen in continuation to My Mitzvot, which I command you today, to love the Lord your God and to serve Him with all your heart and all your soul, then will I grant rain for your land in season. . . . thus shall you eat your fill. Take care not to be lured away to serve other gods and bow to them, for the Lord's anger will flare up against you. . . . Therefore take these words to your heart and soul, bind them as a sign upon your hand, let them be for frontlets between your eyes, teach them to your children, rehearsing them every one when thou sittest in thy house, and when thou walkest by the way, when thou

liest down, and when thou risest up; and thou shalt write them upon the doorposts of thy house and upon thy gates, to the end that you and your children may endure on the soil which the Lord has pledged to your fathers to give to them, as long as there is a heaven over the earth.

God-Torah-Mitzvot-Land form an indivisible unit, safeguarding survival. As the text shifts from an appeal to the people as a whole to a direct plea to every individual, the collective future of the people is placed in the hands of every single person; it is his responsibility. Yet he assures himself of his own survival only as he remains linked in duty, obligation, and kinship to the whole.

Jews have been fully aware of the significance of these words; they recite them twice daily and have bound them upon their hands and foreheads and written them on the doorposts of their homes, as we shall see.

As children of God, the people are warned against self-mutilation, enjoined once more to abide by the dietary laws. In His service they are to tithe themselves, and, equally in His service, remit the debts of debtors every seventh year, to allow the debtor a new start in life on equal footing with all the others.

The festivals are once again reviewed, and the organization of government and proceedings in court are outlined, followed by a most significant statement: In all disputes the people shall be guided by the decision of their magistrates, duly appointed at any given time (Deuteronomy 17:8ff.). The rabbis saw in this injunction the basic justification for the evolution of Torah. Bound by conscience and tradition, the ordained leaders have the right and duty to adjust Torah to the conditions of the times. Thus Torah could not become ossified; by being keyed to life, it kept the people alive.

The king, if there was one, was to read the Torah throughout his life, that he might never come to rule by his own whim or regard his position as a tool to autocratic government. Later, Moses will command that the king read the Torah to the whole people once every seven years, in order that they know what the law is, thus preventing the ruler from deviating from it. Arbitrariness and self-centered individualism were thus excluded.

Laws of war are enunciated; no action may be taken without a preceding offer of peaceful settlement (Deuteronomy 20:10). Greater emphasis, however, is placed on laws of peace, the relationships of man to man. The concern is shown in such detail as this: When you build a new house, you shall make a parapet for your roof, so that you do not bring bloodguilt on your house if anyone should fall from it (Deuteronomy 22:8). You shall not turn over to his master a slave who seeks refuge with you from his master (Deuteronomy 23:16), a law of great significance in ante bellum days in the United States when it was a source of controversy in practice between North and South.

With a solemn blessing, Moses parts from his people. Like Jacob before him, he has an individual benediction for each of the tribes, based on his deep knowledge of their abilities, shortcomings, and potentials, and assigns to them those tasks which equip them best to make their contribution to the whole. Then Moses steps up to Mount Nebo, is given a glimpse of the Land which he is not to enter, and is called to rest. God Himself buries him, that no one may know his grave. Israel is not to make saints of anyone, even Moses: the living spirit is the monument.

The rabbis find an additional message in this final story. Torah begins with charity, as God Himself fashions clothes to cover the nakedness of Adam and Eve; it ends with charity, as He buries His servant Moses. All of Torah is thus wrapped in the spirit of divine charity, and in seeking God through Torah, man must imitate Him.

This interpretive synopsis of Torah does not take into account the conclusions of Biblical criticism, which ascribes its origin to various authors and various ages. It is based rather on Torah as reflected in the consciousness of the Jewish people throughout the ages—Torah, the heritage of the congregation of Jacob, the force that fashioned it.

Nevee-im

Nevee-im (Prophets), the second section of the Tenakh, is divided into two basic parts: *Early Prophets,* including the books of Joshua, Judges, Samuel I, II, and Kings I, II, and *Later Prophets,* including the preserved records of the messages handed to the people by the literary prophets.

Only portions of these writings are regularly used in the worship of the synagogue. On holy days and special occasions, a portion of Prophets is appointed to be read after the reading of Torah. It is called *Haftarah,* and its subject matter is chosen either in relationship to the Torah portion or to convey the special significance of the day. For instance, on the Sabbath Day when the story of the death of Jacob is recited from the Torah scroll, the Haftarah deals with the death of David. On the Day of Atonement, the meaning of the fast is explained in the words of Isaiah 58. Social action is the message of the fast: "to loose the fetters of wickedness, to undo the bands of the yoke. . . . to share thy bread with the hungry, and that thou bring the poor that are cast out to thy house; when thou seest the naked that thou cover him; and that thou hide not thyself from thine own flesh."

Early Prophets contains the historical books, whose events we have

discussed, covering the period from the people's arrival in the Land of
Canaan through the destiny of the two kingdoms. The struggle they
have to engage in is a twofold one: with the nations they have to conquer
and enemies they have to repel, and with themselves. They arrive before
the mighty walls of Jericho and make them fall without raising a hand
in battle. Preceded by the Ark containing the tables of the Ten
Commandments, they surround the mighty fortress in procession,
invoking the name of God, and the walls tumble. It might be a symbol to
them that God is to be their king, that in serving Him they will prevail.
The symbolic message fails. The unity of the people breaks down under
the strain of self-centered antagonism; the spirit of the people erodes as
they yield to the idolatrous and licentious practices of their neighbors.

In the end, the Ark itself—carried into battle as a magic means of
victory—is even captured by the enemy. Their first king, Saul,
forgetting his ordination through Torah and setting himself up as
absolute ruler, carries the people to disastrous defeat. In David, the
struggle of a man with himself parallels that of a king against the
outward foes of the people; his victory is a twofold one, the outward one
the result of his ever-renewed inner regeneration in repentance.

But then, after Solomon's rule, decay sets in once more, resulting in
political and spiritual division and in weakness, defeat, and destruction.
The people fail to see that the land is to be a laboratory of the spirit;
settledness is to be a challenge. Their failure does not mean that they are
worse than other nations, but not better. Theirs is but a kingdom, when
it should have been a kingdom of priests; they desire to be simply a nation
when they are supposed to live as a holy nation.

Again we have interpreted the events not as the historian might, but as
the authors and editors of Scripture did, who were frequently slanting
events to convey an ethical message and spiritual idea. We have followed
this interpretation, for this has been the way in which the Jewish people
have come to understand these events as a lesson for themselves
throughout the centuries.

This period is distinguished by the emergence of the prophets, who
have, therefore, given their name to these books. The movement started
as a kind of school, as men banded together, linked to each other by a
certain spirit of ecstasy. To the people, the prophets were just diviners
who could foretell the future. But out of their bands there emerged
individuals who rejected the narrow scope of the organization. They did
not wish to be "fortune tellers." They had a message to deliver; they had
a burden placed upon them by God; they stood out as individuals in
strength and indomitable courage.

The Hebrew word for prophet is *Nabee,* which William F. Albright
explains from its Accadian source to mean "the one who is called" (by
God) (*From the Stone Age to Christianity.* New York: Doubleday

Anchor Book, 1957, p. 303). The prophet thus receives his call from God. He has to rebuke the people; has to warn them; calls for rebirth of spirit, return, and repentance; and assures them of the ever-present love of God and His everlasting willingness to receive them back into His grace.

In this spirit, Samuel faces the people who want a king, warning them against dependence on human leadership and advising them to place their faith in God. He yields when God acquiesces in the fact that they have denied Him (I Samuel). Emboldened by his divine mission to rebuke if need be, the prophet Nathan approaches David at the height of the king's power, accusing him to his face of having committed a shameful crime deserving death (II Samuel 11–12). (David had seduced his neighbor's wife, Bathsheba, and sent her husband to his death in battle.)

In scathing words, Elijah predicts doom to the sinful king of Israel, and has to flee from King Ahab's wrath. Yet later he returns to face all of Israel, including the king. The people, smitten by a drought, have made their appeal to both God and Baal, a compromise of expediency that called for "other gods before Him." There can be no compromise, Elijah makes clear: "How long halt ye between two opinions? If the Lord be God, follow Him; but if Baal, follow him!" (I Kings 18:21). For the people in their weakness, Elijah provides a visible sign of God's power, but the prophet himself learns that it is not in storms or quakes that God makes Himself manifest, but rather in the still, small voice of conscience and inner vision that God is revealed, and this voice man must follow (I Kings 19). The vision of the divine may be granted more poignantly to the prophet, but it is granted to all mankind. The prophet, like the midwife, releases that which lies implanted in every human being, placed there by God Himself. This will be evident in the Later Prophets, whose utterances we possess, at least in part. Of the speeches of the earlier ones, we have no verbatim record.

Later Prophets. Traditionally, we count three major prophets and twelve minor ones. Those of whose works major portions have been preserved are called major prophets; they include Isaiah, Jeremiah, and Ezekiel. Those of whose works only minor portions are left are called minor prophets, yet they are of equal significance. They include: Hosea, Joel, Amos, Obadiah, Jonah, Micah, Nahum, Habakkuk, Zephaniah, Haggai, Zechariah, and Malachi. (The Book of Daniel, being quite late, is included in the third portion of the Tenakh.) We know that some of the books ascribed to these men were written by several authors, such as Isaiah. We also know that some of the names were not the true names of the authors. (Malachi simply means "My Messenger.") We shall be concerned here only with some of their major ideas, as they interpret, adapt, and evolve Torah.

These prophets came from all strata of society. Isaiah came from the

ranks of the highest nobility, Amos was a lowly farmer, Hosea belonged
to the middle class of comfortable burghers, Jeremiah and Ezekiel were
priests. The northern as well as the southern kingdom were their spheres
of action; and, like Ezekiel, they served as pastors to the people in
Babylonian exile.

Amos (c. 750), compelled by the urgency of his call to lay down his
plow, applies farmer's logic to his message: As ye sow so shall ye reap. If
you plant righteousness your harvest will be good; if you sow wickedness,
evil will befall you. This is universal, hence Amos is aware of the fact
that the providence of God which rests equally upon all the farmers' toil
throughout the world extends in equal measure upon all his children,
regardless of their race. "Are ye not unto me like the children of the
Ethiopians?" (Amos 9:7). He speaks of dark-skinned Ethiopians and
lighter-skinned Philistines and Israel in the same terms. Humanity is one.
If Israel holds any specific place, it is to set an example of true living
under God and to assume higher responsibility for which it will be held
to account. "You only have I known of all the families of the earth;
therefore will I visit upon you all of your iniquities" (Amos 3:2). The
"chosenness" of the Jew does not spell privilege, for all mankind is
equally privileged before God; it demands higher performance. In this
sense, every nation is chosen to contribute to the very best of its strength
those goods which by endowment and education it is best equipped to
give to humanity.

Hosea (c. 745) emphasizes divine love in an unsurpassed manner.
The prophet takes back his errant wife after she has had many
adventures. This act of forgiveness symbolizes God's never-ceasing love
for His people, though they may have gone astray. His call to repentance
(Hosea 14) is read in the synagogue as Haftarah on the Sabbath
between Rosh Hashanah and Yom Kippur, the period of repentance:
"Return, O Israel, unto the Lord, for thou hast stumbled in thine
iniquity. Take with you words, and return unto the Lord. Say unto
Him: Forgive all iniquity, and accept that which is good, and we will
render instead of bullocks (the words of) our lips" (Hosea 14:2–3).
Prayer—the words of the lips—is better than animal sacrifices; thus
has Judaism interpreted the verse.

It is possible that Hosea wished to soften the sternness of Amos'
words, whose contemporary he was. Yet the verse quoted points to
another direction as well: Hosea feels that repentance alone is full
return because he is primarily concerned with Israel's turning away from
God. Sins against God can be forgiven if the sinner expresses his sorrow
and his pledge of a new life in silent communion with Him. Amos is
primarily concerned with the perversion of social justice and its extension
in the life of nations, namely imperialistic war and oppression of others.
These can only be forgiven if restitution is made in addition to

repentance—and which nation is willing to do that? Hence his gloom.

It is with social injustice that both the *First Isaiah* (742 B.C.E.) and *Micah* (740) are concerned. (First Isaiah comprises chapters 1–39.) In scathing words, Isaiah condemns ritual that is merely empty performance of rites and is not undergirded by social justice; if it is carried out by the very same people who oppress their fellows, then ritual turns into blasphemy, blessing into a mockery of God. He will have none of it. Isaiah demands not only penitence but "wash yourselves clean; remove the evil of your doings from before My eyes; cease to do evil, learn to do good; seek justice, correct oppression, defend the fatherless, plead for the widow" (Isaiah 1:16–17). Only then will the prayer of contrition have meaning. Micah has the same message.

The whole tenor of Isaiah's prophecies appears already in the account of his call:

> I saw the Lord sitting upon His throne, high and lifted up, and his train filled the Temple. Above Him stood the seraphim. . . . And one called to another and said: 'Holy, holy, holy is the Lord of hosts, the whole earth is full of His glory.' And the foundations of the thresholds [of the Temple] shook at the voice of Him who called. and the house was filled with smoke (Isaiah 6:1–4).

God is *not* in the Temple, He is in the whole earth; the actions of society have to proclaim His holiness. The hope that Temple ritual will be meaningful to Him without social responsibility in leading the world to holiness is a vain hope. The same theme will be taken up at the very end of the second Isaiah:

> Thus says the Lord: Heaven is My throne and the earth is my footstool; what is the house which you would build for Me, and what is the place of My rest? . . . . This is the man to whom I will look, he that is humble and contrite in spirit, and trembles at My word. . . . He who sacrifices a lamb [is] like one who breaks a dog's neck (Isaiah 66:1–3).

The true response is for mankind to offer itself, to unite under God's kingship, to establish peace and justice. Then God will choose His priests from among all nations. The whole world will have become a kingdom of priests, a holy people; only thus can ritual—the symbolic expression of true worship—be meaningful and acceptable. This world, the time of the Messiah in Jewish tradition, is foretold by both Isaiah (2:2–4) and Micah (4:1–5):

> And it shall come to pass in the end of days, that the mountain of the Lord's house shall be established as the top of the mountains, and shall be exalted above the hills; and all nations shall flow unto it. And many peoples shall go and say: 'Come ye and let us go up to the mountain of the Lord, to the house of the God of Jacob; and He will teach us of His ways,

and we will walk in His paths.' For out of Zion shall go forth Torah, and the word of the Lord from Jerusalem. And He shall judge between nations, and shall decide for many peoples; and they shall beat their swords into plowshares and their spears into pruning hooks; nation shall not lift up sword against nation, neither shall they learn war any more.

As this time is not yet, Israel has the task to prepare it by example: "O House of Jacob come ye and let us walk in the light of the Lord" (Isaiah 2:5). All this will take place simply as the result of mankind coming to its senses. It calls for no miracles, only a simple awareness on the part of men and nations that God is the center, justice mankind's best weapon in the struggle for survival, and peace the most precious goal and treasure. Yet it may bring about a complete transformation of habits, practices, and attitudes. It will be like the wolf dwelling with the lamb, as national jealousies will depart. Thus it will come to pass under a truly chosen ruler, and Isaiah finds him in thinking of David:

There shall come forth a shoot out of the stock of Jesse (David's father) . . . and the spirit of the Lord shall rest upon him, the spirit of wisdom and understanding, the spirit of counsel and might, the spirit of knowledge and of the fear of the Lord (Isaiah 11:1-2).

In such manner is the Messiah seen, and the messianic age conceived; there will be no obstacles to Torah and Mitzvot in their widest meaning. This portion of Isaiah is traditionally recited as Haftarah on the very last day of Passover, the festival of redemption from bondage. It makes the march through history a pilgrimage of free men toward universal freedom, and it releases the Jew from holy days to daily rounds with a challenge and obligation.

In a similar spirit, Isaiah 58 has become the Haftarah in the morning service of Yom Kippur, the Day of Atonement. Not in chastisement, or in one-day prayer can God truly be worshipped, or even in the house of worship, but only through social justice. In this way, the fast can be of purpose, and Israel be that holy nation which leads mankind to holiness.

Micah truly sums it up: "Wherewith shall I come before the Lord. . . . Shall I come before Him with burnt offerings? . . . . It has been told thee, O man, what is good, and what the Lord doth require of thee: Only to do justly, and to love mercy, and to walk humbly with thy God" (Micah 6:6-8).

The theme is carried through all the prophets. *Jeremiah* (626–587 B.C.E.) tells the people in no uncertain words how meaningless the Temple really can become, how its existence holds no magical power of survival; that power lies in the conduct of the people (Jeremiah 7). In spite of terrible persecution, Jeremiah never gives up his faith in the regenerative powers that lie within the people, and neither do any of the other prophets. But he has to face trials much more severe than any others, and, in the end, witnesses the destruction of the Temple, which he well foresaw. He transforms defeat into victory: Exile may be the challenge which will bring about the regeneration, hence his letter to the Jews in Babylonia (Jeremiah 29:1–7). With the fall of the Temple— the loss of the unifying agency—individual responsibility grows. The people no longer constitute a nation, are no longer able to act collectively or to pass responsibility from the individual to the "government."

Thus *Ezekiel* (593–573) becomes the preacher of individual and mutual responsibility, every one for his own destiny, yet accountable for the conduct of those whom he may influence. Ezekiel is a visionary and has powerful revelations in Babylonia, as if to say, God's glory is indeed filling the whole earth; He reveals Himself everywhere. "Blessed be the glory of God from *His* place" (Ezekiel 3:12). Through the spirit of God, the dead bones of a decayed society can be made to live again; the hopeless can restore their trust, and even the land can be restored to them (Ezekiel 37:1–15). This chapter, too, is recited as Haftarah on Pessah, the festival of regeneration; striving for rebirth, we can earn it if we open ourselves to His spirit.

The *Second Isaiah,* Chapters 40–66 (c. 540) is a prophet of hope. "Comfort ye, comfort ye my people, says your God" (Isaiah 40:1ff.) is the Haftarah recited after the mournful fast of Ab, commemorating the fall of the Temple. Israel is God's witness in the world (Isaiah 43:10–12), "a light to the nations to open eyes that are blind" (Isaiah 42:6–7) by its example. This entails suffering, as the servant of God— despised, disfigured, and mocked—upholds his ideals; may their heart be strong for God will redeem them, and the entire human family will be benefited (Isaiah 53). True to his belief that the Jew serves the world, Isaiah welcomes converts who have joined the people and cleave to God; they, too, have a share in the future of Israel (Isaiah 44:5–56:3).

To the homecoming people, *Haggai* is the gadfly. He wants a Temple, a second one to be rebuilt, to be a symbol of the people's willingness to sacrifice. May they give of their substance, even though it hurts, to restore a visible center of divine presence; and may they be undismayed at the smallness of the new building, for its true glory may surpass the splendor of the ancient one.

Zechariah makes it clear that victory comes, "not by might, nor by power, but by My spirit" (Zechariah 4:6).

Malachi points out the way and the goal. The goal is attained when "the hearts of the fathers are turned to their children, and the hearts of the children to their fathers" (Malachi 4:5). Even the natural conflict of the generations will have ceased.

The road is Torah: "Remember the Torah of my servant Moses" (Malachi 4:4). Before redemption there will be conflict, nations will be arrayed against each other. Zechariah no longer shares the hope that reason alone will lead mankind to brotherhood. Here we find one of the eschatological prophecies. Yet victory and peace are assured those who fight with God (Zechariah 14:1–21), and Israel will dwell in safety amidst a reborn humanity. This portion is read on Sukkot, the festival when God's protection is symbolized.

Of *Jonah* we have no historical background. His mission was placed by the book's author in the early part of the seventh century, since the setting is Nineveh at the time when Assyria was still a mighty power. (Nineveh was destroyed in 612.) Jonah is told to call the Assyrians to repentance, but he refuses to go, for this would mean redeeming Israel's enemy by his appeal. After many adventures (including three days in the belly of a great fish) Jonah agrees to do God's will. He calls for repentance, the king and people of Nineveh listen, they have a change of heart, and the city is saved.

What is truly significant is the way in which Jews have come to think of their enemies and of God's concern for non-Jews; they are all His children, they are all deserving of life and a second chance, especially those "who know not their right hand from their left hand" (Jonah 4:11). It is the Jew's task to extend his help, his insights, his strength, and life to them; and if a Jew refuses, God will see to it that it is done anyway through him, if he has the power to influence others for good.

The story is recited as Haftarah on the afternoon of Yom Kippur. It reminds the Jews that they are not singularly chosen for God's special attention and mercy, which He extends to all. The Jew must consider himself the world's servant, in affirmation of his tradition, though he suffer in serving humanity. Judaism's concept of God and mankind is universalistic.

The prophets of Israel are no philosophers. Calm, critical analysis is not theirs; they are moved by great and overpowering emotions which spring from a dual source: the absolute conviction of God's mastery of the world (for He has created it and He shapes its history) and the equally strong conviction that man can serve the purposes of the divine only by raising the standards of ethical conduct toward the absolute of complete social justice. Without this, ritual is meaningless mockery.

But these men do not speak in generalities. They address themselves to concrete situations in life, rebuke the people for failing to live up to the highest ideals in everyday conduct, and call on Israel to be holy, which means to be an example. They rebuke Israel not for being worse than other peoples, but for being no better than the rest, for not being an example. For this, Israel was created, hence it must endure, and endure it will, to find its reward in God's own time. Setting for all mankind the highest ethical goals and speaking in language of supreme grandeur, the prophets have remained the world's greatest—and, in fact, only—heralds of the truly good society under God, a society in which conviction will overcome expediency. They do not abrogate Torah and Mitzvot; they clarify their purpose.

Ketubim

Ketubim (Collected Writings) constitutes the third portion of the Tenakh. As the title states, it is composed of a variety of different works. It includes: The Psalms, Proverbs, Job, Song of Songs (Song of Solomon), Ruth, Lamentations, Ecclesiastes, Esther, Daniel, Ezra, Nehemiah, Chronicles I and II. They are used in Jewish worship at a variety of occasions, which we shall mention in connection with the works themselves.

The *Psalms* are a collection of 150 poems, some of them lengthy, others very short. A good many of them have the names of the supposed authors attached to them, ranging from Moses to the Sons of Korah and Solomon; the majority, however, are ascribed to David. A number of them have musical annotations, including the instruments to be used in accompaniment when recited in public worship.

Several poetic forms are employed. "Parallelism" is used frequently (as it is in other Hebrew poetry); that is, the second verse is a paraphrase of the first: "Lord, who shall sojourn in Thy tabernacle? Who shall dwell upon Thy holy mountain?" (Psalm 15:1). The alphabetic acrostic is also frequently employed, with each verse beginning with a letter of the alphabet (Psalms 34 and 145). In Psalm 119, each letter is used eight times. Some psalms are arranged for antiphonal responses (Psalm 24). In the "Psalms of Ascents" (120–134) the title indicates that they were sung when the people ascended in solemn procession to the hill on which the Temple stood.

In content, the Psalms range from glorification of God to outcry and lamentation, from meditation to jubilant praise, from individual prayer to choral hymn, "Hallelujah, Praise ye the Lord." They speak of "foes" encompassing us, and as the foe is not characterized, every individual may substitute his own need and distress as the "foe" when the psalm is offered as prayer. They may be framed in the singular form, yet the "I" may stand for an individual person or for the people as a whole.

Thus the Psalms have been guide and comforter, a source of strength and renewed faith for the Jews and for mankind throughout history. The Psalms have upheld the people in sickness, distress, and trial, expressed the deepest yearning of their hearts, instructed them in the way of God, and put in words the spirit of gratitude welling up in human souls, which less-gifted persons might never hope to express to equal perfection.

In Hebrew the Psalms are called *Tehillim* (praises), for even the outcry, directed to God, affirms Him as ever present and ever powerful to rescue; it affirms man's trust in Him, that He does right, even though we do not understand the reason for His actions. Thus Psalms are praise in affliction as in victory.

Jewish tradition has divided the Psalms into five books, corresponding to the Five Books of Moses. Actually, they are our response to Torah, witnessing to the fact that we have understood it, accepted it, and made it our own.

In the ancient Temple a special psalm was assigned for choral presentation every day of the week (they are still used in the worship of the synagogue) including Psalm 92, sung on the Sabbath, which reflects on God's work of creation, too deep for man to understand, yet culminating in the victory of the good man, who shall be planted in the house of the Lord. On holy days, Psalms 113–118, called the *Hallel* (Praise), are recited in synagogue worship: God is recognized as God of nature and of nations; He rescued Israel from Egyptian bondage, may we give thanks to His Name; calling on Him in distress we shall always find rescue, hence need not fear the devices men have in mind for our undoing; as we move in His direction we shall be blessed from His House; praise ye therefore the Lord, His goodness endureth forever.

Jewish worship always opens with Psalms, and the Sabbath is especially welcomed with them. Our affirmation of God as our Sustainer is expressed daily by reciting Psalm 145. The Scroll of Torah is removed from the Ark and returned to it as Psalms rise in glorification of its Giver. Psalm 6 expresses the spirit of contrition and our hope in Him, as we preface it in daily prayer by the words: "Merciful and compassionate God, I have sinned before Thee."

In prayer for the sick, the name of the afflicted is presented to God as those verses of Psalm 119 which spell his name are being recited. Verses of the Psalms are woven into the prayers of the liturgy. But beyond that, thousands and millions have turned to the Psalms in hours of need and of joy. In opening their hearts to God, they found comfort in the knowledge that He is "my shepherd, I shall not want" (Psalm 23).

The Psalms have sustained the Jew, his faith and his hope, even as they are one of Judaism's greatest gifts to mankind.

Proverbs, Ecclesiastes, and *Job* offer worldly wisdom or philosophical discussion and are therefore called Wisdom Books. Wisdom (*Hokhmah*) is actually personified at times. This worldly wisdom was equated with Torah; Torah is wisdom, and all wisdom, as Jews have seen it, is an extension of Torah, enshrined in it. Proverbs is a collection of short maxims, affording guidance in life. Ecclesiastes is a pessimistic reflection on life's vanity, redeemed only by the concluding sentence, added later, affirming God's ever present will. Job is a dialogue of a man with his friends. Job's faith is tried by terrible afflictions. The friends feel that he must have sinned, for why else would God punish him so severely? Job denies any guilt and affirms his faith in God whose will must prevail, though it be hidden. He is vindicated by God Himself.

The Song of Songs is one of five books originally written on special scrolls (including Ruth, Lamentations, Ecclesiastes, and Esther), hence called the Five Scrolls. A fervid love song, it was interpreted as symbolic of God's love for Israel. It is recited on Pessah, the festival of spring. Nature, like a bride in all her beauty, forecasts rich blessings; God is the groom. Should not Israel and all mankind equally prepare themselves, link themselves to God's love, and bring to fruition the blessings He has implanted within them?

Ruth, the second Scroll, is recited on Shabuot, the festival commemorating the revelation at Sinai, the giving of Torah. It is an idyllic poem. Ruth, a Moabite convert, cleaves to Torah and to the people of Israel, and no adversity can weaken her determination: "Whither thou goest I will go." A desperately poor immigrant from abroad, she is eventually permitted the peaceful life of the happy farmer's wife in the Land, but this is only one part of her reward. Marrying a man of distinction, she becomes the great-grandmother of King David.

The poem reveals to us that Torah does indeed go forth from Zion, to embrace all who wish to place themselves under it. In the happy farmer's life of which the book tells, a foretaste is given of a future linked to a Messiah of the House of David, when plowshares will cut the soil rather than swords penetrate humans, when people of all backgrounds will find through Torah both peace and happiness. The faith of Ruth in adversity thus becomes a guiding light to the people of Torah, who, like her, must hold on to it with all their heart and soul and might. The reward Ruth receives rekindles the hope that the ultimate consummation of history in divine victory is a reality: the age of David, the Messiah, will come if we persevere.

Lamentations, the third Scroll, is recited on the Fast of Ab, commemorating the fall of the Temple; it expresses the numb terror and despondency as well as the hope that springs eternal within the eternal people, even as disasters grow to unbearable proportions.

Ecclesiastes, the fourth Scroll (also one of the Wisdom books, as we have seen), recited on Sukkot, reflects and mitigates the sense of frustration and pessimism we may feel at the approach of a bleak winter's season. Obey His commandments, it says, and you will be a man: "Remember now thy Creator in the days of thy youth . . ."

Esther, the fifth Scroll, is recited on Purim. It is a strange book, a rather fantastic and quite thrilling story, which never mentions the name of God, and whose scene is laid outside of Palestine, in Persia. Perhaps it tells us that God does work everywhere, though we may not be aware of His presence. The Jews in the story transgress against Torah. Even the story's chief protagonist, Esther, marries outside her faith. Yet as they return to Him in repentance, willing to give their lives for Him, they are spared, and a vicious plan to exterminate them comes to naught. The book gave hope to many in modern extermination camps, for they knew that they might perish, but the Jewish people would surely survive.

Daniel's faith and prayer have served as inspiration to the Jews, never to abandon their holy tradition. The eschatological portion of the book has generally had no impact on Jewish thinking. The prophets' remarks, dealing with cataclysmic events at the end of days (eschatology) have however inspired many speculations by Christian faithful—not shared by Jews—and seem reflected in the New Testament Book of Revelations.

Ezra and *Nehemiah* relate the trials of the people in rebuilding their land and Temple after the Babylonian Exile. Surrounded by the dangers of corrosion, Jews withdraw from contact with the world, renewing their covenant with God and Torah and Land.

Chronicles I and *II* review history once more, emphasizing the line of tradition that has come down through the generations and the religious significance of the events of Jewish history.

Collection of the Tenakh

The books of the Tenakh were collected, edited, and approved by the Pharisees. The Hebrew Bible is what the Pharisees decided that it should be. They saw themselves as the successors of the prophets, and rightly so: theirs is the same spirit. "Moses received the Torah at Sinai and handed it to Joshua, who handed it to the Elders; the Elders handed it to the prophets, the prophets to the Men of the Great Assembly" (the masters of Oral Torah) (Abot I, 1).

Some of the material presented to the rabbis for consideration was rejected either as irrelevant or repetitious, or because it was felt that its message was not significantly in line with the educational objectives of Torah. These books were not lost, however. Some of them had already been translated into Greek by the Septuagint, and hence we have them. They are called Apocrypha, the hidden books, as they were not generally accessible to the ancient reader.

8 OF ORAL TORAH

ORAL Torah is the tradition which was handed down from master to disciple. Generation after generation added to its content. Even after it had been laid down in the Talmud, its evolution continued. The relationship of Written and Oral Torah is explained in a simple parable, found in a medieval Jewish work, *Seder Eliyahu Suta* (82). To a doubter in the validity of Oral Law, the rabbi answers:

> Both were given at Sinai, as a king presents a gift to faithful servants. Once there were two servants, a wise one and a foolish one, and both received from their king a measure of wheat and a bundle of flax. The foolish one put them away in a chest, that they remain forever unchanged; the wise servant spun the flax into a cloth and made precious bread out of the wheat. Placing the bread on the cloth, he invited the king to be his honored guest.

Thus, human concern, wisdom, and love of the Supreme King transforms divine gifts of Torah into *Shulhan Arukh,* a well-prepared table. Without oral law, evolution is impossible, and God is not served.

This task of evolving Torah calls for integrity, humility, knowledge and wisdom, and a deep love of God and men. The Pharisees, their disciples, and the rabbis of the Talmud possessed all of these; theirs is indeed the spirit of the prophets, whose successors they are in both time and spirit. We recognize this spirit in the teachings and maxims of their lives. As it says in Shabbat 88b:

> The Rabbis taught: Those that accept humiliation without ever humiliating others, hear their disparagement without retorting, act always out of love, and joyfully accept chastisement, of them Scripture says: "They who love Him are like the sun as he rises in his might" (Judges 5:31).

Hillel's love of God and man thus came to be proverbial:

> Be of the disciples of Aaron, loving peace and pursuing peace, loving all men and leading them to Torah.

He who aggrandizes his name destroys it; he who does not grow (in knowledge and wisdom), decreases; he who does not wish to learn deserves death; and he who puts the crown (of Torah and position) to selfish use shall perish.

If I am not for myself (doing the work, if need be alone), who will be for me? If I am for myself only, what am I? (My work is without meaning.) And if not now, when (will it be done)? (Abot 1:12–14.)

Rabbi Eleazar places a good heart above all other qualities, for all of them are included therein (Abot 2:13), and Rabbi Eliezer counsels:

Let the honor of thy fellow man be as dear to you as your own; don't be easily angered; return [to God in repentance] one day before your death (that is, every day) (Abot 2:15).

Rabbi Gamaliel warns against selfish ambition as he pleads for civic responsibility: "May all who work in behalf of the community work *with them* for the sake of Heaven" (Abot 2:2).

"The decisive thing is not study but the deed" (Abot 1:17), is Rabbi Simeon ben Gamaliel's word of advice. He also pointed out: "The world rests on three things: truth, justice, and peace" (Abot 1:18). And Shammai, Hillel's intellectual antagonist, proclaimed as the rule for his life: "Make thy study of Torah a well-appointed practice, say little and do much, and receive every person with a cheerful face" (Abot 1:15). Yet the decision in all religious matters follows the School of Hillel:

A heavenly voice was heard at Jabneh: "The words of both are the words of the living God, but the decision must follow the School of Hillel." In discussion it was asked, "If both are the words of the living God, why was the decision accorded to the School of Hillel?" The answer was: "Because they were kindly and peaceful, always studied both their own views and those of the School of Shammai, and even presented the words of the School of Shammai before their own," which teaches that he who humbles himself God raises up, and he who looks for aggrandizement, God humbles. He who chases after recognition finds it runs away from him; he who strives to avoid it finds it follows him. He who pushes his objectives will find himself pressured by them, he who puts them aside finds himself aided by destiny (Erubin 13b).

Life, as the rabbis saw it, must be imitation of God.

Rabbi Hama, son of Rabbi Hanina, said: "Follow none but the Lord your God" (Deuteronomy 13:5). But can man follow God? It means that we must follow God's acts. As He clothes the naked, so do thou clothe the naked (Genesis 3:21); as the Holy One—Blessed be He—visited the sick (Genesis 18:1), so shalt thou visit the sick. Even as He . . . comforts those who mourn (Genesis 25:11) so shalt thou comfort those who are in mourning. As the Holy One . . . buries the dead (Deuteronomy 34:6) even so do thou bury the dead. . . . The Torah begins with deeds of kindness—as God made clothes for Adam and Eve—and it ends with kindness, as it is written: "He buried [Moses] in the valley" (Sota 14a).

These were the principles held by the men who developed the Talmud, the *Tannaim* (Teachers) who were the masters of the Mishnah and the *Amoraim* (Speakers) who carried on the discussions and made the decisions laid down in Gemara (the Completion). By their ordinances (*Takkanot*), they erected the fence around Torah; by their preachments, they conveyed ethical teachings. Their legal decisions, directing the Jew's "walk" in life, are called *Halakhah*, meaning walk; their preaching became known as *Haggadah*, which means preaching. In Mishnah and Gemara they are interwoven, but we find Haggadah also in separate works arranged as a commentary to Scripture, called *Midrash* or the "Search" for meaning. Law and ethics, Halakhah and Haggadah, actually cannot be separated. Judaism, as a religion of action, has always seen the law as an instrument of ethics, and as an ethical ideal to be pursued. The Torah does not say, for instance, "Ye shall love your enemies." It says instead, "If you see the ass of your enemy lying under its burden and would like to refrain from raising it, you must nevertheless help him to lift it up" (Exodus 23:5). This is not a nondescript, general injunction to love, but a concrete, specific act, which, in turn, cannot help but promote love among two former enemies. As a piece of general legislation, it will eventually create a society whose members feel an inner obligation to help each other, thus overcoming animosities.

Halakhah is practical and practiced ethics and must be understood as such. Mitzvot become Torah, namely instruction. Judaism denies the often-heard argument, "You cannot legislate morality." We may actually have to start with legislation, that out of its observance— disagreeable as it may appear to us at the beginning—a new spirit may emerge. Halakhah fortified by Haggadah may achieve it.

Organization of the Talmud

The Talmud is divided into six *Orders*. Each order consists of a number of Tractates. The Tractates are subdivided into chapters and paragraphs. An individual Mishnah constitutes a paragraph, therefore simply called *Mishnah*.

1. The first order, *Zeraim* (Seeds), deals with the laws of agriculture. Since it is our duty to give thanks to God for the gifts of nature, the order opens with the tractate *Berakhot* (Blessings), dealing with worship in general.

2. The second order, *Moed* (Appointed Times), discusses the rules and regulations pertaining to holy days. Among its tractates we find *Shabbat* (Sabbath), concerning the observance of the Sabbath; *Yom Tob* (Holy Day), dealing with the rules regulating the other holy days; and several

tractates laying down Halakhah regarding specific holy seasons, such as *Yoma* (The *Day* of Atonement), Sukkah (Festival of Sukkot), and Pessahim (Feast of Passover).

3. The third order, *Nashim* (Women), contains marriage and divorce laws. Among its tractates are *Kiddushin* (Sanctification of Marriage), *Ketubot* (civil laws of marriage), and *Gitin* (laws of divorce).

4. The fourth order, *Nezikin (Damages)*, forms the code of civil and criminal law, which were public laws when Israel was a nation of old, and during the Middle Ages, when Jews had their own civil jurisdiction.

5. The fifth order, *Kadashim (Holy Things)*, deals with laws of Temple sacrifices in times of old and also lays down the dietary laws (*Hulin*).

6. The sixth order, *Taharot (Purifications)*, states the laws of ritual purity whose observance was required as prerequisite for entry and service in the Temple of old.

In opening one of the heavy tomes of the Talmud, we shall find first of all that, regardless of edition, its pages are numbered identically. Otherwise we would never find an indicated quotation or discussion. At the beginning, we shall find the *Mishnah;* it will be followed by the *Gemara,* which discusses and analyzes it, to be in turn followed by another *Mishnah.* This text is found in a column in the center of the page, surrounded on the inner margin by the commentary of Rashi, and on the outer, by Tosafot (the additions made by Rashi's successors). Supercommentaries and cross-indexes may be found on the side or bottom of the page, witnessing to the fact that Torah and Talmud are not a closed book but are continuously developing.

Continuing Oral Torah

Oral Torah did not come to an end with the compilation of the Talmud. It led to further commentaries and to codes such as that of Maimonides, the Turim (see p. 37), and the *Shulhan Arukh.* On the basis of the accumulated material and precedences, the Orthodox rabbi has to decide individual cases brought to him. Throughout the ages, a number of these decisions, called *Responsa,* were collected, and serve a rabbi in the same manner as court decisions guide judges and attorneys. The authority to hand down these decisions is granted the rabbi by his ordination. Modern rabbis are trained in many fields, and serve in many facets of life, such as in being teachers, preachers, and counselors. The ancient and medieval rabbi was simply a scholar and teacher, and above all, the vested authority of Jewish law. Traditional rabbis still fulfill this function, but (as in England, and also occurring in the United States) a group of rabbis who are specialists in Jewish law may also be appointed to deal with the more difficult cases. Such a body is called a *Beth Din* (Court of

Law). The Israeli rabbinate operates almost exclusively as an agency of religious law.

Example of Use of Commentaries and Codes: We shall now follow the development of one small item of law from its source to the codes. This is what we will have to do: (1) Get the source in the Written Torah and study it; (2) study Rashi's commentary to the verse in Written Torah; (3) turn to the Talmud and first study the Mishnah; (4) follow the comments of the Gemara. At each of these steps, Rashi's commentary will aid us. We may study additional commentaries, such as Tosafot.

Now we (5) turn to the Codes, which give us the accepted decisions. (It is not always necessary to consult all of the codes. In easy cases it may be sufficient to turn to the *Shulhan Arukh,* or even to one of the digests written later. In difficult cases, however, a rabbi may consult other codes and commentaries as well.) We can choose the Code written by Maimonides, his *Mishneh Torah.* We may follow it by the *Tur,* the code of Rabbi Jacob ben Asher, who arranged the law in the four "Rows" or *Turim.* We shall certainly consult the *Shulhan Arukh* by Rabbi Joseph Karo, which is the authoritative code for traditional Jewish practice. [Following the *Tur,* Joseph Karo also arranged the law in four sections. These are: (a) *Orah Hayim* (The Way of Life), containing laws of worship and holy days; (b) *Yore Deah* (The Teacher of Knowledge), dealing with dietary laws; (c) *Eben ha-Ezer* (The Stone of Help), containing the rules of family relationships, marriage, divorce, and others; and (d) *Hoshen Mishpat* (The Breastplate of Judgement), dealing with civil laws and similar items.] We turn to the volume dealing with our subject matter.

Our selection deals with the recital of the Affirmation of Faith, beginning with the words, "Hear O Israel, the Lord our God, the Lord is One." The first word, "Hear," is *Shema* in Hebrew, hence the whole paragraph is called the Shema.

Our source in Written Torah is Deuteronomy 6:4-9, quoted here with the usual verse numbers to aid in the discussion:

4. Hear, O Israel, the Lord our God, the Lord is One.
5. Thou shalt love the Lord thy God with all thy heart, and all thy soul, and all thy might.
6. And these words which I command thee this day shall be upon thy heart.
7. Thou shalt teach them diligently unto thy children, and shalt speak of them when thou sittest in thy house, and when thou walkest by the way, and when thou liest down, and when thou risest up.
8. And thou shalt bind them for a sign upon thy hand, and they shall be as frontlets between thine eyes.
9. And thou shalt write them upon the doorposts of thy house, and upon thy gates.

Rashi explains, citing midrashic and talmudic sources:

"Thou shalt love" (Verse 5): Do His bidding out of love, for he who acts out of love cannot be compared to him who acts (only) out of fear. . . . "With all thy heart": With both thine inclinations (toward good or evil), or another explanation: do not act half-heartedly in relationship to God. "And with all thy soul": Even if He takes thy soul (life). "And with all thy might" [citing Talmud Berakhot]: With all thy substance or money. There are people to whom their money is more precious than their person, hence it is stated: "and with all thy substance." Another explanation: With all thy capacities. . . . And how does this love express itself? "These words . . . shall be in thy heart" (Verse 6); through it, he recognizes God and cleaves to His ways. . . . "Speaking of them" (Verse 7): Your basic talk shall be about them. Make them your basic concern and not merely a side issue. "When thou liest down": I might have thought even if he lies down in the middle of the day [he would have to recite them], hence Torah says: "When thou risest up." I might have thought, even if he rises up in the middle of the night, hence Torah says: "When thou sittest in thine house and when thou walkest by the way." The Torah speaks of the customary usage, the usual time of lying down and the usual time of rising up.

As we turn to the Talmud, we find the Mishnah in the Tractate Berakhot, Chapter 1, Mishnah 3. This is followed by the Gemara. The Mishnah and the following discussion of Gemara are found on pages 10b and 11a in all editions of the Talmud.

In Tractate Berakhot, Chapter 1, Mishnah 3, we read:

The School of Shammai teaches: In the evening one must recite the Shema in a reclining position, and in the morning standing up, for it is said: when thou liest down and when thou risest up. The School of Hillel teaches: One may read it in any position, for it also says: When thou walkest by the way. [Torah simply says, you must recite it wherever you are and whatever you do.] Why does [Scripture] say: When thou liest down and when thou risest up? This refers to the hour of the day when people lie down, and the hour when they rise up. Rabbi Tarphon told: "Once, when on the road, I reclined to recite the Shema in accordance with the teachings of the School of Shammai, and I was almost attacked by robbers. They retorted: "You deserved to get into trouble, having transgressed against the words of the School of Hillel."

And in the Gemara we find:

The School of Hillel has indeed explained its reason and refuted the School of Shammai; but why, then, did the School of Shammai refuse to yield? It could argue [from the verse]: Scripture should have stated "in the morning and in the evening" [then the School of Hillel would be right]; but it states "when thou liest down and when thou risest up." It must mean that at the time of evening rest a leaning position is required, and at the time of getting up, a standing position is required.

The Rabbis taught: The School of Hillel says: one may recite it leaning, or standing, or sitting or reclining, or while walking by the way, or during one's work. Once, Rabbi Yishmael and Rabbi Eleazar, Son of Azariah, were together. Rabbi Yishmael was reclining, Rabbi Eleazar standing. When the time for the Shema came in the evening, Rabbi Eleazar reclined and Rabbi Yishmael stood up. Rabbi Eleazar said to Rabbi Yishmael, "Brother Yishmael, . . . while I was standing you were reclining, now that I am reclining you stand." [Why?] He answered, "Because I followed the decision of the School of Hillel [which permits the recital in any position; therefore I stood up, even in the evening]; you followed the opinion of the School of Shammai. Furthermore [had I not stood up], the disciples might have observed it and established Halakhah in that manner." What did he mean by the second statement? According to the School of Hillel, one may recite the Shema while reclining, provided that one finds himself in a reclining position. Until now, you were standing, then sat down and reclined [to recite the Shema]. [I was reclining, and had I continued to recline, the disciples would have seen both of us reclining, and] therefore one would have believed that both of us followed the decision of the School of Shammai. Noticing it, the disciples might have fixed Halakhah permanently" [according to Shammai]. [Hence I stood up.](10b–11a).

[In other words, one had been reclining already and the other sat down before reciting the Shema. According to Hillel, the first one could have remained in his position, but this might have created the wrong impression, that both followed Shammai; hence Rabbi Yishmael stood up. Now the disciples knew that the Shema could be recited in any position.]

The overriding issue was the principle. There must be no doubt in the disciples' minds that the School of Hillel must always be followed because this principle had many implications in numerous fields of Halakhah. In addition, the masters were aware of their obligation to teach not only by their words, but equally by their actions; conduct is instruction. Teaching and practice must go hand in hand. Example is more important than preachment. The disciples would recognize in the performance of their masters that they took in utter seriousness not only the *act* of reciting the affirmation of faith and of love of God, but the *meaning* of their affirmation, as well, in preparation and in recital, in adjustment of body and direction of heart. The two rabbis knew that in the presence of their disciples their action spelled out both a legal precedent and an inspiration in faith. Seen in this manner, the concern of these men does not spell a dwelling on trivialities and hairsplitting, but an act of guidance. No one ever knows how deep the impression of his actions may be, though they may appear insignificant to himself. It is only in this manner that we can fully understand the great concern of the rabbis with the exact performance of every Mitzvah.

Now we turn to Maimonides' *Mishneh Torah*, Book 2, and find the following:

Twice a day one must recite the Shema, in the evening and in the morning, as Scripture says, "when thou liest down, and when thou risest up," at the hour when people lie down, namely at night, and at the hour when people rise up, namely at daytime (Chapter 1, Par. 1).

He who recites the Shema without directing his heart [to God] . . . has not done his duty (Chapter 2, Par. 1).

Everyone may recite it in his prevailing position, standing or walking or sitting or riding on an animal. Yet it is forbidden to recite the Shema stretched out, facing downward or upward; but he may recite it resting on his side. If he is obese or sick and cannot turn on his side, let him turn a bit sidewise and recite it (Chapter 2, Par. 2).

If he is walking, he shall stop during the first verse; the rest he may recite walking. If he is asleep . . . one must wake him up (Chapter 2, Par. 3).

He must wash his hands before he recites it . . . (Chapter 3, Par. 1).

The regulations regarding the Shema will be found in the Orah Hayim section of *Tur* and *Shulhan Arukh*. In the Orah Hayim of *Tur*, Chapters 61 and 63, we read:

He shall recite it in awe and attunement to God . . . everyone shall consider it a new royal proclamation, newly issued, whenever he recites it. . . . It is God's proclamation. Thus do we find it in the Midrash . . . when a king of flesh and blood issues a proclamation to his provinces, all the people receive it standing up . . . but the Holy One . . . said to Israel: . . . I will not burden you by commanding you to stand up when you recite it . . . you may do so even while walking by the way, but must do so in awe and reverence.

He may read it either walking or standing or sitting down, but not lying down on his back, as Maimonides points out [here Maimonides is quoted]. Anyone who wishes to impose upon himself a special burden by standing up when he had been sitting down does wrong, and is actually called a sinner.

[Commentary by Joseph Karo]: For in daytime he transgresses against the decision of the School of Hillel and appears to be following the School of Shammai . . . and at night he follows neither school. He is called a sinner, for we find in [Tractate] Shabbat [40a] that he who transgresses against the rulings of the Rabbis is called a sinner.

Finally, we read in the Orah Hayim section of the *Shulhan Arukh* by Joseph Karo, Chapters 61 and 63:

He must recite the Shema with attunement to God, in awe and reverence. "Which I command thee this day" [is cited in Scripture] to tell you that it must be new to thee every day, and not be like something often heard and habitual. It has been a custom to recite the first verse aloud, in order to arouse the "Kavanah" (attunement).

It has been a custom to place the hands over the face during the recital of the first verse, in order that he may not be distracted from his Kavanah by extraneous impressions.

He shall prolong the pronouncement of the letters of the word "One" in reflection on God's Kingship in heaven and on earth and to call to mind that God is One and Only in the universe, ruling over its entire expanse.

After the first verse he shall recite: Blessed be His Name, His glorious Kingdom is for ever and ever. (This sentence is not part of the verses in Deuteronomy.)

After these first verses he shall pause for a brief instant (before continuing "and thou shalt love . . .") to indicate (and reflect on) the distinction between "Acceptance of the Kingdom of Heaven" (contained in the first and second verse, which, as the foundation of Jewish life, is basic) and the Mitzvot ("thou shalt love", which derive from it). He may recite it walking, or standing, reclining, or riding on an animal, but not lying stretched out, facing downward or upward; yet he may recite it lying on his side (note: if he is lying down already, and it would be a burden for him to get up). If he is obese and cannot turn to his side, or sick, let him turn a bit to the side and recite it.

He who wants to make it hard on himself and stands up after he has been sitting, to recite it standing up, he is called a sinner.

If he is walking and wants to recite the Shema, he shall stop at the first verse.

If he is asleep one must wake him up, even if it troubles him.

In these developments, we see the respect for Written Torah; every word in it is regarded as significant. Fluid interpretation at the beginning of the development yields to terse regulation at its end. We should remember that Hillel and Shammai lived at a time when the Land constituted a unifying force. Maimonides balanced strictness in observance by freely speculating in philosophy, as Torah permitted. The *Shulhan Arukh,* at the end of the development, was written to unite the people and strengthen their will to live through Mitzvot. Immersion in Mitzvot gave the people the sense of closeness to God and to one another. The elements of God-Torah-Land-Mitzvot are all there, yet emphasis is placed differently as outward conditions have weakened the Land as living soil of a living people, and as persecution has drawn them ever more deeply into the shell of minute performance.

DEFINITIONS AND SYMBOLS: 9
GOD, MAN, AND ETERNITY

God

IN his vision of God at the burning bush, Moses is given a definition: "I am He Who Brings Into Being" (Exodus 3:14). A contraction of this term is found in the name of God, spelled *YHWH*. Pious Jewish tradition forbids the pronouncement of this word, and in the reading of Torah and worship it is read: *Adonai*, "Lord." God, Creator and Master of nature and history, is thus seen as so completely unfathomable that even a proper name would confine Him. The name is not used; God is simply Lord. To the patriarchs, this knowledge of God was not yet vouchsafed. To them He was *Shaddai*, a term which has been interpreted as God who is self-sufficient, who needs no other force or assistance. (Some scholars of the school of Biblical criticism explain the term as meaning "God of the Mountains"; Jews have given it a different etymological derivation.) God also bears the name *El*, which stands for Power, and *Elohim*, which might define Him as the Sum of All Power: As Elohim He is envisioned as mankind's supreme Judge. Jews have applied yet other terms to Him, such as *Makom*, The Every-Place, and *Shalom*, meaning Absolute Perfection. (Shalom means peace, which is the sum of perfection.) In search for a term which might contain all the elements of divine omnipotence, Jews have also used the term King. God is King.

With the attribute of power goes that of love. The rabbis note that two names of God are used in the story of creation. "In the beginning God (Elohim) created" (Genesis 1:1). Later, beginning with the second chapter, a double term is used, the Lord God (YHWH-Elohim); finally, only the term the Lord (YHWH) is used. This particularity was also observed by those scholars who undertook the scientific investigation of the authorship of Scripture beginning in the nineteenth century. The difference between the scholarly results of the "Higher Biblical Criticism" (that school and movement, comprising

127

Christians and Jews, dealing with Scriptures as a human work, and subjecting it to critical analysis—historical, linguistic, archaeological, etc.) and the conclusions drawn by the rabbis is highly revealing of Jewish thought. The modern researchers found in the different names for God an indication that different authors had composed the various parts, which had then become fused. They speak of a *Jahvist* (a writer who uses YHWH as God's Name, spelled in German with a J) and an *Elohist,* who uses Elohim; and they found additional authors, one composing the *P* (priestly code) of Leviticus, and *D,* a Deuteronomist, the author of the fifth book of the Pentateuch, etc. With these investigations, modern Biblical research got under way.

The rabbis see Elohim as the Name of God, who uses His power as stern judge; Elohim in Hebrew also means judge; YHWH, the God of History, reveals to us His compassion, which makes life bearable in history. The rabbis explain as follows: In the beginning, God decided to rule the world by strict justice, but He realized that it could not exist when judged by the absolute standard of justice. He added the attribute of His compassion, prepared to permit mercy to mitigate justice, hence the two Names. Ultimately He found that even tempered justice was too much for man and world, and He based His rule entirely on mercy. We find, therefore, that in the pronouncement of His attributes (Exodus 34: 6–7), the term El, God of justice, is intimately linked to *Rahum,* a term derived from *Rehem,* the mother's womb. He is concerned with justice but He is abundantly compassionate, sheltering His people in absolute loving security.

Rabbi Johanan says in Megillah 31a:

> Whenever you find the greatness of God expressed in Scripture, you equally find expressed His humility. Thus it is recorded in Torah, repeated in Nevee-im, and again, for the third time, in Ketubim. In Torah (Deuteronomy 10:17–18) we read: "For the Lord your God, He is God of gods, and Lord of lords, the great God, the mighty, and the awesome, who shows no favor and takes no bribe. . . . but upholds the case of the fatherless and the widow." In Prophets (Isaiah 57:15) we read: "For thus says the High and Lofty One that inhabiteth eternity, whose Name is Holy: I dwell . . . with him that is of a contrite and humble spirit, to revive the spirit of the humble, and to revive the heart of the contrite ones." Repeated a third time in Ketubim (Psalm 68:5–6), it reads: "Extol Him that rideth upon the skies, whose name is the Lord," followed by, [He is] "a father of the fatherless, an advocate of the widows."

The Jew, recognizing the holiness and absoluteness of God, is confidently sure that God's power will be but the instrument of His mercy. This synthesis is expressed in the designation of God as "our

Father." A father has power and dominion, which is exercised in behalf of his love. "Blessed art thou, O Israel," exclaims Akiba, "for He who cleanses you of all your sins, and before Whom you cleanse yourselves, it is your Father who is in heaven."

On the Days of Awe, the great prayer of petition (in which Jews ask for a year of health, sustenance, forgiveness of sins, and blessings), appeals to God as "Our Father, our King." We trust in Him as our Father, secure in His eternal love, we appeal to Him as our King, all-powerful to supply our needs.

As King He must judge us and all mankind, for without justice the world could not endure; as Father he waits for us and urges us to repent, and never ceases pleading with man to the moment of his death that he may return. And if man does repent, He will immediately receive him in affection as His beloved child. Even in judging us, He is aware of our frailties and deals with us kindly, as the Father who has given us life and knows our weaknesses. Therefore, Jews have realized that divine love is never withdrawn from them in prosperity or in adversity; they praise Him even in moments of deepest sorrow and distress.

As has been explained, Judaism is aware that no definition can encompass God. Thus it has been free to define Him in different ways, as we have seen in our discussion of Maimonides, Hermann Cohen, Mordecai Kaplan, and others. Two things are forbidden the Jew: he may never see God as anything but absolutely one, and may not confine Him to any image. The liberty accorded otherwise by Judaism may equip its liberal thinkers with the freedom to find those definitions of God which make Him meaningful and acceptable under changing conditions, including our scientific age. This has not yet been fully done for our time and is leading some Christian (and Jewish) thinkers through the potentially very dangerous stage of atheism, the rejecting of the old without new affirmations. But it may eventually constitute a contribution to a God concept meaningful to "honest-to-God" moderns. So far the "God-is-dead" theology has resulted in confusion.

The living God is truly found in imitation—in Mitzvot—rather than speculation. In this sense, Martin Buber is right when he maintains that God is found in a dialogue. I must listen to Him, understand what He demands of me, and act upon this call in my relations to my fellow man. In the course of existing before Him, I shall find Him unfolding before me. The Talmud points out, [If there were a choice] "better they forgot Me [says God] but kept My Mitzvot" (Jerushalmi, Hagiga I:7). For in keeping the Mitzvot, we make Him manifest. Though we forget His definition, we establish Him. God and Mitzvah thus are linked inseparably as Call and Response. He who responds cannot forget the Caller.

Man

Rabbi Akiba used to say, "Beloved is man, as he was created in the image [of God], and an even greater love was accorded him in being made aware that he is created in the image of God" (Abot 3:18). Thus he becomes God's co-worker, and all men are equal. The creation of but one man underscores this fact: no one can say that his ancestors were better than those of his neighbor (Sanhedrin 4:5). Created in the image of God, and endowed with a divine soul, man has worth and dignity beyond any other work of God's creation, even though he is a product of the earth to which he must return, weak, frail, and insignificant. This dual character is expressed by the Psalmist:

> When I behold the heavens, the work of Thy fingers, the moon and the stars which Thou hast established; what is man that Thou art mindful of him, and the son of man that Thou takest account of him? Yet Thou hast made him but little lower than the angels, and hast crowned him with glory and honor. Thou hast made him to have dominion over the works of Thy hands . . . (Psalm 8:4–6).

Man thus is "son of man," but he is also "son of God" (Deuteronomy 14:1) ; the choice is his. Man bears the characteristics of his divinity and the characteristics of his animal character, the rabbis point out. Like any animal, he eats and drinks, excretes, multiplies, and dies. As a divine being, he stands erect, speaks, reasons, and sees straight. If he is worthy, he precedes the angels, as the Psalmist has pointed out ; if he is unworthy, every insect may remind him, "I was created before you and take precedence over you."

Man's soul is given him pure; Judaism does not accept the concept of original sin. It would not be just, and contrary to God's goodness, to burden the innocent with the guilt of the past. Yet man has the capacity to sin. It is a prerequisite of freedom; only he who has the power to sin can voluntarily do good. "The inclination to do evil" thus is an instrument of human creativity, a challenge to holiness; it gives man his freedom and with it his dignity, for it sets him apart from all the rest of nature. "All is in the hands of Heaven [God] except reverence for Heaven" (Berakhot 33b). This freedom must find a twofold expression: we must keep away from evil, and we must actively promote good, "to set aright the world under the Kingdom of the Almighty" (daily prayer). This creative act is Mitzvah.

Out of this awareness of man's inherent equality and dignity, our relationships to one another must be established in the spirit of love. "Love thy neighbor, his is like thee: I am the Lord" (who created him like thee, and who watches over his dignity as He watches over thine)

(Leviticus 19:18). Hence the first questions addressed to man as he appears before God in final judgment of his life are these:

> Hast thou dealt faithfully with thy fellowman; hast thou appointed regular periods for [the study of] Torah [that it be a guide to conduct]; hast thou brought children into the world; hast thou looked forward to redemption . . . ? If the fear of God is his treasure, it will be well with him, otherwise not (Shabbat 31a).

Man's work in the world, his striving for redemption, and his actions in behalf of God as he carries out his daily rounds—these assure his life of worth. Not in Mitzvot toward God, but in those toward his fellow man does man primarily earn his salvation. This entails a decent love for one's own self. Of Hillel it is said that he considered the care of his body a Mitzvah. Judaism has never believed in the merits of asceticism and has even stated that man must account for the decent joys in life which God has placed in his way and which he declined (Jerushalmi Kiddushin 4). Joined to this self-respect must be humility. Moses was deigned worthy by God to receive the Torah because he was humble (Shabbat 67a).

These principles entail also an unconditional love of neighbor, even of enemy. We must help him and may not even bear any grudge against him (Exodus 23:4–5; Leviticus 19:17). We must consider every man's dignity and may never put him to shame. Only in secret may we give our support to the poor, lest he feel embarrassed. Charity in Hebrew is called *Tzedaka,* righteousness; it is simply right living that we support those with whom destiny has dealt harshly:

> Better than charity is the loan given to the needy, which helps set him up; better even a partnership with him, that allows him to draw on your experience as well as your resources (Abot deRabbi Nathan 41:66a).

> Let the honor of your fellow man be as dear to you as your own; and let the property of your fellow man be as dear to you as your own (Abot 2:15, 17).

This applies not only to Jews, but to all people, regardless of faith or race or color:

> I call heaven and earth to witness that on every person, be he Jew or non-Jew, man or woman, or servant, the divine spirit rests on him according to his deeds. The heathen is thy neighbor, thy brother, to do him wrong is a sin (Tanna debe Eliyahu 207, 284).

The Jew, therefore, respects the right of all to find their way to God in their own fashion. Judaism did exclude the heathendom of old with its immoral practices, but solemnly declares that "the righteous among the peoples of the world will have a share in the world to come" (Yalkut Shimoni to Prophets 296). "The just among the peoples of the world are priests of God" (Eliyahu Sutah 20).

Judaism accords respect to all ethical faiths, and—finding that they all lead to salvation—does not engage in missionary work. Nevertheless, Judaism would consider it unfair to any person were it to deny him the right to join the faith and destiny of the Jewish people. If, in full conviction, a person feels that Judaism gives him true spiritual fulfilment, he has a right to find it. Having thus affiliated himself, the convert becomes a full-fledged member of the Jewish people, beloved by God and his newly found brethren in faith.

In Judaism, not one single soul is considered expendable. God is the Father, and every human being is a son of God upon whom the holy spirit rests. Only through sin may the holy spirit depart from him, as David found out. Involved in grievous sin, he therefore cries out: "Do not take Thy holy spirit from me" (Psalm 51:13). In return to God through repentance, man finds this spirit restored to him.

Angels

Malakh (Angel) simply means messenger. Whoever carries God's message in the world becomes His angel. Significantly, the messengers of God in the narrower sense of His Angels are simply called "man." Three men (angels) appear to Abraham to predict, among other items, the birth of Isaac (Genesis 18); Samson's mother, to whom an angel predicts a son who will rescue his people, recognizes him simply as a man of God (Judges 13:2-6).

In time, angels came to be considered special creatures, serving as specific messengers of God, surrounding Him as a heavenly court (Isaiah 6), performing functions specifically entrusted to them by God Himself. The names given them give evidence of their functions: *Raphael,* God heals; *Uriel,* God is my light; *Michael,* Who is like God. It is an angel who relays God's message to Abraham, telling him not to sacrifice his son (Genesis 22:11ff.).

In later writings, the idea of guardian angels is developed. Michael is Israel's guardian angel, who will lead Israel in the conflict with the enemies of God in the battle at the end of days (Daniel 12).

The fact that Jewish thought recognizes angels nevertheless should not obscure their minor position, as it is to God that we offer prayer and from Him alone that we expect help. "For His angels will He put in charge over thee to guard thee . . . because he has set his love on Me, *I* will deliver him" (Psalm 91:11-14). This shows clearly in a verse offered in prayer at bedtime, one of the few prayers that mention angels at all:

In the behest of God, the Lord of Israel, may there be Michael at my right, Gabriel at my left, Uriel in front of me, Raphael behind me; but over my head may there be the presence of God.

Satan

From Persian thought, the concept of Satan entered Jewish beliefs. The Persian Zoroaster believed in a conflict between light and darkness, good and evil, which would continue throughout the ages, until, at the very end, God, the light of the world, would triumph over the forces of darkness and evil. God was thus seen surrounded by a heavenly host, the angels, and His adversary, Satan, by his minions of evil.

This form of dualism was attacked by Jews. The second Isaiah makes it clear: God alone creates light and darkness, fashions peace as well as evil (Isaiah 45:7). Satan was demoted and became a kind of prosecuting attorney, as in the book of Job, where he levels his accusation against Job and is given the right to test him. From then on he no longer appears in the book. It is God who settles the issue and determines Job's fate. Yet, even as the accuser, doing his duty, Satan is rebuked. Has he no compassion with the remnant of Israel, "a brand plucked out of the fire?" (Zechariah 3:1ff.).

The concept of Satan thus has had little significance in Jewish thought; God, and He alone, is their merciful and living shield, protector, and guardian; he may chastise, but only in love, and He will redeem.

The Messiah

Plagued by adversity, setbacks, and disappointments, subjected to tyranny, yet convinced that God, Master of History, would lead the world to redemption, the Jews came to envision the day when peace and brotherhood would reign, when no further obstacles would prevent the full enjoyment of the Land and the wholehearted response to the divine call in Mitzvah. This was the day of the Messiah. As David once had been Israel's ideal king, so would his descendant establish a perfect society. Isaiah's utopia, the time when the lion and lamb would dwell together, and the "shoot of the trunk of Jesse" would rule in righteousness (Isaiah 11), was transposed into the future as both goal and challenge. In the forecast of Malachi, this Messiah, God's anointed (messiah means anointed) would be preceded by Elijah, the prophet, who had never died but gone bodily to heaven (II Kings 2:11–12).

Elijah had been the foe of compromise, the champion of integrity; he would create the unity of love between the generations which would assure the coming of the messianic age (Malachi 3:23–24).

The idea of the messianic age has been fundamental to Judaism, and its most creative force in their dedication to social justice.

When will he come? "Today, if you will hearken to my voice," quote the rabbis (Psalm 95:7). Maimonides warns against any eschatological predictions. The times calculated by man for the end of days, Maimonides points out, will pass without fulfilment; the end is concealed, speculation regarding it prohibited by the rabbis. "For the vision is yet for the appointed time. . . . Though it tarry, wait for it; because it will surely come, it will not delay" (Habakkuk 2:3). Thus the messianic age is not a subject for calculations, but an eternal task, challenging us to grow toward it. What will this end be? Again, Maimonides answers:

> The world will not change its accustomed order, but Israel will dwell se-cure, and mankind will find that true faith which will prevent them from making war and carrying destruction. Israel will not become exalted over mankind, or yield power, but will be undisturbed to follow Torah, study it, perform its Mitzvot. No longer will there be war in the world; all man-kind will enjoy peace and prosperity; and all will search for that wisdom which God alone can give (Maimonides' Mishneh Torah XI, XII).

Orthodox Jews believe in a personal Messiah, a man who will actually arrive; Reform Jews see in the messianic age the symbol of a future in which all mankind will be united in brotherhood. The modern philoso-pher Hermann Cohen, eliminating the belief in a personal Messiah, yet considers the Messiah idea as the most powerful lever in history and Judaism's most significant contribution to the vision of the future for all mankind. As Cohen puts it:

> The future, which the prophets have painted in the symbol of the Mes-siah, is the future of world history. It is the goal, it is the meaning of his-tory . . .

> It is humanity itself which has to bring about this age of the Messiah. Men and cultures must learn to think and hope for the ideal of human life, the ideal of individuals and nations, the future of the Messiah as something in the *future* of the human race. The realization of morality on earth, its tasks and its eternal goal, this, and nothing else is the meaning of the Messiah for us . . .

> The Kingdom of the Messiah is the kingdom of God. Not a personal ruler is this Messiah, not a hero, but the spirit of God rests upon him and he brings justice to the peoples . . . (Jüdische Schriften III, p. 173ff.).

The significance of the messianic idea in Judaism can hardly be overemphasized. It differs from the Christian idea, as it is directed to the future. It has sustained the Jew in times of trials and inspired him to work for the kingdom of God on earth, not for himself but for all mankind.

Resurrection

Many pious and devoted workers for this great consummation of history will die before the event happens. Should they not be rewarded? These considerations may have prompted the belief in Resurrection. Daniel (12:2) mentions the awakening of those who sleep in the dust, some to their rewards, others to their punishment. The idea is not found in the Five Books of Moses, but the Pharisees believed so firmly in the Resurrection that they interpreted the Song at the Red Sea (Exodus 15:1) to refer not only to the rescue which Israel had just felt, but also to the future. "Then sang Moses and the children of Israel" can grammatically be construed also as, "Then will Moses . . . sing," and this refers to the day of their resurrection, according to rabbinic comment.

But Judaism has not been concerned too much with the question of resurrection. Reform Jews denied it at one time. As far as punishment is concerned, Jews, in the words of Hillel, maintain that God is altogether too merciful to impose eternal punishment for the temporary aberrations of weak human beings during their lifetime. He will be gracious to all mankind.

The World to Come

As Judaism firmly believes in the God-given soul, bestowed pure on every man, it also maintains a firm faith in *Olam Haba,* the world to come. This is not the same as the time of the Messiah, or the Resurrection. It is the sheltering of souls in God's eternal dwelling forever. There they will share the joys of their closeness to the divine Glory.

Again, Maimonides warns against the formulation of any picture. As we do not know God, we know not what He has in store for us. But Judaism does not devote excessive thought to the question of the "salvation" of souls. "All of Israel will have a share in the world to come." "All the righteous of the peoples of the world have a share in it."

The idea of a temporary punishment or purgatory can be found in Judaism. It would expiate the sins of our temporary stay on earth (but sinners will find rest every Sabbath). But the task is here, and now. May we devote ourselves to it, and leave to God the ultimate determination of our future.

Some Symbols

A symbol is a visible object or an act that conveys a message greater than itself. Every Mitzvah is, in a sense, a symbol. It stands for the presence of God to whom we respond and it links us to the community of Israel, past, present, and future. It speaks of Torah, upon which it is based, and reveals the sanctity of life. A few special symbols will be mentioned here.

The *menorah* is the seven-branched candelabrum which was once the lamp in the sanctuary (as ordained in Torah) and is now the coat of arms of the State of Israel. Zechariah sees a seven-branched menorah in a vision, and is told, "Not by might, nor by power, but by My spirit" [will ye prevail] (Zechariah 4:6). The seven branches reflect the seven directions of the universe, East, West, North, South, Above, Below, and man's place itself. All of them are to be illuminated by the light of the holy spirit.

The windows in the Temple of old were so constructed that the light did not fall into its precincts from the outside, but was shed abroad from the menorah within. The menorah thus stands for the illumination that shall go forth from Zion; it represents Israel's function as a light to the nations; it envisions the day when all mankind will walk in God's light; and assures the Jew that by the spirit of God he will prevail against the forces of adversity. The menorah is symbol of Israel's historical mission and of the world's redemption when it is ready to accept the spiritual illumination that goes forth from God, who is everywhere, but who considers the place and condition of the individual—every individual—as a primary source of enlightenment.

The *Magen David*, Shield of David, is a six-pointed star. We do not know if David's shield had this form. As symbol, the Shield of David emerged later than the menorah. The synagogue in Capernaum, Israel (second century), features the menorah prominently and the Magen David only incidentally. It may have been a charm, repelling evil spirits, even as the five-pointed star was so used in the Middle Ages. The explanation which Franz Rosenzweig offers (p. 59) holds a great deal of poetic meaning: The points signify God-World-Man and Creation-Revelation-Redemption; the rays stand for the road which links each of these three, combining all of them into an eternal unity. The Star formed of the two triangles becomes symbol of the goal (the Messianic Time) and of the road, the unification of all the elements which humanity must bring about, and which Judaism calls for.

The *Wearing of the Hat* is a late symbol. For many centuries the practice was fluid. It might signify the fact that "the glory of God resides above" and I humbly cover myself before it, indicating the limitations of the human mind (Kiddushin 31a). Yet it may also stand as a symbol of Jewish self-respect and hope. Upon the medieval Jew, the world forced a grotesque, horn-like hat, to symbolize his demonic character; the Jew—son of the devil—wore horns. But the Jew, never doubting the love of God and convinced of his redemption in the day of the Messiah, wore it proudly. First he wore it only during worship, then always. He was a prince in God's sight, and like a prince, might let his head remain covered in the presence of the King of Kings. To the degree that degradation increased, the wearing of the hat became universal. As a symbol of self-respect, it was truly Mitzvah, enshrining God's presence, Torah, and commandments, and a permanent reminder of redemption.

No custom has had a firmer hold on Jews than the wearing of the hat. None created more controversy than the ruling of Reform Judaism that it need no longer be worn in worship, as times, customs, and symbols had changed. Many laws of Torah were quietly discarded, but the hat, expressing Jewish self-affirmation, remained.

As symbol of self-respect and affirmation of human dignity and rights, the hat or the skullcap (often called *yarmulke*) has recently acquired a new and significant meaning. In their battle for civil rights, the Negroes of the American South found support from many whites, who came from all parts of the country to join the marches and demonstrations and give whatever help they could. A large number of clergymen, including rabbis, were among the demonstrators. While the clergy of the Christian denominations was recognizable by their clerical garb, the rabbis, who wear no distinctive clothing, decided to wear *yarmulkes* in order to be recognized. The Negroes, instinctively recognizing in this head-covering a symbol of freedom, immediately began to clamor for it, and hundreds of skullcaps were actually sent by the rabbis to the South and its Negro people. The symbolic meaning of the hat thus found a practical application in our time, and may lead to its reintroduction at least to some of the Reform congregations who previously abandoned it.

LIFE AS MITZVAH III

10 PRAYER AND THE HOUSE OF THE LORD

IDEALLY, the totality of life is to be a witness to God, an all-encompassing Mitzvah through which God will be made manifest and the people of Israel sustained.

The *Shulhan Arukh* states it clearly:

Man shall make himself strong as a lion as he arises in the morning to serve his Creator. [Note by Rabbi Moses Isserles: "I have set the Lord always before me" (Psalm 16:8) is one of the basic principles of Torah; it is one of the virtues of the righteous who walk before Him at all times. . . . "Let man take to heart that the Great King, God—whose glory filleth the whole earth—stands over him and watches over all his actions. . . . This awareness will immediately fill him with reverence, humility, and awe before Him, Blessed be His Name. . . . May he never feel ashamed before those people who make mock of him on account of his service to God, His Name be Blessed" (Orah Hayim 1:1).]

If he cannot study without an afternoon nap, let him take a nap, but not drag it out. . . . Even in as small a matter as that, may his intentions be not to give pleasure to his body, but to return his body to the service of Him whose Name be Blessed. The same applies to all the enjoyments in this world; not pleasure be his intention, but service to his Creator, Blessed be He, as it is written, "In all thy ways recognize Him" (Proverbs 3:6), to which our sages have commented: "May all thy actions be for the sake of Heaven" (Abot 2:12). Even his unregulated actions, such as eating and drinking, walking and sitting, standing, intercourse, talk, and all the needs of the body, every one of them should be directed to the service of his Creator, or as a means leading to service unto Him. Thus, if he be hungry or thirsty and eats or drinks simply for his enjoyment, his acts are not praiseworthy; rather shall his intention be to eat and drink for the preservation of his life, in order that he may serve his Creator. . . . The same goes for intercourse, the marital duties ordained in Torah. If he performs them to appease his desires or for the enjoyment of his body, he should be ashamed; even if his intentions are to have children who may eventually help him and ultimately take his place, that too is not praiseworthy. His intention shall be to have children who will serve his Creator; or better yet, his intention shall be to fulfil the command-

140

ment of marital duty like a man who pays a debt. The same applies to talk. . . . All in all: He must turn his sight and heart toward his road, weigh all his actions on the scales of his intellect. If he sees something leading him to an opportunity of serving his Creator, Blessed be He, let him do it; otherwise, may he not do it. He who conducts himself in this fashion serves his Creator always (Orah Hayim 231:1).

We may readily admit that such a life is impossible for the average person. We recognize that Mitzvah had become *the* pillar of Judaism by the time the *Shulhan Arukh* was written; we may see in its statement a guideline and goal affecting every action, and affording a yardstick by which daily routine may be measured. We note that nothing is excluded from being a Mitzvah, there is no dualism of spirit and flesh. All depends on the intent. Sex may be a Mitzvah, while simple rest, under certain circumstances, may not be.

Since everything from enjoyment to suffering must be given a meaning in God's plan, it is essential that man be aware of his actions as he performs them; then they will become Mitzvah.

The Berakhah (Blessing)

The rabbis of the Talmud ordained, therefore, that every act be preceded by a spoken affirmation that it is done "for the sake of Heaven," every pleasure must be savored in adoration of its Creator. Thus the unit of prayer was formulated in order that the Jew might clothe the promptings of his heart in a structured garment. This unit is *Berakhah,* the Benediction. The Psalmist had used it: "Blessed art Thou, O Lord, teach me Thy statutes" (Psalm 119:12).

The Talmud teaches:

Over fruit growing on trees one says [before eating them]: "Blessed art Thou, God our Lord, King of the Universe, who createst the fruit of the tree". . . . Over wine one says: "Blessed . . . who createst the fruit of the vine". . . . Over fruits of the ground one speaks: "Blessed . . . who createst the fruit of the ground." Over bread one pronounces: "Blessed . . . who bringest forth bread from the earth." Over anything which does not grow from the earth one says: "Blessed . . . by whose word all was created". . . . After a meal everyone shall say grace (Mishnah Berakhot 6:1, 3, 6).

Over comets, earthquakes, thunder, storm, and lightnings, over mountains, hills, oceans, rivers, and deserts [a blessing is pronounced by the beholder]. . . . Over rain and on getting happy news one says: "Blessed . . . who art good and art doing good." On receiving evil tidings one recites: "Blessed . . . the true judge". . . . It is man's duty to bless God for the ills that befall him holding hidden good, even as he gives

blessing for the good that comes to him, though it hold hidden ills. . . .
Has he built a new house or bought new clothes, he shall pronounce
praise: "Blessed . . . who hast kept us alive, hast sustained us, and has
brought us to this time" (Mishnah Berakhot 9:2, 3, 5).

Man's thoughts thus revolve constantly about God. The world is
truly the Lord's, and the fullness thereof. What man owns may be
legally his; ideally, it is God's. The Berakhah is man's request for
permission to use it, joined to man's pledge to make use of it for God's
glory, in order that God may be made manifest. The totality of life thus
becomes worship; it is Mitzvah.

Understanding the character and purpose of Berakhah, we may arrive
at an understanding of Jewish prayer in general, which is built on
Berakhah.

Prayer and Its Structure

Prayer is not so much petition, but affirmation of God. Petition emerges
in form of an adjunct. We know the greatness and omnipotence of God,
we affirm His love, hence (aware of His power and of His compassion)
we present our needs to Him, trusting that His response to our plea will
always be for our best, regardless of whether we can grasp it or not.
Many petitions thus open with the words: "May it be Thy will,"
meaning if it not be Thy will, then Thy will be done, not ours, for Thy
will is good. Prayer, therefore, must be offered not as routine recital of
words, but as a plea, an outpouring of the heart (Berakhot 4:4) with
Kavanah, attunement of the heart. Nor may it be an ever-repeated,
overindulgent appeal; this would make it cheap, and diminish our respect
for God (Tanhuma). Nor may we approach God in formal prayer,
unless we have attuned ourselves to it through meditation; only thus can
prayer fulfil its function to link us to God and to unify ourselves as we
overcome inner conflicts through the act of relating our total being to
God.

This applies specifically to formal, structured prayer. For every day of
the week Jewish law has appointed three orders of prayer: *Shaharit,* the
morning prayer, *Minhah,* the afternoon prayer, and *Maariv,* the evening
prayer. On holy days, a special prayer, the *Mussaf* (Additional Prayer),
reflecting on the significance of the day, is added. These prayers are
uniform throughout the year, as far as their core is concerned; morning,
noon, and evening prayers are the same for every day. This is significant.
Structured prayer, first of all, expresses the feelings of the individual
person better than he could in his own words. It offers the vehicle for his
own thoughts, as he fills the familiar words with ever-renewed meaning.

The repetition of identical prayers actually corresponds to the eternal course of time, always the same, from sunrise to sunset, yet ever renewed. The worshipper who endows the unchanging words with ever new meaning is thus drawn to the fact that life is uniform, but may not be routine, that day follows day, but each day is a new creation, challenging him to renew himself in spirit and in action, and never to lose his wonderment at the miracle which is evident in the orderliness of nature. This finds clear expression in one of the Berakhot that is part of every worship:

> We gratefully acknowledge unto Thee that Thou art the Lord our God, and the God of our fathers unto all eternity; Thou art the Rock of our life, shield of our salvation from generation to generation. We give thanks unto Thee and declare Thy praise for our lives committed unto Thy hand, for our souls entrusted unto Thee, for Thy miracles that are with us daily, Thy wondrous deeds and acts of goodness that are with us at all times, evening, morning, and afternoon. Thou art good, for Thy mercies never fail; compassionate, for the acts of Thy loving kindness never cease. We hope in Thee forever. For all this Thy Name be blessed and exalted, Thou, our King, always and forever. May all the living offer laud unto Thee, and praise Thy Name in truth, God of our salvation and of our help. Blessed art Thou, O Lord, "The Good" is Thy Name, and to Thee it is proper to render thanks.

Under God every moment of life becomes a miracle. In Him we gain strength. The knowledge that He *is* gives us hope. All that lives expresses His praise, being witness to His creative power. In this spirit we must approach structured worship.

Of the three prayers, the morning and evening prayer have their source in the Shema itself: Rehearse ye the words of God's unity and the call to love every evening and every morning. Morning prayer prepares us for the road in life; evening prayer bids us to give account. The afternoon prayer, at the time when the afternoon offering was once presented in the Temple, calls us to pause and reflect: how much have we achieved, where have we failed, what may we yet do to transform the work of the day into a Mitzvah?

We may compare our appearance before God in worship to an audience before a king. Its structure reflects this thought.

Shaharit (Morning Prayer)

1. On arising, the individual, grateful for his reborn strength, prepares himself for the meeting; even as he puts on his clothes, he is aware of God's beneficence in clothing him, in feeding him, in giving him bodily vigor.

2. In meditation and psalm, the worshipper puts himself in tune with the occasion.

3. Individuals form a group to meet the King. Public worship opens with the call to worship, "Bless ye the Lord to whom all blessing belongeth." The congregation responds, "Blessed be the Lord to whom all blessing belongeth, unto all eternity."
4. The people affirm God's greatness, love, and majesty:
He is the Creator of day and night, the Lord of nature;
He is the source of all wisdom, who has given his Torah to His people.
He is One, calling for our love: the Shema Yisrael is recited.
He is the God of history, who has rescued us from all enemies, and will help all mankind.
5. Trusting in Him, we offer our petitions to Him, asking for wisdom, health, forgiveness of sins, our daily bread, and restoration. But we begin and conclude with praise. This prayer is recited standing and is called *Amidah*. The petitionary prayer is first offered in silent devotion and then publicly, repeated by the Reader (during morning and afternoon worship) with an insertion of the sanctification proclaiming His divine majesty: "Holy, holy, holy is the Lord of hosts, the whole earth is full of His glory." The wording of the final petition closely resembles the affirmation of faith in its wording. The affirmation had started with: *Shema Yisrael, Adonai Elohenu*, "Hear, O Israel, the Lord our God." The petition begins with: *Shema kolenu, Adonai Elohenu*, "Hear our voice, O Lord, our God . . . and accept graciously our petition." The same rhythm that proclaims Him, expresses our plea, for it emerges out of His recognition and simply evokes reciprocal love.
6. The individual confesses his sins in awareness that he is truly unworthy to petition, much less to receive the divine mercies for which he has asked.
7. The word of the King is heard. The Torah is read on appointed days of the week and on special days.
8. With a final affirmation and remembrance of the departed (that their memory be a guide), we take our leave.

Minhah (Afternoon Prayer). The afternoon prayer is short. Since the recital of the Shema is not ordained, it is omitted. By reciting Psalm 145 (which speaks of God's goodness to all), we put ourselves in tune. He sustains us; may we be mindful of it whether the day so far has been successful or a failure. Then the Amidah is recited and repeated. Confession of sin and final affirmation conclude the worship.

Maariv (Evening Prayer). Parallel to morning worship, the evening worship, after an introductory psalm, starts with the call to worship. God is praised as Creator of night and as author of Torah, source of all wisdom. Then the Shema is recited. God is revered as Master of History, and now a special prayer for protection throughout the night is included.

The Amidah is recited silently, after which, with affirmation, we take our leave.

A prayer at bedtime concludes the day.

On Sabbath days and holy days, all petitions are omitted; sheltered in God's peace, the Jew should forget his cares on these days. Confession of sin is also omitted; nothing should dim the joy of God's day, not even the knowledge of our sinfulness.

On festivals of joy, the Hallel (Psalms 113–118) are recited by the people in gratitude for God's special dispensations of help.

Mussaf (Additional Prayer). To commemorate the special festive occasion in remembrance of the ancient service in the Temple, a special prayer is added on holy days, the *Mussaf,* Addition. It is recited after the reading of Torah and keynotes the special occasion. (Reform Judaism has eliminated it.)

The prayers are not simply read, but rendered in the form of a recitative, which is very old. The reading of the Torah and Haftarah follows a prescribed pattern of modes, which the Reader must know. While every Jew with ability and moral character may serve as "the congregation's messenger" leading them in prayer, Jews have always had a great love for music (a dynamic force in contrast to sculpture), and demanded well-trained cantors with good voices, who might endow the words with added meaning, expressing in song the yearning of the heart and conveying in music the message of a special day. Thus a great body of liturgical music was developed. Each holy day has its own theme song. Compositions were frequently influenced by the musical taste of the general environment. Today, leading Jewish composers are writing liturgical music in modern idiom.

The Prayer Book

In the morning two [Berakhot] are to be recited before [the Shema], and one after [the Shema]; in the evening two before [the Shema] and two after [the Shema] (Berakhot 1:4).

We have seen that this formal arrangement is still followed, and we can recognize in it the great age of formal Jewish prayer. Indeed, the text is very old; *tradition* traces the origin of its key skeletal portions to Ezra, his contemporaries, and immediate successors, a body of unidentified teachers called "The Men of the Great Assembly." The Prayer Book is thus the second oldest literary work still in constant use in the Western world, the oldest being the Bible (and both of them are of Jewish origin). Transmitted by word of mouth, the prayers were edited in the ninth century, and various different editions with slight variations appeared throughout the centuries.

Actually, the *Siddur* (the Prayer Book) reflects the evolution and destiny of the Jewish people. The fate of Sefardic and Ashkenasic Jewry is reflected in the variations between the Siddur used by either group. Yet the variations are small and do not prevent a worshipper brought up in one tradition from finding his way easily in the prayer book of the other, or from failing to feel at home in either worship. While the basic core always remained unchanged, poets and singers throughout the Middle Ages were free to add poetry of their own, especially for worship on holy days. Thus variety in uniformity was achieved, the new tied in with the old. It was the printing press that gave the Siddur its unchanging character; prayers and poems included in the printed Siddur found the widest acceptance, and, once printed, could not easily be changed.

Throughout the ages, the Orthodox prayer book has undergone hardly any changes, although modern translations have been produced, and a number of additional and optional readings have recently been included in some editions.

Reform and Conservatism, however, effected certain basic revisions. Reform was the most radical. Realizing the inability of the people to understand Hebrew, it emphasized prayer in the vernacular, leaving only a few basic Hebrew prayers, and arranging the book itself to read from left to right following the English, rather than from right to left, which would have acknowledged the primacy of Hebrew, as Hebrew is read from right to left. The prayers for the Land of Israel were eliminated in the belief that Emancipation had brought full freedom for all Jews in the countries where they lived, and a hope for restoration of Zion could be safely abolished. The Mussaf, dealing with the sacrifices of ancient times, was eliminated. In recent years, however, new editions of the Reform prayer book have reintroduced numerous traditional portions, including prayers for Zion.

The Conservative prayer book shows only slight changes in the Hebrew text. The hope for the rebuilding of the Land of Israel is powerfully expressed, but not the anticipation of a resumption of the former sacrificial service in the Temple, as of old; it is presented merely as a recollection of the pattern of worship which once prevailed. A great many English responses are added, to offer variety in the service and permit it to be keyed to special religious as well as civic and national American observances.

The Reconstructionist prayer book, following basic Conservative principles, has adjusted the text to naturalistic Reconstructionist theology; references to the "chosenness" of Israel are also omitted. The link to the Land of Israel and to Hebrew is as strongly maintained as in the Conservative Siddur.

Numerous efforts have been made, and are being made, to key the Siddur to the needs of the people and to the philosophy of modern man.

None has fully succeeded. In none of the prayer books, however, has the basic pattern, hallowed by tradition, been broken.

It cannot be denied that the use of different prayer books has split Jewry, yet there is still sufficient uniformity transcending the differences to make the prayer book a unifying element within the Jewish people.

The Congregation

Prayers may be offered by every individual in the privacy of his chamber. Yet it is better if they rise from a united congregation. The congregation is symbol of a united society before God, rendering homage to Him, and accepting His word. The congregation thus forecasts the united society of mankind under God. In addition, the congregation sustains the individual; each worshipper aids, upholds, and strengthens his neighbor; selfishness departs; responsibility grows.

To constitute a congregation for the purposes of public worship, a quorum of ten men is required. It is called *minyan* or the quorum. Why ten? The ordinance goes back to ancient times, and gives us an insight into the scriptural interpretation by the rabbis of the Talmud. Twelve men were sent out by Moses to scout out the land; ten came back with an evil report, and only two were confident that God's help would permit Israel to overcome the enemy. To the ten, who had conspired for evil, God calls out in indignation, "How long shall I bear with this evil *congregation*?" (Numbers 14:26). Ten once formed a congregation of rebellion; may ten form a congregation expressing faith and obedience, upholding each other in this spirit.

Physical Reminders

The *Tallit*. The ancient Jews, like the Bedouins of today, used to wear a large, four-cornered robe, which they wrapped about themselves. It was their only garment. To remind them of the constant presence of God and keep them from going astray in their daily pursuits, Torah commanded that they place fringes, like tassels, on the corners of the garment, which, swaying at every step, would remind them of God's presence. Thus life could and should be a Mitzvah, they were to remember. "Ye shall see them and remember all of God's Mitzvot and do them; and not go astray . . . and be holy unto your God" (Numbers 15:37–41). We no longer wear such a garment, but it became the *Tallit*, a four-cornered robe, with tassels (*Tzitzit*) on it. It is worn in worship during day hours (the time of day when the tzitzit can be *seen* in natural light, as Torah commands). It may be a big garment, which may cover the worshipper entirely and which he may even draw over his head when he wishes to commune with God in complete concentration and absorption, or it may be simply a "stole," a "prayer shawl." The stole in Christian worship is derived from it. The cantor or leader at worship will wear it even at nighttime. He approaches God, symbolically wrapped up in Mitzvah. The Tallit is the garment symbolically clothing the worshipper in the robe of responsibility; his life, in every step, must be walked in His presence.

The *Tefillin.* "Bind them for a sign upon thy hand, let them be for frontlets between thine eyes." These injunctions contained in the Shema (p. 125v.8) simply mean that men's minds and actions must be guided by the love of God. Yet the commandment was also taken literally, and has led to the *Tefillin,* phylacteries, as visible symbols. A small leather container in the form of a cube, containing several selections including the Shema, all of them words of the love of God, is attached to a leather strap and placed on the left upper arm, opposite the heart, and the remainder of the strap is wrapped about the arm and hand. Another container is similarly placed on the head. Thus are head (seat of the mind) heart (traditionally the source of man's will) and hand (the instrument of man's action) encircled by His word and His love. The word of God sets man's limitations and lifts him up.

On Sabbath and holy days, the Tefillin are not worn. These days, in themselves, are reminders of God's nearness. To add more symbols might obscure their true meaning as guides to ideas. This is good educational philosophy.

The *Mezuzah.* "Write them on the doorposts." (See p. 125v.9.) The love of God should guard our going in and our going out. A small scroll, the *Mezuzah,* containing several of the same selections as the Tefillin, including the Shema, is placed on the doorposts. Thus the Shema is the last greeting and admonition to those who leave the house; may their lives be guided by its ideals. The Shema is man's first welcome home; may he place his home, and his thoughts and actions within it, under the instruction of God's Torah.

Like the scroll of Torah itself, the scrolls in Tefillin and Mezuzah must be handwritten on parchment by pious men who dedicate their lives to this holy art; they also make the containers and straps of the Tefillin, following special regulations. No special rules apply to the container in which the Mezuzah is kept, and many artistic designs have recently been fashioned for it.

The House of the Lord

We have seen in Chapter 2 that the Jews were the first ones to transform the small dwelling place of the deity in ancient times into a meeting place where people met in the presence of God to sustain each other as they affirmed Him in solemn assembly. The religious meeting house is a Jewish invention. Originally, it was called *proseuche,* the term *synagogue* standing for the gathering of the people rather than for a building. Eventually the term was applied to the building, subtly reminding the congregation that it is the people who give it meaning and purpose. The term *temple* came to be used in modern times under the influence of Reform. It was to indicate that the individual synagogue had now assumed the place of the ancient temple, once and for all, as no restoration of the Land was anticipated. In the course of the years, however, the term lost this connotation, and we find "temple" and "synagogue" used interchangeably without any real difference between the terms.

In ancient Israel, during the period of the second Temple, we find synagogues in many communities operating simultaneously with the national sanctuary. The synagogue was the House of Prayer (*Bet ha-Tefilah*), it was House of Study (*Bet ha-Midrash*), and the ancient synagogue of Capernaum in Israel shows a large educational annex attached to the central sanctuary. Finally, it was the House of the People (*Bet Am*), their assembly hall. This threefold function has been retained and has actually been strengthened in modern times. All synagogues have religious school facilities, and most of them are equipped for social gatherings in a religious atmosphere.

Structurally, the synagogue translated some of the features of the ancient Temple into its different character and purpose, while diverging from them in others. At the same time, individual traditions and general taste have made for variety of design in various countries. The ancient Temple had three sections: the court where the people assembled, the sanctuary where the menorah was found together with other holy vessels, and the holy of holies, separated from the sanctuary by a curtain, containing (during the period of the first Temple) the Ark with the Tables of the Ten Commandments, and entered only once a year by the high priest. The synagogue, too, has three sections: the people's pews, the pulpit, and the Ark, Aron hakodesh, the shrine where the Torah scrolls are kept, frequently separated by a curtain, in which the Torah Scrolls are kept.

The differences, however, are equally significant. In ancient, and many Orthodox synagogues, the *Bimah,* or reading pulpit for the Torah, is found in the center, and the scroll is carried there for reading. Thus, the people once again surround it, as they did when it was first bestowed upon them at Mount Sinai. Modern synagogues have placed the Bimah in front of the Ark, primarily to save space. Traditionally, the reader of the service, facing the Ark, stood on the same level as the people. He was not a priest, but one of them, their "messenger" offering their prayers while standing in the midst of the people. In Conservative and Reform congregations he generally faces the people, to be better heard. Only the Torah was elevated; steps lead up to the Ark, in which it is kept, and to the center Bimah (when it is retained) from which it is recited as divine instruction. Some modern synagogues have two reading desks in front (one sometimes of higher elevation). One is used for the reading of the Torah, while the other (lower one) is used by the reader, offering the congregation's petitions and homage to God. Ark and Bimah thus are the centers of worship, combined into one in modern synagogues. As once in the Temple, an eternal light burns in the sanctuary, signifying the presence of God, and the eternal illumination going forth from His word. The menorah may also be in use, as in the Temple. But there is another, invisible, worship center. Synagogues should be so oriented that the worshipper faces Jerusalem in prayer. God-People-Torah-Mitzvah-Land thus are fused into an indivisible unit, their oneness symbolically expressed.

The entrance hall was designed for the people to put themselves in the mood of reverence. A wash basin and water pitcher may be found there in traditional synagogues for the worshipper to cleanse his hands symbolically before entering the sanctuary. (This is not holy water, however, although the font may be derived from it; in addition, water once used may not be used a second time.) From this hall, a step would sometimes lead into the synagogue proper (although we do not usually find it today), to signify, "Out of the depths I call upon Thee, O Lord!" (Psalm 130:1). The synagogue has to have windows. It is not to be removed from the world, but rather a place from which the world is to be re-viewed in the light of God's design.

In line with a practice emerging during the time of the Mishnah, it became customary to separate the men from the women by placing the women in a gallery (which was eventually curtained) in order to eliminate worldly temptations during worship. Conservative and Reform synagogues have seen a greater value in keeping families together in worship and have instituted mixed seating.

While the rabbis ordained quiet and grave decorum in the synagogue, their advice was frequently not followed. This was the people's place, their second home, here they celebrated the joyful events of life and reflected on their afflictions; here they gathered for many purposes; and, above all, here the voices of children and adults could be heard in study, recital, and discussion. To this day, a synagogue is called a *Shul,* a school, by the people. Thus conduct was rather informal, and some of it has remained so, in spite of efforts by Reform and Conservatism to give the meetings that solemnity which modern man considers esthetically essential to express his reverence for God in the House of God.

By Jewish law, the synagogue must rise above the roofs of the houses in the town. During the Middle Ages this was specifically prohibited by the Christian authorities. As a symbol, Jews might, therefore, attach a high pole to the roof of their house of worship, surmounting it by the Star of David, a practice which may have brought the star into widespread use.

There are, however, no specific rules regarding synagogue architecture. Old synagogues frequently followed the general style of the time. Often we find the use of Moorish architecture to distinguish synagogues from Christian houses of worship. In modern times, this freedom from restrictions has inspired architects to fashion buildings in a modern style, some of them of great beauty and of daring design. Life and worship are thus synchronized, and God is worshipped in beauty reflecting the spirit of the present.

11 THE MITZVAH OF PHYSICAL CONSECRATION: DIETARY LAWS

DAILY worship and study of Torah bring mind and soul to attunement with God, and the dietary laws consecrate the body. Judaism has never made the distinction between body (as being weak) and soul (as being strong and divine); both must serve God, both are holy.

The dietary laws may well have emerged from numerous taboos of antiquity or from health considerations; their hygienic character is in many instances self-evident. Pious Jews have looked at them in a different light. The truly devout Jew sees in them simply God's law; He has commanded their observance, to "sanctify us by His commandments," and He knows their purpose. Yet these laws may also be considered a means of preserving Israel's uniqueness, linking the members of the Household of Israel to closer unity. Jews could and would associate only with those who shared the practices of life and table, and were barred from primary contact with those who did not. These laws may additionally be viewed as symbolic expression of belonging to a group, binding the members in fellowship (as a handshake may bind the members of a fraternal order), reminding them of their tradition, history, and aspirations.

Depending on the emphasis placed by individual Jews on these various points of interpretation, patterns of observance have varied among modern Jews. The Orthodox Jew will make the greatest sacrifices, denying himself many contacts with friends in order to observe strictly the God-ordained rules. Others may wish to uphold them without being concerned about minute details, but true to their basic principles, as unifying bonds to God and fellow Jew. Again, many Jews may observe them in their homes, in order that any Jew may join their table, yet feel free to disregard them when eating out. Their homes must be hallowed; in the home, Israel's eternity under God must be expressed, symbolized, and transmitted. Some Jews will observe but a few of the laws as a matter of discipline and a symbol of belonging; they may refrain, for instance, from eating pork. Finally, there are those who see no purpose and spiritual meaning in the dietary laws and do not feel bound by them in any way; they cannot accept the doctrine that Torah was literally dictated by God and cannot see any spiritually sustaining symbolic power in the dietary regulations. Of course, there are many who are simply backsliders, lax in any observance. But to millions of Jews, the dietary laws are precious; they will deny themselves food rather than break them, even under difficult conditions, and will cheerfully accept the many sacrifices, including comparative isolation in society, they entail.

Prohibited Foods

There is no prohibition against any vegetables. Regarding animal food, the Scripture sets definite rules (Leviticus 11, Deuteronomy 14):

1. It permits whatever animal that "parteth the hoof and is completely cloven footed, and cheweth the cud" (Leviticus 11:3), listing among the permitted ones the ox, the sheep, the hart, and the gazelle (Deuteronomy 14:4–5). If either of these two characteristics is missing, the animal may not be eaten. This forbids the pig, which has cloven feet, but does not chew the cud, and the rabbit, which chews the cud but has no cloven feet.

2. It prohibits a number of birds. Since the exact meaning of the ancient Hebrew terms for the birds is not known, only those birds which have traditionally been eaten may be consumed. This includes chicken, ducks, geese, pigeons, and turkeys as "clean."

3. Fish must have fins *and* scales (Leviticus 11:9, Deuteronomy 14:9), excluding all shellfish as well as eel and sturgeon.

4. "Swarming things" are equally prohibited, from mice to crocodiles to most insects. Certain locusts and grasshoppers were once scripturally permitted, but today no insects are permitted, as the identity of those mentioned in scripture is no longer clear (Leviticus 11:20–23, 29–30).

Thus, all animals which live by destruction of others are excluded, as are birds of prey—a reminder, perhaps, to strive for peace.

Restrictions on Permitted Foods

Even permitted animals may be consumed only under certain conditions. The following are prohibited: animals that have died on their own (Leviticus 11:39, Deuteronomy 14:21); animals that have been torn by others (Exodus 22:30); all blood (Leviticus 7:26), certain animal fats (Leviticus 3:17); certain sinews (Genesis 32:33). None of these restrictions, or any of those following, apply to fish.

Preparation of Meat. Any animal not slaughtered by a method approved by Jewish law, or found diseased, thus is not suitable for consumption.

1. Animals must therefore be slaughtered by a man trained in Jewish law, a *Shohet.* Using a very sharp knife which may not have any nicks in it, he must cut the animal's throat, severing arteries, veins, and windpipe in one continuous stroke without exerting downward pressure. In this manner the brain is so rapidly drained of blood that no pain sensation occurs. (It takes some time to feel pain, as we know when we cut ourselves with a very sharp knife. Physiological research has shown that the Jewish method of slaughter is the most humane one; in addition, rapid drainage of blood makes the meat better fit for preservation.) After the slaughter, the shohet must examine the animal for disease, and if he finds damage in the lungs, an ulcerated stomach, or discoloration of the brain, the animal may not be eaten.

2. The Jewish butcher, who must also be responsible, then removes the sinews. Since those of the hindquarters are difficult to remove, this part is frequently not used at all, unless the butcher has special, certified skill in preparing it.

3. Elimination of the blood becomes the task of the housewife. The meat must be fresh; if it has been stored for three days, the blood has congealed to the point where it cannot be removed and the meat cannot be used (unless it has been soaked once in water during this period, to keep it soft). The housewife soaks the meat in water for about one-half hour, then covers it with salt on all sides, leaving it in the salt for about one hour, and then washes off the salt. Another method is to broil the meat over an open fire, permitting the blood to flow out freely; this method must be used for liver. After this procedure the meat is "kosher," which means it is "all right."

4. Kitchen utensils which have been used in connection with forbidden foods cannot be used in a kosher household. Neither can foods that have admixtures of non-kosher ingredients. Soap containing animal fats thus cannot be used for washing dishes; detergents, being inorganic chemicals, can be used. The Union of Orthodox Congregations, therefore has a service of certification. On many products regularly obtainable in food stores, a "U" in a circle— Ⓤ —certifies that they can be used in kosher households.

Meat and Milk. At three different places in Scripture we find the injunction: "Thou shalt not seethe the kid in the milk of his mother" (Exodus 23:19, 34:25; Deuteronomy 14:2). This was interpreted as containing three prohibitions: against eating meat and milk products together, against cooking them together, and against using any mixture of them.

These products may therefore not be served together; for example, butter and milk may not be found at a meal that offers meat. After eating meat, a person has to wait several hours before eating milk products.

Not only may they not be cooked together, but different utensils have to be used for meat and for milk. This requires a kosher family to have two complete sets of dishes, silverware, and cooking utensils. (A third set for neutral food, such as fruit, may also be found in the home.) If these have become mixed up, they may occasionally be cleansed either by boiling or burning out the food by bringing the utensils to red heat. Otherwise the utensils become useless. The decision in this matter rests with the rabbi, whom the family will consult. In addition, the kosher family will need two complete sets of dishes for Passover, when those having come in touch with leavened food during the year may not be used.

The laws of kashrut (kosher laws) call for thoroughly trained rabbis to supervise and decide problems, learned shohetim and conscientious butchers, and vigilance and devotion from every housewife (although practices become second habit with the years). Above all, they set God always before every Jew, as he disciplines himself to accept or deny himself the pleasures of food, and even its life-sustaining gifts. This is Mitzvah, a daily and constant response to God, promoting inner strength, and the joyful conviction in the observant Jew that he follows the will of God with his body as with his soul.

12 SABBATH, DAY OF RE-CREATION

DAILY observance is the pulse beat, supplying the individual Jew with the lifeblood of the divine. The Sabbath re-creates him, giving him the strength for meaningful daily living. It is linked to God's creative act itself (Genesis 2:1–4). God rested from His work and hallowed the Sabbath. It is the only holy day ordained in the Ten Commandments, both in Exodus (20:8–11) and in Deuteronomy (5:12–15). But God needs no rest; the meaning of the term lies deeper. God ceased from making the world all by Himself; henceforth man must be His co-worker. As Creator, God is the world's owner, and may ordain rest for those who toil in His domain. As we obey this command, we acknowledge God's ownership of the world and constitute ourselves not its masters but its stewards. We become aware that we are called to carry on His work during the six days of labor. This task has two distinct features: First, nature and all its produce must be utilized for beneficent purposes; we may neither squander its riches nor selfishly claim them all for ourselves. Hence the commandment emphasizes that God is nature's creator. Secondly, society and every one of its members is equally God's; it is our duty to see to it that all mankind be given that dignity which comes for being God's children. Servants, too, must be allowed to rest, as is doubly emphasized in the version of the Commandments found in Deuteronomy, "that thy servants may rest as well as thou." The meaning of the Sabbath thus synthesizes the religious element and the social element, the spiritualizing of daily work and the promotion of humanity's basic rights. Judaism considers one without the other to be meaningless.

To the Jew, the Sabbath has become not merely a day of rest, but a day of spiritual re-creation to the tasks which it enjoins, and which form the functions of the week's labor. As such, it has given the Jew strength, hope, and confidence. Truly man, so charged with a divine duty, is dear to God. The Sabbath became a covenant between God and Israel (Exodus 13:12–17); its desecration spells denial of God Himself, and

156

His creatorship (Numbers 15:32–36). It guarantees Israel's eternity, for the servant's life has meaning as long as the Master's work needs to be done; and this work is eternal. It has given the Jew the strength to endure and preserved his mental balance. In the terms of Heinrich Heine, the German poet (who was of Jewish background), a dog during the week, the Jew is restored to his true character as a prince of God one day a week. If he must, he can return to the degradation the world may impose upon him, for he knows his true identity. According to the rabbis, the Sabbath thus provides the Jew with "a taste of the world to come." Sagely they remark: "As Israel has kept the Sabbath, the Sabbath has kept Israel alive."

Prohibition of Work

The meaning of "rest" had to be defined, lest a person rationalize that his work, or that imposed upon his servants, could not really be called "work." A simple yardstick was used in this definition. All of God's world is His sanctuary; as His co-workers, Israel once built a sanctuary in the desert, a small symbol of His presence, though He pervades the entire universe. All types of work, once connected with the building of the tabernacle in the desert, are therefore prohibited; in this manner the principle of rest in God's behest is realized by those who are called to build the greater sanctuary of a God-centered society.

This led to the prohibition of 39 basic kinds of work, arranged under several general principles: (1) the growing and preparation of food (eleven prohibitions), (2) clothing in all its processes (thirteen prohibitions), (3) leather work and writing (nine prohibitions), (4) the building of shelter (two prohibitions), (5) the use of fire (two prohibitions), (6) work completion, the final hammer stroke (one prohibition), and (7) transportation (one prohibition). Around these primary prohibitions the rabbis added secondary ones to prevent violation of the basic ones. Thus, the Sabbath became a day of complete spirituality. The toil of daily living fell away and thoughts and preoccupation with daily events were completely banished. A truly divine peace settled upon those who fully observed it.

Observance of the Sabbath

The Jewish Day of Rest always starts with the preceding evening. As Scripture states: "It was evening and it was morning" (Genesis 1), putting the night before the day. This is a natural arrangement also for the farmer and artisan, whose days end when the sun sets; their thoughts then turn to the morrow. All Jewish holy days begin with the preceding evening.

Friday evening thus becomes a night of solemn observance. The food is prepared during the day, the body beautified. A festive table is laid out. As dusk settles, the mother, guardian of the home, kindles the Sabbath candles, blessing God and invoking His blessing upon her household in silent meditation. There must be at least two candles on the table, a double portion of light compared to the single dim light that once offered scant illumination during the days of the week. On returning from worship, the parents bless their children, placing their hands upon their heads and offering the Biblical blessing: "The Lord bless thee and keep thee . . ." (Numbers 6:25–26). On the table stands the cup of wine. The father raises it, proclaiming the sanctity of the day, and the family partakes of it. Two loaves of bread (*Hallah*), covered by a cloth, are also placed before him. It is a double portion of sustenance, even as Israel in the desert was given a double portion of manna on Friday, in order that they need not work on the holy day (Exodus 16). The manna was covered by a layer of dew, symbolized by the sheltering cloth. After the blessing for bread, a *hallah* portion is given to each member of the household.

Wine and bread are indeed the most precious gifts resulting from the partnership of God and man. The divine gifts of nature are transformed into perfect food through the ingenuity of man. In raising the cup of wine, the head of the house proclaims an even deeper meaning. *Kos,* the Hebrew word for cup, is derived from *kosas,* to measure out. It stands therefore, for the gifts God has measured out to us, be they plentiful or scanty, pleasant or full of sorrow. We give thanks for all of them as we raise the cup. Thus we witness to God's power and surrender to His will as we sanctify the Sabbath with the cup of wine, in the prayer of sanctification, the *Kiddush*. After wine and bread, the meal follows, concluded by Sabbath hymns and grace.

Significantly, the husband does not forget the greatest human blessing he possesses, his wife, guardian of his home and of its spirit. In her honor, he recites the praise of the "woman of valor" (Proverbs 31: 10–31).

Traditionally the Sabbath is ushered in at sunset on Friday. For convenience's sake, and for those who no longer observe the Sabbath in the home, a late Friday night service has been instituted in many American congregations, followed by *Oneg Shabbat,* a fellowship hour, but it is at best a pale replica of true, leisurely family celebration.

In the morning, the family attends worship; the Torah is read and explained. On their return, they recite once more the Kiddush, preceding a joyful meal. The rest of the day belongs to man, even as the morning has belonged to God. There should be some study of Torah, but the festive meal and afternoon nap, designated as "delight," and a leisurely walk, are also firmly established folk patterns of traditional observance. For Judaism is down-to-earth, it is not ascetic; it recognizes the beauty of decent bodily enjoyment.

During the afternoon service, the Torah is read once more; this time the beginning of next week's portion, already projecting the next Sabbath across the week of labor and possible disappointments. With the rising of the stars, the evening prayer is offered, followed by a special ceremony of farewell, *Habdalah,* the prayer of separation of the holy day from the days of the week. Again the cup is raised, filled to overflowing: may the week mete out to us God's blessings in fullest measure. A box containing various sweet-smelling spices is passed around, that all may take a last whiff of the Sabbath smell into the week. This box is often fashioned in the form of a little silver tower, for God is the tower of salvation. A twisted candle, held during the ceremony, gives special light; after all, the end of the Sabbath marks the beginning of the first day, when the light was created (Genesis 1). After blessing God for the gift of light, the leader of the service watches the play of light and shadows on his hands, making practical use of the light: we must use the gifts given us to practical purpose. Finally, the candle is extinguished in the overflow of the wine; the Sabbath is over. As people had greeted each other on Friday night with the wish, "A good *Shabbos,*" or the Hebrew *Shabbat Shalom,* they now extend to one another the hopeful salutation in the ancient Yiddish, "A good Woch," a good week.

The best expression of the essence of the Sabbath is perhaps found in the following paragraph from the Mussaf prayer:

> They who observe the Sabbath and call it a delight rejoice in Thy kingdom. The people that hallow the seventh day are all sated and given delight out of Thy goodness. For upon the seventh day Thou has poured out Thy grace and hast hallowed it; Thou hast called it the most precious of days, in remembrance of the works of creation.

13 THE JEWISH CALENDAR AND HOLY DAYS

As man walks through the year, the seasons of nature and the events of Israel's historical march from slavery to freedom under God are all remembered and given meaning simultaneously in the observance of the Jewish holy days. In order to understand how these days of remembrance are fixed, we must briefly look at the Jewish calendar.

Jewish Calendar

The Jewish years are numbered from the date of creation, arrived at by the ancients by adding up the years of the generations of man in Scripture. While we know that the report of Scripture does not coincide with scientific knowledge of the world's origin, there has been no change in the numbering; it reminds us of God's creatorship. Thus the year 1000 of the general calendar is equivalent to the year 4760 in the Jewish one, except that the Jewish years start in the fall, as we shall see.

The year itself is a lunar year, based on the phases of the moon. When Israel dwelt in its own land under its own sovereignty, the Supreme Court (Sanhedrin) solemnly proclaimed the beginning of each month, upon receiving testimony that the first sickle of the moon had appeared in the sky. Messengers were then sent out to all communities to give them the exact date, which was important for the observance of the holy days. But these messengers could traverse only the land of Israel itself in sufficient time before the festivals; the Jews in the Diaspora had no certification. These Jews, therefore, observed two days of each holy day, to be certain that one of them was the correct one.

To this day, Jews in Israel observe only one day of festivals, whereas Jews in the world observe two, even though we have a firm calendar and know the exact dates. Only Reform Judaism has felt that there is no longer any need for a second day, since we know the exact dates, hence it observes only one day of every festival.

The Jewish calendar was permanently fixed by Hillel II (about the middle of the fourth Christian century), and has worked well through the centuries. It is based on a combination of solar and lunar years, in order that all festivals should occur during the same season of the year. The lunar year has only 354 days, ten days less than the sun year; unless adjusted, its dates would recede, and festivals would run through all the seasons. This may not be. To adjust the two calendars, 7 leap years of 30 additional days each (one whole month) were included in every cycle of 19 years. (Nineteen moon years of 354 days equals 6726 days; add to it 7 times 30 days, or 210 days, and we arrive at 6936 days, the approximate equivalent of 19 sun years; minor adjustments take care of the variations in the sun year, such as leap years, etc.) Thus Jewish holy days may move back and forth within the span of 30 days of the sun year, but they will always fall in the same season.

It may help us in our discussion of the festivals which accentuate the course of the Jewish calendar year if we briefly list them in a table, giving their position in the seasons of the year, their length, and their Biblical origin. Those that are observed as major holy days are underlined, and an asterisk marks those that are observed for only one day in Reform Judaism and in Israel. We shall start with the fall month of *Tishri,* beginning between September 6 and October 4 of the sun year.

Name of month	He-brew date	Festival	Biblical origin	Observed In Israel	In Reform
Tishri	1	Rosh Hashanah	Lev. 23:23-25	Yes	Yes
	2	Rosh Hashanah		Yes	No
	3	Fast of Gedaliah	II Kings 25:22-25 Zechariah 7:5; 8:19	Yes	No
	10	Yom Kippur	Lev. 23:26-32	Yes	Yes
	15	Sukkot*	Lev. 23:33-36 Deut. 16:13-17	Yes	Yes
	16	Sukkot		Yes in both, but not as major holiday	
	17-22	Sukkot		Yes	Yes
	22	Shemini Atzeret*		Yes	Yes
	23	Simhat Torah		No	No
Marheshvan					
Kislev	25	Hanukkah	Apocrypha: Maccabees	Yes in both; observed for 8 days	
Tebet	10	Fast day		Yes	No
Shebat	15	New Year's Day of Trees		Yes	Yes

Name of month	He-brew date	Festival	Biblical orgin	Observed	
				In Israel	In Reform
Adar I (additional month in leap years)					
Adar II	13	Fast of Esther	Book of Esther	Yes	No
	14	Purim	Book of Esther	Yes	Yes
Nissan	15	Pessah*	Exod. 12; Lev. 23:4–8	Yes	Yes
	16	Pessah	Deut. 16:1–8	Yes in both, but not as major holiday	
	17–20	Pessah		Yes	Yes
	21	Pessah*		Yes	Yes
	22	Pessah		No	No
Iyar					
Sivan	6	Shabuot*	Exod. 19–20	Yes	Yes
	7	Shabuot	Lev. 23:15–21 Deut. 16:9–12	No	No
Tammuz	17	Fast day	Zech. 7:5; 8:19	Yes	No
Ab	9	Fast day	Jeremiah 52	Yes	No
Elul					

* Observed for only 1 day in Reform Judaism and in Israel.

The days of fasting commemorate tragic events in Jewish history and call us to repentance. They have no specific names and are simply called by the calendar date. The names of the months are of Persian derivation; Torah simply calls them "first month," "seventh month," etc., counting them, however, from Nissan (Exodus 12:2), the month of liberation, the beginning of Israel's freedom.

Days of Judgement and Accounting

Every day in the life of the Jew must be a search for meaning, a response to God. Prayer and Mitzvot combined with study (the search for meaning through Torah) serve this goal. The Psalmist's words are daily guides:

> Create in me a clean heart, O God; and renew a steadfast spirit within me. Cast me not away from Thy presence, and take not Thy holy spirit from me. Restore unto me the joy of Thy salvation, and let a willing spirit uphold me. Then will I teach transgressors Thy ways, and sinners shall return to Thee (Psalm 51:10–13).

Renewal is the watchword; not the striving for something new and untried, the disorderly rush from excitement to excitement, but a restoration of personality and society in ever-renewed effort. God's holy spirit dwells in us as we strive for these aims. The Sabbath teaches us that the world is orderly, well established under Him, not a chaotic accident. This it must be for us, regardless of what science tells of its origin. Thus man stands in judgement at all times; judged by God, and judging himself. In the end, the eternal hope is held out to him by the prophets that, through God, all will have a new heart and a new spirit, permitting them to walk in God's statutes joyfully, and assuring them of inner security and outward stability in their land. (See Ezekiel 11:19–20 and 36:26–28.) A new heaven and a new earth will emerge, as all mankind will serve God as His priests (Isaiah 66:19ff.).

The days of the year challenge man by their uniformity: his life must not become routine. The seasons of the year call him to judgement by their diversity; he must judge himself as he is being judged by the success and failure of each season's harvest.

Days of Awe

This fact stands out most clearly in the fall of the year, when the harvest of the farmer is gathered. He ponders: If his harvest is poor, where has he failed to sow and irrigate? If his harvest is good, how can he apply the same procedures again, and in other parts? He judges himself, he makes his accounting. Translating this approach into spiritual terms, Judaism has appointed special days in the Fall as days of judgement, divine and human. As the accounting at harvest time is a universal task, so is spiritual judgement seen as universal. The Mishnah states:

At four seasons of the year the world is judged: on Pessah, regarding the harvest; on Shabuot, regarding the fruits of the trees; on Rosh Hashanah, all those who have come to be in this world pass before Him as a flock of sheep [pass before the shepherd one by one], as it is stated: "He that fashioneth the hearts of them all, considereth all their doings" (Psalm 33:15); on the festival [of Sukkot] they are judged regarding the water [to be allotted to them] (Mishnah Rosh Hashanah 1:2).

As the farmer's day ends at nightfall, the calendar day in Jewish count ends similarly; and as the farmer's year ends at harvest time, the Jewish year renews itself at the moment when the new task is being considered by the results of the past.

Fall marks *Rosh Hashanah, the Beginning of the Year,* New Year's Day. "On the first of Tishri the calendar year begins" (Mishnah Rosh Hashanah 1:1). By its challenge to twofold accounting, the opening period of the year becomes a time of great solemnity, sober judgement, and awesome awareness of God's power and our trusting faith in Him. It is a period of repentance, of return to God, of renewal. These are the "Days of Awe."

Pious tradition linked this moment of renewal with the supposed date of the creation of the world; it must be a creative moment for us, as we rebuild our world. The Days of Awe open with the festival of Rosh Hashanah, followed by a week of repentance (when in daily pursuits we are bidden to put into action the resolutions we have made), and culminate in Yom Kippur, the Day of Atonement, when—in complete separation from the world, united with God for a full period of a night and day—we confess our shortcomings and ask for forgiveness, not only of God but equally of our fellow man, to return to daily living with new confidence and a new purpose.

Rosh Hashanah

To awaken us from the slumber of unexamined living, the *shofar* (ram's horn, the oldest musical instrument in use at any worship service in the Western world) is sounded in daily worship for an entire month preceding the festival. Special services of intercession call the worshippers at early morning hours to *Selihot* (prayers for forgiveness) in the days before Rosh Hashanah. On the holy day itself, however, no confession is heard, no plea as yet offered. Before we recite our sins, we must affirm to Whom we confess them; Rosh Hashanah is the day of affirmation. God is proclaimed as King, Judge, and Redeemer of all mankind, and the shofar is sounded in His honor.

Evening services are simple. On returning to his festive meal in the evening, the Jew finds several symbols on his table in addition to the usual wine and bread. The *hallah* may be round, in the form of a wheel, for a wheel goes through the world, and those who are on top may be down before long and those who are low may be raised soon, as God's will may be. May we put our trust in Him rather than our own strength. A sweet apple is dipped into honey and consumed by the members of the family: may our year be sweet.

Early in the morning the people return to worship. Curtains, Torah covers, pulpit coverings are all white, symbol of purity. In Orthodox synagogues, the men wear the white garments in which they will some day be buried, a reminder of human frailty, and equally of human equality. (Before God we are all alike, weak mortals: yet our very weakness evokes divine mercy and must lead us to be tolerant with one another.) The morning prayer is followed by the scriptural reading. It tells us of Abraham, prepared to give his son in obedience to God's will, and of how God kindly set aside the sacrifice. If we do our utmost, God will not demand more of us than we can bear.

Now the shofar's voice is heard. Its sound is weird, primitive, just like the outcry of the human heart. In its piercing sound is enshrined the full message of the day. Maimonides explains it:

> Wake up, ye sleepers, from your sleep; and ye that are in daze, arouse yourselves from your stupor. Reflect on your actions and return in repentance. Remember your Creator. Be not as those who forget truth in their chase after shadows, wasting their year wholly in vanities which neither help nor bring deliverance. Look into your soul, and mend your ways and deeds. Let everyone forsake his evil ways and worthless thoughts (Teshubah 3, 4).

Four signals are sounded in succession: *Tekiah,* a long-drawn sound; *Shebarim,* a three-times broken sound; *Teruah,* a whimpering, nine-times broken sound; and again, *Tekiah.* As the rabbis point out, Tekiah is the wakening call, Shebarim the sobbing of the contrite heart, Teruah the weeping of a heart aware of its guilt, and Tekiah, the straight, awakening sound again.

Samson Raphael Hirsch has meaningfully elaborated on the meaning by comparing the sounds to the signals alerting the people during their wanderings in the desert. Tekiah called them to attention in their daily routine: thus it calls us. Shebarim and Teruah were signals commanding the people to break up camp: thus it bids us to break with the past and with its errors. Tekiah once again called the people to start marching in a new direction: it enjoins us to change the direction of our life and to pursue holier goals ("Chorev," *Versuche über Jisroels Pflichten* [Altona: 1837], pp. 182ff.).

In the Mussaf prayer, the affirmation reaches its climax. Before the congregation proclaims God's holiness in Isaiah's words, "Holy, holy, holy is the Lord of hosts, the whole earth is full of His glory," it reflects —in symbolic terms—on God's power in a hymn by Calonymus ben Meshullam of Mainz (though ascribed by him to one of the earlier medieval martyrs of faith):

> Let us speak of the great holiness of this day, for it is indeed a day of awe and dread. On it Thy kingdom is exalted, Thy throne established in mercy, and Thou sittest upon it in truth. In truth, Thou art judge, accuser, and all-knowing witness . . . And all that live Thou makest pass before Thee as a flock of sheep . . . On Rosh Hashanah the sentence is inscribed, on Yom Kippur it is sealed: how many shall pass away, and how many shall be born; who shall live and who shall die. . . . But Repentance, and Prayer, and Works of Goodness annul every severe decree . . . for . . . Thou desirest not the death of the guilty, rather that he turn from his way and live. To the very day of his death Thou waitest for him. If he returns Thou wilt right away receive him. In truth, Thou art their Creator, Thou knowest their urges, that they are but flesh and blood. After all, man's origin is dust, and his end is dust . . . but Thou art King, the Living, Everlasting God.

Then the Mussaf moves to the threefold proclamation of God, using appropriate verses from Scripture:

Malhiot: God is King. We pronounce the Shema (Hear, O Israel) in acknowledgement of His Kingship. Then the shofar is sounded in royal proclamation.

Zikhronot: He is the Judge who mercifully remembers His creatures even while judging them, as He has done from Noah's days to ours. The shofar is sounded, calling us to His Court.

Shofarot: He is Redeemer, who, by the sound of the shofar, once gave His Ten Commandments, and who, by the sound of the shofar, will redeem mankind. The shofar is sounded once again, expressing our trust in His redemptive power.

In the afternoon a quaint custom is observed, which may possibly stem from Christian usage (at least Petrarch tells us of having observed it in the City of Cologne). The people go to the river, reciting the verses from Micah, "And Thou wilt cast their sins into the depth of the sea" (7:19). May God do so unto us, as we symbolically express our desire to abandon them to the waves.

The week following Rosh Hashanah is a period of implementation. Selihot are offered every day, early in the morning. The day immediately following Rosh Hashanah is a day of fasting, when no food or drink may be consumed. It is called the Fast of Gedaliah. Gedaliah was the Jewish governor placed in charge of the community in Palestine by the Babylonians after the destruction of the first Temple; holding him responsible for their unhappy fate, the people murdered him, bringing the wrath of the king upon them, which forced them to give up their homeland in flight. It is not known if Gedaliah was murdered on this day, yet the message is obvious. Let us not blame others for our troubles, but let us look into our own hearts. Let us not project in callous denial of our own guilt, nor let us find scapegoats for our own fate, for the end of such an attitude spells disaster. In every evil that comes to us we are involved in some degree, and to the measure that we are at fault, we must purge it from our souls.

Yom Kippur

With these concerns, and through Mitzvot indicating our preparedness to respond to God, we approach the holiest day of the year, the Day of Atonement, Yom Kippur. We dare not usher it in without having made up the wrongs committed to fellow man, for without reconciliation among men there can be no forgiveness from God. The rabbis ordain that we must seek out our enemy again and again and, being approached by others, must show generosity in forgiving and forgetting fully and graciously. Then we are ready for Yom Kippur.

For 24 hours no food or drink may touch the lips of the Jew, no earthly concerns enter his mind as he stands before God. In token of castigation, some people may wear soft shoes instead of leather ones, memorial lights are lit that the memory of the departed inspire us, and the men stand in the garments of death. The evening service starts with the *Kol Nidre* prayer, well known for its haunting melody. In itself, the prayer is simply a declaration of dispensation from ascetic vows once made but not kept. The tune, however, expresses all the longing for God, the agony of those who pledged their lives to Him yet found it cut short in martyrdom; from distress it soars to triumph: our faith in Him is undiminished. Immediately, our cry finds answer: God says, "I have forgiven."

All prayers during the 24-hour period include the confession of sin. It is recited privately, only for God to hear, but it is also repeated in unison, as we acknowledge our mutual responsibility for one another. Whenever we failed to direct our neighbor on the right road in life we bear part of the guilt. The confession thus renews within us the spirit of the responsible kinship of all men.

We appeal to "Our Father, our King" (as we have done throughout the Ten Days of Awe) to grant us health and sustenance, forgiveness, and peace.

The worship of the day includes in the prophetic reading of the morning a passage from Isaiah (58:5–7) as the message of the fast:

> Is not this the fast that I have chosen, to loose the fetters of wickedness, to undo the bands of the yoke, to let the oppressed go free, and to break every yoke? Is it not to share thy bread with the hungry, and that thou bring the poor that are cast out to thy house; when thou seest the naked that thou cover him, and that thou hide not thyself from thine own flesh?

The message fits in well with the confession of sins, for we mention in the formal confession not those toward God, but only those toward our fellow man.

With these thoughts, the congregation enters the Mussaf prayer. In it, the ancient ritual of the service in the Temple is recited. As we reach the portion which tells of the people prostrating themselves before God, the congregation kneels, and proclaims, "Praised be His Name, His glorious Kingdom is forever and ever." During the year, the Jew may not kneel, for it might be misunderstood. Is he kneeling before God or is the burden of his life pressing him down? Now, in solitude before Him, away from the world, but having understood the message of Isaiah, the congregation becomes the symbol of a humanity unitedly bending the knee before Him. Trusting that this future will become a reality, pledging to work for it, the people kneel.

To make clear that God's love and forgiveness and His kingdom is not reserved for Jews but given to all mankind, the Book of Jonah is recited as part of the Scripture reading immediately following the Mussaf. All are God's children, as Jonah learns:

> Should I not have pity on Nineveh [says God], that great city, in which there are more than a hundred and twenty thousand people who cannot discern between their right hand and their left hand, and much cattle, too? (Jonah 4:11.)

The Minhah (afternoon) prayer follows. Its purpose throughout the year is to give us pause to reflect on the course of our day so far. On Yom Kippur it brings to mind those whose lives had been lived truly to the fullest, the martyrs. Together with a memorial service for our own departed, which is part of the Yom Kippur service, it extends the link to the past from which we must learn as we march toward a future that is equally envisioned. The individual thus stands between past and future, a link in an eternal chain, part of a household under God, and must find his way back unto the highway from the bypaths to which his own inclination may have led him.

Ne'eelah (the closing prayer) sums it up: we have heard the message, we wish to return. It is a special prayer for Yom Kippur:

> Open unto us the gate, at the time that the gate is being closed,
>   as day has almost waned.
> The day is waning, the sun is setting fast,
>   let us enter Thy gates!

We hope that our prayers may find the gate; we hope that our lives may lead to the gate toward a future that is attuned to God. As the stars rise in the sky, and the day is completed, the congregation stands in silence. This is the moment of affirmation, the moment of the vision of God's kingdom. Slowly, word by word, the people recite before the open Ark:

> Hear, O Israel, the Lord our God, the Lord is One!
> Blessed be His Name, His glorious Kingdom is forever and ever!
> The Lord, He is God!

The Ark is closed. The shofar is sounded, Tekiah! Onward into life! Finally, Habdalah is recited.

The road leads directly to *Sukkot,* the Festival of Thanksgiving, as we account for the earthly goods which God has bestowed upon us, rendering unto Him our joyful thanks. Sukkot follows five days after Yom Kippur.

Sukkot: Thanksgiving for Harvest and Shelter

The spiritual stocktaking of the Days of Awe has prepared us to take account of the physical blessings bestowed upon us in a spirit of gratitude to God rather than in simply economic terms; hence Sukkot immediately follows, a festival of joy before God who has blessed and "will bless all your crops and all your undertakings, and you will have nothing but joy" (Deuteronomy 16:15). Sukkot is observed for seven days (eight days in the Diaspora) and followed by a concluding day, a total of eight (or nine) days. Of these, the first two and last two are full holy days with work prohibition, except for the preparation of food, which is permitted on festivals though not on the Sabbath (Exodus 12:16).

Sukkot is one of the three festivals, the *Shalosh Regalim,* for which pilgrimages to the Temple of Jerusalem were ordained in times of old (Pessah and Shabuot are the other two). These three gave expression to the indivisible unity of the Jewish people under God. By their physical response to God's call, they expressed and deepened the thanksgiving for the Land in whose holiest spot they assembled. The pilgrimage festivals clearly represent the unity of God-Torah-Mitzvot-Land. But their message rises to universal significance as if to state that only on the foundations of self-dedication and the will to meaningful survival can a people fulfil its universal task.

These three festivals have been adapted by Christianity; Pessah and Shabuot became Easter and Pentecost, Sukkot, of course, Thanksgiving. Christian doctrine translated the social idea into individual terms, however. It has linked Easter to the personality of Christ and his redemptive work for mankind, whereas Judaism connects Passover with the redemption involving every individual person, people and society, in the act. Shabuot is dedicated to the giving of the Ten Commandments to all, whereas Pentecost recalls the outpouring of the Holy Spirit upon the disciples. The Thanksgiving observed in America by all faiths has been turned into a rather secular feast. It originated with the Puritans, who were well aware of the Biblical holidays, hence may have drawn on Sukkot. (The great holy days of Rosh Hashanah and Yom Kippur have no counterpart in other religions.)

The Symbols of Sukkot: The Festive Bouquet. Scripture (Leviticus 23:40) ordains that a bouquet of four plants be brought to the sanctuary, citron (*Etrog*), a branch of the date palm (*Lulab*), myrtles (*Hadassim*), and willows of the brook (*Arabot*). These four represent the variety of the produce of the earth. Citron, an edible fruit of pleasant taste and smell; the date (the branches of which are presented), an edible fruit tasty without smell; myrtles, tasteless, but of sweet smell; and willows, which have neither taste nor fragrance, but are of use. All of these are essential for life; without any one of them, the bouquet is worthless. The rabbis saw in them a symbol of mankind itself: there are those who have both intelligence and human kindness (taste and smell), others who have but intelligence nourishing society without fully relating to their neighbors, those whose kindness sweetens the atmosphere about us, though they be far from brilliant, and finally, those who are in no way distinguished, yet needed in the framework of our society. No human being is expendable.

In worship the produce of the Land is hallowed unto God and the service of society, as Torah ordains. These four plants are brought to the synagogue, and during the recitation of the Psalms of Thanksgiving (Psalms 113–118, the Hallel), they are pointed in six directions (the four directions of the compass and above and below) as we recite: "Praise the Lord for He is good, His goodness endureth forever." This expresses symbolically that God is found in all the directions of the universe, whence our blessings flow. We may see in this observance one of the reasons for the significance of the number seven; there are six directions, forming the sources of divine blessing, and finally man, the seventh point, who must gather them to make good use of them.

This function of man is expressed at the end of the Mussaf service. Now, preceded by the Scroll of the Torah, the congregation with their bouquets in hand, marches in procession through the sanctuary, as once they surrounded the altar in the Temple. (Guided by Torah, we take in hand the gifts of the world in our procession through our days, which must be centered about God.) The congregation intones, "Hoshanah, Save us, O God, we beseech Thee." (It is Jews and mankind on the move, in the best sense of the word, invoking God's help that their work be accomplished.)

The Symbols of Sukkot: The Sukkah. As God must be our Mover, He equally provides us with shelter and rest. This is expressed in the *Sukkah,* a small hut or booth covered with a roof of branches and leaves, in which the family takes its meals during the holiday, if the weather is good. Originally a shelter in the harvest fields, the Sukkah was endowed by Torah with a deeper meaning: God made the people dwell in booths when he took them out of Egypt (Leviticus 23:42–43). He gives us rest on our march toward the future. As long as twigs and branches form the roof, permitting us to see the stars as witnesses to God's creative power, we may hope for peace, something our concrete shelters implicitly deny. Rabbinic wisdom has explained that we go into the Sukkah in the fall, when others return to their homes, to show that we do so not for the sake of comfort in summer's heat but in obedience to Mitzvah. How truly this expresses the fate of the Jew, so often homeless and driven about when others dwelt secure, yet feeling protected by God. This spirit is underscored by the "guests" whom we invite symbolically to dwell with us in the beautifully decorated hut, that their spirit inspire us. There are seven, one for each day: Abraham, Isaac, Jacob, Joseph, Moses, Aaron, and David. All of them rose to greatness through homelessness, for their homelessness never weakened their faith in divine protection or in their divine mission; it strengthened it. It is only a custom, but a truly symbolic one.

The Message of Torah for Sukkot. The scriptural readings chosen for the festival make its meaning explicit, underscoring the lesson taught symbolically by the Sukkah and the Festive Bouquet. In Torah we hear the ordinance of the feast, and, in addition, God's attributes of love and mercy are brought to mind. He is merciful and gracious. Though no one can see His face, we may recognize Him as He has passed through the events of history (Exodus 23:12–24, 26). In the Haftarah we review the story of Solomon's Temple, its construction and completion, and its dedication as a house of prayer and instruction for all mankind (I Kings 8:2–21, 55–66). But we also read of conflicts and battles in world history, eventually to end in victory and the gathering in of the dispersed (Zechariah 14, Ezekiel 38:18–39:16). In this manner we are given a review of history, its bitter struggles and agonies, and the suffering it has brought to so many innocent. Eventually it will result in the day when evil will have vanished. In the meantime, we must remain mindful of God's sheltering hand, never despair, but imitate His attributes of love in our daily lives.

On their march through the desert, God gave Israel Sukkot, sheltering huts, the Scripture says. The Tent of Meeting, like the Sukkah, reminded them of His providence. He sustained them with food and shelter. Eventually, desert conditions led to settled life, and the tent was replaced by Solomon's Temple, followed again by homelessness and struggle. The day may come when "God will be King over all the earth; in that day shall the Lord be One, and His Name be One" (Zechariah 14:9). All the nations of the world will recognize Him and come to Him. "I will magnify Myself and sanctify Myself, and I will make Myself known in the eyes of many nations; and they shall know that I am the Lord" (Ezekiel 38:23). These verses were taken over into daily worship, the first (from Zechariah) to conclude the three daily prayers; the second (from Ezekiel) to form the great affirmation of God, the *Kaddish,* which we shall discuss. And when this utopia has become a reality, mankind will no more start all over again, no new horror will emerge from man's own accomplishments, as modern writers from H. G. Wells to Aldous Huxley have feared. Rather, "they shall go up every year to worship the King, the Lord of Hosts, and to celebrate the feast of Sukkot" (Zechariah 14:16), "and there shall be inscribed on the bells of the horses, 'Holy unto the Lord'" (Zechariah 14:20). The Sukkah becomes symbol of mankind's highest hope, of mankind's trust in God, when even war horses are turned into animals used for sacred service.

Two elements are thus combined in the lesson of Sukkot. In our own time we recognize how closely they are linked together. In ancient days, man's greatest enemy was nature. It might withhold sustenance from him; failure of crops, storms, and natural disasters might lead to famine; epidemics might strike. In the Festive Bouquet, thanksgiving is expressed for bounteous harvest out of God's gracious hand, and with it for the preservation of life amidst the natural hazards of life. In modern times, mankind has largely mastered nature, assured itself widely of abundant food, at least in Western countries, defeated many diseases. Technology has provided us with the means. But a new danger has arisen as a result of our technological progress; it is man himself. Locked in conflicts while distances have shrunk, armed with the latest weapons of world destruction, he is to be feared greatly. As the Haftarah seems to express it, wars are getting to be ever more frightful and all-encompassing. The Sukkah, therefore, calls for a new outlook; it makes it clear that mankind can and must live together in an open society, finding shelter in the spirit of love, which is the imitation of God. Then it will dwell secure. Sukkot is more than a thanksgiving for bounteous harvest. It teaches strength, provides hope, envisions the future, and shows the way. In a truly universal manner, it includes all of humanity in a future under God for which all mankind is to strive. The Jew is to maintain mankind's hope by his steadfast endurance throughout his historic wanderings.

Yet the very brilliance of the vision of the future may lead to skepticism: Can it ever come to pass? The people may well argue, "We have heard the message, but in a few days the festival will be over, and we will be back to the eternal, hopeless round of dreary toil and suffering." Fall and the onrush of winter together with the events of the day may speak more loudly than Torah and Mitzvot and holy days could. With psychological insight, the rabbis permitted the people to express these thoughts. On Sukkot the Book of Ecclesiastes is read: "vanity of vanities, all is vanity," all is hopeless. As the feelings are given vent, an opportunity for an answer is also given:

> The end of the matter, all having been heard: fear God, and keep his Mitzvot; for this is the whole man. For God shall bring every work into the judgement concerning every hidden thing, whether it be good or whether it be evil (Ecclesiastes 12:13–14).

As nature presents one danger, we answer by pleading with God for the greatest gift of nature, rain in right measure. On Sukkot the prayer for rain is offered, for on these days, according to the Mishnah (see above) the world is judged in regard to rain. In Temple days a solemn offering of water was presented at the altar amidst great joy and jubilation. In the gift of water we may see God's eternal and loving presence in nature, and need not despair of future sustenance.

If we are afraid of man, including ourselves, then let us return to

Torah. It holds the answer for the skeptic and shows the way to those lost in conflict. On the last day of the Sukkot Season (called *Simhat Torah,* Joy in Torah), the annual cycle of scripture readings from the Torah Scroll is completed and the new cycle started immediately. The Scrolls are carried in procession, followed by the children, who receive sweets. There is no end, there is always the beginning; it can be on a higher level, if the message of the past has sunk in, and it is linked to ever new hope with every succeeding generation. Through Torah and Mitzvot the Jew can find shelter in both winter storms and the upheavals of history. He revives himself and all humanity. With the Torah in his arms (literally), the Jew steps out of the holy day season into the winter and the new year.

The Beginning of a Month

By Biblical command, the beginning of a month is observed in special worship (Numbers 10:10, 28:11–15). It is announced on the preceding Sabbath with a prayer for divine help. In the ancient city of Mainz, where I grew up, this announcement was always recited in the theme song of whatever holy day might fall during the period of the next month. In announcing the month following the fall festivals, the melody was adapted from the recitative usually employed in the study of the Talmud. The month of Heshvan has no holidays; the announcement set the key for the month and the winter: the study and practice of Torah is to give it light. Only a few minor festivals occur during this period.

Hanukkah

In midwinter, the festival of Hanukkah is observed for eight days. It is a very minor holiday, the only one that has no Biblical source, as it is based on the story of the Maccabees, related in the Apocrypha. In the year 167, Antiochus IV, Epiphanes, overlord of Syria (to which Judah belonged), introduced the worship of Greek gods as the state religion, ordained for himself divine recognition, desecrated the Temple, and prohibited the exercise of Jewish religion. A small band of heroic fighters arose against him, led by Juda the Maccabee; they were prepared to give their lives for freedom of religion, as far as I know the first time in history that men rose in a concerted, organized, popular movement in defense of their faith. They overcame the enemy and re-consecrated the Temple; Hanukkah means dedication. This is the background of the observance, yet it does not celebrate a victory of arms, but that of the spirit. The rabbis tell a story: When the Maccabees entered the Temple they found the menorah out of order; they took their spears, fashioning out of them a makeshift menorah, transforming the weapons of war into the implements of peace. They also found that there was left only one small cruse of oil, still bearing the seal of the high priest, just sufficient to light the menorah for one day. It would take eight days to prepare new oil, which was required for it by Biblical injunction (Leviticus 24:1-4;—see also Numbers 8:1-4). Miraculously, the oil burned for eight days, until a new supply had been prepared (Shabbat 21). It was then ordained that every year in every home the light be lit in memory and as inspiration.

A nine-branched menorah is used. There are some types of menorah in which oil is used, but candles are permitted and usual. The center light, set apart, is the *shamosh,* the serving light, with which we kindle the others. It represents man. Every evening an additional candle is lighted, beginning with one, and eventually reaching eight, even as the miracle grew from day by day. Again, it is the spiritual aspect that matters, not victory in war; and this is brought out in the Haftarah of the Sabbath during Hanukkah: "Not by might nor by power but by My spirit [will ye prevail]." (Zechariah 4:6.)

The festival is minor, there is no work prohibition. While the candles are burning, the family might thus engage in work which really is not work, such as playing cards. For children there was the little *Dreidel* (top, from the German *drehen,* to turn, spin). Four letters were engraved on it: N (which gave the child *n*othing), G (which allowed him to *g*et all out of the kitty), H (which gave him *h*alf), and S (which compelled him to *s*et or put one—a nut or a chip or a penny—into the kitty). But the letters also form the initials of the sentence: *Nes Gadol Hayah Shom,* a Great Miracle Happened There. The children might get a few coins to play the game. This was the extent of gifts.

In our time, Hanukkah has for many become a "substitute" for Christmas. This is deplorable. Christmas, with its symbol of the Christmas tree, is a Christian religious holy day, and should not be profaned by being rationalized away as a universal observance. The Jewish child may well partake in the joys of his Christian neighbor and friend, even as he may invite him to all of his observances, yet he should learn that every religious tradition has its own observances and ideals out of which it contributes to the welfare of all. The Maccabees fought for the right of men to worship freely in their own fashion; in doing so they proclaimed the duty for the faithful of the various religions to be true to their own, even if it involves some sacrifices and nonparticipation, as in the case of Christmas for the Jew. It is dangerous to make religion simply "fun," and to take observances from all sources; only if we permit it to strengthen our character have we fully understood it.

Hanukkah reveals another side of Jewish religious practices as well. By permitting card playing and games at an appointed time, the rabbis built them into the structure of the faith itself, decreasing their temptation, which a blanket prohibition might increase. We shall see this again in connection with Purim, the Feast of Lots, to be discussed shortly.

Other Holy Days

The *Tenth Day of Tebet,* a fast day, commemorates the siege of Jerusalem. Actually, it may also serve to sober the revelers and return them to their duties. In the city of Mainz, card playing was permitted up to this date, then life in its seriousness took over to replace a spirit that might regard life simply as a game of chance.

The *Fifteenth of Shebat,* planting season in Israel, is observed by giving children various fruits, while the youth in Israel goes out to plant new trees. The link to the Land of Israel is thus made manifest.

About one month (in a leap year, two months) later, Purim is observed, preceded by the *Fast of Esther,* a day of reflection before merrymaking. Esther was called upon, according to the Biblical book that bears her name, to plead for her people, whom a wicked enemy, Haman, had planned to destroy. She had to go to the king, unbidden, which might cost her her life, even though she was his wife. In prayer and fasting she prepared herself, with courage she approached to plead the cause of her kinfolk, was graciously received, and permitted to bring deliverance to her brethren, while Haman was hanged. We have no historical evidence that the story ever happened, yet the spirit deserves emulation and, in fasting and repentance, we dedicate ourselves to it before entering the day of revelry.

Purim is the Feast of Lots because Haman cast lots to ascertain the best day for the massacre of the Jews. Since it falls during the Christian carnival season, it has acquired many of its characteristics. In the evening and morning, the Book of Esther is recited from a special scroll. Children, armed with noisemakers, are permitted to rattle them whenever the name of Haman is mentioned, for the joyful sound of children dwelling in the house of God has always overcome the designs of Israel's foes. The morning is given over to the exchange of gifts. Esther commanded that every one send gifts to his friends and to the poor; thus only can deliverance be celebrated. The poor cannot reject the gifts, for they are handed to them, not because they need them, but because they are friends. No one can feel ashamed. The afternoon brings merrymaking. Masquerades were introduced. In Israel there are great carnival parades. But Purim is specially set aside as a day when getting drunk becomes a Mitzvah:

> He shall drink until he no longer knows whether Mordecai (who planned the rescue with Esther) is to be blessed or cursed, or whether Haman (the villain) is to be cursed or blessed (*Shulhan Arukh*).

In Israel, the feast is therefore also called *Ad delo Yoda,* "Till he knows no longer." Again, we note the psychological insight of the rabbis. By permitting drunkenness on one day, they eliminated the temptation of alcohol. Jews have always used alcohol, but always with a prayer, transforming the taking of a drink into a Mitzvah, toasting each other with the words *L'hayim,* may it be unto life. Alcoholism, however, has never been a problem among them. Where permissiveness eliminated temptation, moderation prevailed. On the other hand, we find that many of the strict dietary laws regarding food have been widely discarded by modern Jews.

Pessah (Passover): The Birth of Freedom

Pessah, the festival of spring, comes one month after Purim and marks the rebirth of nature in renewed strength and promise. In the Land of Israel it is the season of the beginning harvest: the grain has grown, the lambs have developed to usefulness for human needs. From the earliest times, mankind has marked this moment in celebration, rejoicing in the harvest of early grain. The farmer linked his feasting to that of the shepherd, who saw his flock blessed. Pessah has remained a festival of nature, of gratitude for the Land and for its yield, but Torah gave it greater and deeper meaning. It has become the festival of freedom, commemorating the deliverance of Israel from Egyptian bondage, that they be servants of God and not of men. The fusion of these ideas into the unity of God-Torah-Land-Mitzvah is most clearly expressed in Deuteronomy 16:1–4:

> Observe the "month of the green corn," and prepare a Passover unto the Lord thy God, for in the month of green corn did the Lord thy God lead you out of Egypt by night. [We note the linking of agriculture to a historical event.] Offer a Passover sacrifice of the flock and the herd in the place which the Lord will choose for His Name to reside there. [The shepherd's thanksgiving is fused with Mitzvah, a response to God.] Thou shalt not eat leavened food with it; for seven days shalt thou eat *matzot* [unleavened bread], the bread of affliction; for in great hurry didst thou go forth from the Land of Egypt. [The historical significance of the feast is added to its agricultural and pastoral one.] Thus shalt thou remember the day of thy departure from Egypt all the days of thy life. [The event in all its implications calls for a commitment.] And there shall not be seen any leaven in all thy domain for seven days . . .

Pessah makes God manifest as God of Nature and of History. Unless the gifts He grants us in nature are freely made available to all of mankind, humanity is not free. Freedom and our commitment to it is the principal message of Pessah. As the Talmud proclaims, on Pessah man is judged in regard to the harvest (as quoted, p. 163), social conduct must make him deserving of it. Pessah and the Exodus from Egypt are therefore the key event and key challenge to the Jew. The Ten Commandments establish God as Him "who brought you out of the Land of Egypt, out of the house of bondage." Every Sabbath and holy day worship includes the words "in remembrance of the Exodus of Egypt." Daily worship contains this remembrance as well. The Exodus revealed God as Master of history, making us His co-workers; it gave us freedom, in order that we might extend it to all. "The stranger . . . you shall love . . . as yourself, for you were strangers in the land of Egypt: I am the Lord your God" (Leviticus 19:34).

It is too easy to forget this, and it is quite common for the poor man, become affluent, to *wish* to forget, and to think only of himself. This, under God, may not be; on the festival of deliverance and harvest joy, the Jew may not feast himself on pastry, but on matzah, the unleavened bread, consumed in Egypt when slavery permitted little time to prepare decent bread. This Matzah is the bread of liberty as well, symbol of freedom "because they were thrust out of Egypt and could not tarry" (Exodus 12:39) to bake real bread. Remembrance of enslavement provides the incentive to promote liberty. The ancient philosopher Philo sees in matzah a symbol of purity. Matzah consists simply of flour and water baked quickly into a flat substance like a cracker, for it must not rise. The admixture of spices, which wealth can produce, is forbidden, an admonition that prosperity may never lead to that selfishness which becomes self-centered, making us forget to love the stranger and further human welfare. God is always present, the verse in Leviticus points out, to watch and to judge, and to adjust the evil; whatever is ours comes from Him, to use and to share with all men. By linking God-Torah-Mitzvah-Land, Judaism has made of a nature and historical festival a powerful call to righteousness. Pessah celebrates the redemption of a people.

In preparation for the festival, all leavened items must be removed; this leaven, *hametz,* includes a great many varieties, bread and pastry, products made with starches and grain alcohol. No hidden traces may be left. This called for a complete spring housecleaning, which may well have promoted health among the Jews of the Middle Ages, when the general population permitted dirt to accumulate and become a breeder of diseases. On the night before Pessah "one must search for hametz by the flame of a light" (Pessahim 1:1). It is a custom still observed, a joyful march through the house, when children might gather small pieces of hametz (left on purpose), and be happy in this opportunity to share, learning the meaning of the feast by doing. Since the dishes used throughout the year have become permeated with hametz, the Orthodox

Jew will replace them by special ones which are used only during the holiday, and stored throughout the year.

So significant is the message of Pessah, immediately directed to every person, especially the child, that observance in removal of hametz and in the worship of the synagogue is not sufficient. "When, on this day at a future date, thy child asks, 'what does this mean?' thou (individually) shalt *tell* him" (Exodus 13:14). A specific family celebration has thus come into being, truly a Lord's Supper, dedicated to Him on the eve of the holiday. It is based on the family gathering preceding the Exodus (Exodus 12:1–14) when God passed over (hence the name of Passover) the homes of the Israelites while punishing the Egyptians. Ordained as a perpetual observance, it led to the offering of the paschal lamb in Temple days, which the family shared during the evening meal. Sacrifices are no longer offered in Judaism, but otherwise the *Seder* or "Order" of the family service, outlined in the Mishnah (Pessahim), has remained.

The Seder

The Symbols on the Table. To make the meaning clear to the child, symbols are used:

1. At each seat is a little book containing the story in its right order; it is called *Haggadah,* the story.

2. There is also a cup at each place, which will be filled with wine four times. We find four promises of freedom in Exodus (6:6–7); four times the cup of deliverance is therefore passed. God says: "I will bring you out from . . . Egypt; will deliver you from their bondage, will redeem you . . . , and will take you to Me for a people."

3. An additional cup is placed at the hand of the leader, the father, who conducts the Seder. It reflects a fifth promise of ultimate redemption for all mankind. Traditionally, Elijah is the messenger of this blessed day (Malachi 3:22–24; Malachi 4:4–6, according to King James' version); the cup is thus called "Cup of Elijah." We do not drink from it, but use it only as a reminder to "remember the Torah of Moses" to speed the coming of the universal day of peace. The past reaches out to the future.

4. At the head of the table, three matzot are placed, symbol of the three groups in Israel's community: priests, Levites, and common folk. They were all redeemed equally; they must all be mindful of the message of the matzah. These three matzot are covered with a cloth.

5. A roasted shankbone is a reminder of the Pessah offering of old (the Passover lamb) combining joy in nature with the spirit of dedication. It is not eaten; there are no more sacrifices.

6. An egg, symbol of nature's awakening, is placed next to it. It, too, is not eaten.

7. A dish of green vegetables (parsley) and a dish of salt water come next; the beauty of nature once was made bitter by the tears the slaves shed in their toil, and again made glorious as, by God's help, they marched dry-shod through the salty waters of the Sea of Reeds [the Red Sea].

8. Bitter herbs, including horseradish, reminders of slavery, and a dish containing a brownish-colored mixture of nuts, apples, wine, and cinnamon (*haroset*) is placed nearby, a reminder of the mortar which ancient Jews had to make for Pharaoh.

The Service. Candles are lighted as on every festival; the members recline in comfort; the Kiddush, sanctification of the day, is recited over the cup of wine. The parsley is dipped into the salt water and distributed; it is a symbol of wealth, as ancient meals always would start with an aperitif, but woven into it is both the idea of spring and of redemption and the memory of enslavement.

The Father breaks the middle matzah, putting aside one portion for later use, even as a poor man would reserve some of his bread for the future. He shows the rest to the family: "This is the bread of poverty our fathers ate in the land of Egypt." Immediately, he draws the relevant conclusion: "May those who are still cast out in the street come and join us in our celebration," that through it we may promote that spirit of brotherly hospitality which will make men free.

Now the child asks the questions of the day: Why is this night different from all others, as we eat matzah and bitter herbs, dip herbs in condiments, and sit in special comfort? With these questions the actual story begins. The *past* is reviewed, a tale briefly interrupted by the father in an admonition to the adults. There are different kinds of children, bright ones, and wild ones, average ones and simple ones; treat every child in accordance with his personality and abilities, then the past will become relevant, and the future of tradition will be preserved. Returning to the story of divine rescue in days gone by, the father concludes the first part in thanksgiving, and the second cup, praising God for help in ages past, is consumed.

The *present* enters. The matzah, whose meaning has by now been explained, is shared by all. The bitter herbs are dipped in haroset and consumed. Following the practice of Hillel, we make a sandwich of matzah and bitter herbs, an opportunity of bringing to mind Hillel's way of life and his teachings. He saw the essence of Torah in love of neighbor, and that is the essence of this celebration. The festive meal follows, concluded by the sharing of the matzah previously put aside, the *afikomen,* a reminder of the ancient paschal lamb. But previously the children have been permitted to steal it, perhaps to keep them entertained, perhaps to indicate that they should early "steal" the spirit of matzah from their elders and carry it into the next generation; they will now receive a small reward for returning it. After grace, the third cup is drunk, in gratitude for God's manifold gifts of the present.

Now the thought turns to the *future,* the task ahead. The door is opened to welcome Elijah, symbolically expressing that we shall never despair of ultimate victory. In the Middle Ages, this served an additional, tragic purpose. Jews were accused of using Christian blood for the Seder; this was a calumny once directed against Christians, who were accused by the heathens of using pagan blood in the mass, for the idea of the mass was not comprehended by the world. Now Christians, forgetting that they, too, had been outcasts, leveled it against the Jews, and the Jews looked outside to watch if there were any evil spies. But then the Seder returns to hope for the future in song and praise, and even children's charades, concluding with the fourth and final cup, a toast to the future.

In our own time, the Negro leadership in America has been entertaining plans to appoint a day of annual celebration of Negro liberation from the bondage of racial discrimination. It is to be patterned after the Passover, and a Haggadah rehearsing the arduous steps from slavery to full freedom would be the guide to this celebration of freedom under God. This is a clear indication of the impact Passover has had upon those yearning to be free in all lands and in all periods, and makes explicit the significance of the Haggadah, which transforms the observance of freedom from one of simple jubilation into a challenge to human responsibility for liberty under God.

In 1966 an additional ritual for the Seder was enjoined on all Jews in America by the combined rabbinical organizations of all groups of American Jewry. A fourth Matzah was added to the three traditional ones, the Matzah commemorating Russian Jewry. It was distributed to the participants with the following declaration:

This is the Matzah of Oppression. We set aside this "lechem oni"—this matzah of oppression—to remember the three million Jews of the Soviet Union. Most of them cannot have matzah on their Seder tables tonight. Conceive of Passover without matzah—without that visible reminder of our flight from slavery. Think of Soviet Jews! They cannot learn of their Jewish past and hand it down to their children. They cannot learn the languages of their fathers and hand them down to their children. They cannot teach their children to be their teachers, their rabbis.

They can only sit in silence and become invisible. We shall be their voice, and our voices shall be joined by thousands of men of conscience aroused by the injustice imposed on Soviet Jews. Then shall they know that they have not been forgotten, and they that sit in darkness shall yet see a great light.

Counting of the Omer

Beginning with the second evening, the days from Pessah to Shabuot are counted. This is called the "Counting of the *Omer.*" Omer was a measure; an omer of grain was once offered on this day in the Temple of old; the counting reminds us to use both freedom and the gifts of life as means leading us to Shabuot, the day of divine revelation.

The Days of Pessah. The first and last days are full holy days. The Torah reading tells the story of Exodus, and the Haftarah readings tell us of Joshua's first task upon arriving in the Land of Israel. Torah had been received, the land had been entered. The first act was the Mitzvah of circumcision, not performed in the desert. On the Sabbath during the Pessah week, we learn of God's attribute of mercy:

> The Lord, the Lord, a God merciful and gracious, long suffering, and abundant in goodness and ever true; keeping mercy unto the thousandth generation, forgiving iniquity, transgression, and sin (Exodus 34:6-7).

In imitating Him, we perform the work of freedom. But is there any chance for a lost humanity, inwardly decayed and spiritually dead? The Haftarah gives us the answer. It relates Ezekiel's vision of the dead bones (Ezekiel 37:1-14): As the spirit of God is breathed on dead bones they come to life again. In the same way, the spirit of renewal and deliverance from spiritual bondage and death is available to mankind, if it but permits God's breath to inspire it.

The last day's Haftarah (Isaiah 10:32-12:6), similar to the concluding part of the Seder, leads us into the far future, when the lion shall dwell with the lamb, and we shall say:

> I will give thanks unto Thee, O Lord, for though Thou wast angry with me, Thine anger is turned away, and Thou dost comfort me. Behold, God is my salvation; I will trust and not be afraid; for God, the Lord, is my strength and song; He is become my salvation.

The same verse is recited in the weekly Habdalah, as from Sabbath rest we enter the difficulties of the week.

On Pessah, the Song of Songs is recited; according to Jewish tradition, it symbolizes God's eternal love, expressed both in nature and God's dealing with his people in history. But from the third day of the festival, only half of the Psalms of Praise (113-118) are recited; in compassion with the sufferings of the Egyptians, joy is tempered. The rabbis put the admonition into God's mouth: "The works of My hands are drowned in the sea, and you want to sing?" (Sanhedrin 39b.) Thus is the spirit of Pessah established.

The Period of Counting is considered a time of mourning. By tradition, the disciples of Rabbi Akiba died of a plague during this period. They were stricken as a result of their feuding, in spite of their knowledge. It is also the period of the great massacres of German Jewry in the Middle Ages, even as the second day of Pessah commemorates the heroic uprising of the Warsaw Ghetto against the Nazis. Traditionally, no weddings are to be performed during this period, that in sadness we may remember the decimation of the Jewish people, from external and internal causes, and strive to eliminate the causes for all mankind.

Shabuot

Shabuot is called the Feast of Weeks, as it falls seven weeks after Pessah. With Pessah and Sukkot it is the third of the Pilgrimage Festivals. It commemorates the giving of the Ten Commandments, and is called in the Talmud *Atzeret,* concluding festival. The march to freedom was completed only with dedication to God's Torah. In ancient times, the farmer brought his first fruits to the Temple on this day. It is the day when judgement is given regarding fruits. (See p. 163.) Synagogues are decorated, with trees and flowers, but there are no symbols. Nothing can symbolize Torah, revealed on this day.

The Torah reading is the Ten Commandments. The Haftarah readings of Shabuot tell of the vision of Ezekiel (Ezekiel 1), calling for complete absorption in the divine will. The second day brings us "the prayer of Habakkuk, concerning human error," in deserting Torah:

> O Lord, I have heard Thy message, and I am afraid. O Lord in the midst of [these] years bring it to life; in the midst of the years make it known; in wrath remember mercy (Habakkuk 3:1–19).

We also recite the Book of Ruth, not only because it tells an event occurring during the harvest period of the year, but primarily to tell us that Torah is not only for Jews. Ruth, the Moabite, cleaving to God, becomes the great-grandmother of King David. The Jew knows of no distinction in races; he knows only those who accept the divine charge of creative living and those who reject it. And those who live by it are truly worthy to bring about redemption—symbolized in David—regardless of their background. Liberal congregations have instituted a service of confirmation on this day, when young people (usually after completion of junior high school) confirm their lives in the Torah and tradition of the Jewish people.

Summer Days of Mourning

Two events once took place during the summer months which call for fasting and repentance. On the *17th of Tammuz* the walls of Jerusalem were breached and regular Temple worship came to an end. Three weeks later, the ninth of Ab marks the date of the destruction of both the first and the second Temple.

Tishah b'Ab, the ninth of Ab, is observed in deep mourning. For 24 hours the congregation fasts. All the coverings are removed from Ark and pulpit. The people, like mourners for a dear one, sit on low stools. In the evening, the Book of Lamentations is recited. In the morning, dirges are sung, telling of Israel's tragic fate throughout the centuries.

Yet hope is expressed as well. Tradition will have it that the Messiah will be born on Tishah b'Ab. An understanding of the meaning of suffering will lead to the kind of conduct which will bring mankind's salvation.

Destruction of the Land never meant the end; it called for more mitzvot. Hope for the Land was never abandoned, by God's will the unity of God-Land-Torah-Mitzvot would be restored not only to the Jewish people, but eventually, to the entire human family. Repentance and new resolve show the way.

Three weeks after Tishah b'Ab, the shofar summons the people to prepare themselves for a new year.

14 THE DAYS OF OUR YEARS

EVEN as the days and weeks and seasons of our year hold their meaning and mitzvah, so do the great seasons in the flow of life present us each with a specific task and responsibility. As we have seen, the transition from season to season is marked by special observances, allowing us a truer recognition of our functions in the divine plan. The milestones in human life are similarly set aside for reflection, dedication, and commitment.

The rabbis of old gave clear expression to their conviction that every age group has its specific duty. Rabbi Judah ben Tema outlined it. He used to say:

At five years [the child is ready] for the study of Scripture,
At ten for Mishnah,
At thirteen for [responsibility in performance of] mitzvot,
At fifteen for Talmud,
At eighteen [the youth is ready] for marriage,
At twenty for the pursuit of a livelihood,
At thirty [man reaches] strength,
At forty full understanding,
At fifty the ability to provide counsel,
At sixty he enters his senior years,
At seventy he attains old age,
At eighty [his survival reflects] strength,
At ninety, bent in anticipation of the grave,
At one-hundred, he is as dead and past, withdrawn from the world (Mishnah Abot 5:24).

The life of a Jew starts with Torah, leading to Mitzvot, reaching its first fulfilment in marriage. From then on, his duty is to those around him, the children through whom he perpetuates the household of Israel, the family whose livelihood is his responsibility, and his society, to whom he must impart the wisdom he has acquired, by guidance and counsel. Old age to him is not a period of rest, but of reflection, as he gives thanks to God who has permitted him to attain the span of "threescore years

and ten, or even by reason of strength, fourscore years" (Psalm 90:10).
Aware of his destiny to stand before his Maker, he faces death in calm
submission, and should he live beyond the usual span of life, he must gain
the wisdom of withdrawal, letting new generations face their problems
in their own way, finding new solutions for their own time and needs.

Living in this fashion, he knows that his work on earth will not be
without results, that the traces of his earthly days will not vanish, even
after he himself has passed on. This is symbolically expressed in the fact
that succeeding generations will bear his name, making a name for
themselves by building upon the foundations of the past and the name
their ancestors have made in the world.

Jewish Names

It is customary to give every child a Hebrew name in addition to the
common one he bears; by this name he will be called to the Torah,
recorded in the marriage certificate, remembered in prayer after death.
There are no family names in Jewish usage. A son and daughter are
known by their own and that of their father. Moses thus would be
called: Mosheh ben (son of) Amram; the name of the Biblical Miriam
would be: Miriam bat (daughter of) Amram. King David is known as
"Son of Jesse."

It is customary among Ashkenasim to name a child after a departed
ancestor in order that the example of a fulfilled life may be a guide to
him, and that the eternal chain of the generations may be made visible.
The Sefardim name their children after forebears who are still living, in
order that a child may look upon a living grandfather or grandmother as
his special guides and counselors in life. These names are bestowed upon
boys at the time of circumcision and on girls in a special blessing in the
synagogue shortly after birth.

The civic name given a child may, of course, be the same as the
Hebrew name, as in the case of Biblical names such as David, Ruth, or
Michael. It may be a translation of a Hebrew name or of its meaning:
Johanan becomes John, Miriam is given its Latinized, common form of
Mary; Judah, compared in Scripture to a "lion's whelp," becomes Leo.
Most common, however—and least desirable—is the practice of using
alliterations, making the civic name start with the same letter as the
Hebrew one; thus Aaron becomes Alfred, Samuel becomes Seymour.

Family names were introduced under civic ordinances in the Napoleonic period. Frequently they are based on the cities from which the
family originated, such as Oppenheimer (from the German city of
Oppenheim on the Rhine), or Posner (from Posen, now Poznan in
Poland). Names may indicate the family's descent from the priests or

Levites of old, as in Cohen (priest) or Cahn, or as in Katz, an abbreviation of *K*a*h*en *T*zedek, a pious priest. Segal is an abbreviation of *Seg*an *L*evaya, overseer of Levites.

Hebrew names may be translated into modern languages, and today, in Israel, are being translated back into Hebrew.

In medieval times, various homes were distinguished by signs or special features, and the people dwelling in them were remembered by these. A house with a red shield bestowed upon its inhabitants the name *Rothschild;* one with a large flight of steps in front (a *Treppe,* or *Trepp* in earlier and colloquial German) resulted in the name *Trepp.* A great many names, however, were simply bestowed by government officials upon the Jews, by decree of the governments. This led to abuses, as these officials were frequently corrupt. If a man were willing to pay well, he might get a beautiful name, such as *Blumenfeld* (a field of flowers) or *Rosenberg* (a mountain of roses) ; if not, some hideous name might be given him.

Many Jews whose names might be hard to pronounce in America have anglicized their names and have become indistinguishable. Unhappily, this had also to be done to escape discrimination in employment.

On Joining the Household of Israel

A person becomes a member of the House of Israel either by birth or by conversion. By birth he is considered a Jew if his mother is a Jew. Conversion implies full acceptance of the duties and obligations of the Jewish faith and people. The convert must fully take upon himself "the yoke of Torah and mitzvot" and cast his lot with that of the Jewish people. Judaism has not made conversion easy, although in recent years we find a greater readiness to accept converts.

Preceding conversion, the candidate has to discuss his resolve carefully with the rabbi, for his conversion must be from conviction. The rabbi outlines to him the privilege of joining the Jewish faith, but also the disadvantages that are attached to being a Jew, the duties that it demands, the discrimination to which Jews have been exposed. He points out that from the standpoint of "salvation," a non-Jew is not considered in any way inferior or less privileged than a Jew, but that a Jew is obligated to perform the mitzvot to attain that state which a non-Jew reaches by simple compliance with basic principles of ethics and of justice. Then the rabbi must send the candidate home, to give him an opportunity of a clear analysis without any pressure. Afterwards the postulant undergoes a period of study, in order that he know what it is he is to accept. He is still free to withdraw.

The rite of final acceptance traditionally consists of circumcision for males plus immersion; for women, only immersion is required. The formal rite is completed by a declaration of acceptance of Judaism before a rabbinical court of three. Reform Judaism merely requires the latter. The convert is then given a Hebrew name, usually, in the case of men, the name Abraham; being thus considered a son of the founder of Judaism who brought many converts to the One God, he is called Abraham ben Abraham. Henceforth he enjoys all the rights of a Jew and bears full responsibility for the performance of mitzvot. A certificate testifies to his admission. No one may ever hold it against him that once he was not a member of the family of Israel (Talmud Baba Metzia 58b). On the contrary, "having left the environment of their childhood, they deserve our special respect and kindness" (Bamidbar Rabba 8:2), they are beloved of God. Many of the great leaders of Jewry were themselves either proselytes or the immediate descendants of converts. "He may see his grandson be high priest" (Bereshit Rabba 70), even as Ruth saw her great-grandson David as king of Israel.

When does a Jew cease to be a Jew? This is a question much more difficult to determine. A decision of the Israeli Supreme Court established the principle that a Jew who chooses another religion thereby gives up his affiliation with the Jewish people.

Circumcision

The covenant of circumcision (*B'rit Milah*) is the first mitzvah to which the newborn son is led. Its hygienic character has come to be recognized to the point where some physicians perform it almost routinely on all newborn boys, regardless of religious affiliation, simply as a health measure. (Medical studies seem to indicate that there is a much lower incidence of cancer of the penis and cervix when circumcision has been performed.) To the Jew, however, it is a religious act, patterned on the example of Abraham, into whose covenant the child enters (Genesis 17:10ff.), and ordained in Scripture (Leviticus 12:3). It has been regarded as so significant that it was once performed in the synagogue and in the presence of the congregation. It is sufficiently important that the operation must be performed even on the Sabbath or Yom Kippur, when these days fall on the appointed eighth day after birth. Only when there is danger to a child's health may it be postponed; in no case should it be performed earlier, according to religious law.

Pious men, especially trained in the performance of the operation, are called to conduct it; such a man is called a *Mohel*. It is an honor to be a mohel, and there are distinguished businessmen who, to the neglect of their own affairs, dedicate themselves to this mitzvah, naturally without pay. Lately it has become a paid profession.

Traditional usage calls for a quorum of ten (the legal minimum constituting a congregation) to be present. The grandmother or a close relative brings in the child, thus becoming his godmother; a close relative holds him during the operation, thus being his godfather. The godfather is seated on a chair next to which another chair is placed, symbolically for Elijah, guardian of Israel's covenant with God. With a quick stroke, the mohel removes the foreskin of the penis, then wipes off the blood, and secures the skin so it cannot grow back. The father speaks the blessing: "Blessed be Thou, O Lord . . . who hast commanded us to enter him into the covenant of our father Abraham." The people respond: "As he entered the covenant, so may he enter into [the study and performance of] Torah, into marriage, and [the performance of] good deeds."

The name is then bestowed upon the child as the mohel raises the cup of salvation in prayer that it be a cup of happiness. A drop of wine is passed to the child's lips, and the father finishes it. A festive meal completes the observance.

Today, circumcision has frequently become a hurried affair, celebrated in the hospital with only the closest relatives present. This may be required by the rules of the hospital, but circumcision should not be performed before the appointed time, and its religious character should be preserved. Hadassah Hospital in Jerusalem has a surgical section attached to its synagogue in order that the rite may be performed under highest hygienic conditions, and yet in the tradition of age-old custom of Jewish religion.

Bar Mitzvah

As early as possible, the child should learn his prayers, the affirmation of faith: "Hear O Israel, the Lord our God, the Lord is One," and the pledge to God's Torah: "The Torah which Moses commanded us is the heritage of the congregation of Jacob." Gradually, he is brought to know and understand and practice; the responsibility rests upon the parents.

At the age of 13, the beginning of puberty, he becomes Bar Mitzvah, a (responsible) Son of the Mitzvah; and the first mitzvah he performs is to give allegiance to Torah. Now that he may be counted as one of the minyan, the quorum of ten, he may be called to Torah to witness, or—if able to read Hebrew—read himself a portion of it, to recite the Haftarah, and, above all, to pronounce the blessing which is a pledge to Him "who has given us the Torah of truth, thus planting eternal life in our midst." At this age, a Jewish child automatically enters the state of responsibility. No special rite is required, yet it has been in practice throughout the ages, akin to ancient puberty rites. Today, as part of the worship service, the boy may be addressed by the rabbi. He is then given gifts at the joyful celebration which follows.

All too often, this may be altogether too lavish, and be designed more for the parents and their friends than for the boy himself. It thus becomes the parents' celebration of achievement, meeting their need for recognition. While it may well express the parents' pride in having raised a child to conscious Jewish living, it frequently is totally secular, and worst of all, fails to impress on the youngster that Bar Mitzvah is not the end of his training as a Jew, but very much the beginning. It is the open door to responsible living. A correction of this abuse has been sternly demanded by the American rabbinate.

Recognizing the equality of women in our society, many congregations have instituted Bat Mitzvah (daughter of the commandment) observances patterned after those of Bar Mitzvah.

Following the Christian custom of confirmation, a similar ceremony has also found entrance in the synagogue. It allows the young people after Bar or Bat Mitzvah to continue their education and to confirm their faith at the age of about 16, when they have a greater awareness of their duties. As we have seen, it is held on Shabuot, the festival commemorating the Giving of the Ten Commandments, the holiday of Torah, to which these young people are to give their allegiance.

Marriage

Judaism believes in early marriage, yet feels that a man should be able to support his family at the time when he takes this important step. The Talmud advises careful thought in order that both partners be matched well physically and emotionally, in background and in outlook; the rabbis advise against any marriage in which the woman is of higher social status. They see the best assurance for a blessed home in a mother who is the daughter of a "disciple of the wise" (Yoma 71a) ; she has acquired the spirit of Torah and can transmit it to the children. It is prudent, therefore, even in our day, for young people to obtain the rabbi's guidance together with their parents' counseling before they enter the holy bond of marriage.

In antiquity, the young people were solemnly betrothed to each other one year before their final marriage vows; it allowed the future bride to prepare her trousseau and eliminated the man's fear, "that someone else might get her." This betrothal ceremony has now become a part of the marriage act.

The Wedding Ceremony. In ancient Israel as in modern Israel, the wedding ceremony combined both legal and religious features. Legally, a couple is married if the man gives a precious gift to his bride with the

intent of marrying her, and she accepts it in this spirit. This resulted in
the wedding ring, hence a double-ring ceremony is not essential in
Judaism. A second method of marrying was by contract, and a third by
cohabitation. All these elements are present in the wedding rites. In
addition, God's blessing is invoked.

Traditionally the groom would enter escorted by his father and
father-in-law, the bride escorted by her mother and mother-in-law. They
meet under the *huppah,* the marriage canopy, symbolizing the home in
which they are to dwell together. (This meets the requirement of living
together, at least symbolically.)

Upon ascertaining that the two really wish to marry each other in free
will, the rabbi pronounces the blessings of betrothal, and bride and
groom share in the cup of wine which he has raised. The groom then
places the ring on the finger of his bride, pronouncing the words: "Be
thou consecrated unto me by this ring, according to the law of Moses
and Israel." Thus the second condition is met.

A marriage contract, signed by witnesses, is read in fulfilment of the
third requirement. The couple are legally married. Now the rabbi,
raising a second cup of wine, invokes upon them divine blessings. May
the cup of life, which they will share from now on, even as they share
this cup, be fully blessed by God. With an address (optional) and a
blessing, the rabbi pronounces them to have become husband and wife.

It has become customary to break a glass at the end of the ceremony, a
reminder, even in the fullness of joy, of Israel's suffering, and an act
making the newlyweds conscious of the fact that love is easily broken:
May they treat each other with tenderness. At the festive meal, the
benedictions, spoken under the huppah, are recited once again.

Marriage and Divorce. The Jewish marriage ceremony is called
santification, *Kiddushin;* in the home its spirit was truly fulfilled. The
Jewish home was holy, a haven of peace, for it was a home with a
purpose. The women knew that theirs was the greatest task of all, that
of raising the children in Torah and Mitzvot. "Be fruitful and
multiply" says Torah (Genesis 1:28), and the Talmud comments that
each family should have at least one son and one daughter (Mishnah
Yebamot 6:6). But mutual enjoyment of marriage is equally important,
and the Talmud permits contraceptives under certain conditions, for
instance when a pregnancy would endanger either the health of the
mother or the welfare of a previous child (for instance when the
mother's milk would run dry too soon as a result of a new pregnancy).

Another Jewish law may have added to the permanence of the home.
Torah prohibits intercourse during the period of menstruation and seven
days thereafter; for about twelve days every month, husband and wife
may not even touch each other. Then the wife has to immerse herself in a
ritual bath of purification before intercourse can again be permitted. As a

matter of cleanliness and hygiene, this immersion was of great value, especially in the Middle Ages, when bathing was very rare in most other cultures. This commandment is strictly observed by Orthodox women to this day. Thus husband and wife can hardly get tired of each other physically, a factor greatly contributing to the stability of the home.

The mother became mistress of the home. She kindled the Sabbath light, and her husband honored her by reciting the Praise of the "Woman of Valor" every Friday evening (Proverbs 31:10–31). Legally, however, her position was inferior. From the time of her marriage she covered her hair, sometimes cut it off. Should her husband disappear without a trace, and with no witnesses to his death, she could not remarry. He could divorce her, yet she could not divorce him (although in ancient times the Jewish court would force him to grant her a divorce when conditions warranted). This has created problems for modern Orthodox Jews. Conservative Jews include in the marriage contract a provision binding the man to grant his wife a religious divorce should the occasion arise. Reform Jews require only the legal divorce granted by the state.

Thus today if a marriage does not work out, divorce is permitted. While the rabbis proclaim that the altar sheds tears when a home is broken (Gitin 90b), Judaism has been wise enough to permit divorce without requiring the proof of "guilt" on the part of either partner.

Before a rabbinical court of three, a bill of divorcement (*Get*) is written in accordance with specific detailed regulations, purposely made difficult as a deterrent to divorce. The husband, who must request the Get, then hands it to his wife, and as she accepts it in free will, she is divorced, and may remarry 90 days later (in order to avoid questions of paternity in case of an early pregnancy in her second marriage). A woman may remarry her husband, but only if she has not been married to another man after her divorce from him.

Today, no religious divorces may be granted until the final divorce has been obtained by the couple in the regular courts, in accordance with the law of the state, under the Talmudic law: "The law of The State is *the* [religious] law [as well] (Talmud Baba Kamma 113b).

Sickness and Death

It is man's duty to keep his body in good health, a worthy instrument in the service of God. But sickness is the lot of all of us, and we must seek competent medical aid when it occurs. The Jew may therefore not live in a town that has no physician (Jerushalmi, Kiddushin 4:12). When illness strikes, we turn to God, find strength in friends, whose duty it is to visit, but must also do all that can humanly be done to restore health.

As death approaches, family and, above all, friends stay with the

patient. They recite with him the confession of sins, or if he is too far
gone, do so for him. They repeat the affirmation of faith, "Hear O
Israel, the Lord our God, the Lord is One," making an effort so to time
or repeat the affirmation of faith that the Oneness of God is proclaimed
by the dying with his last living breath.

During these last stages of life, no manipulation of the dying is
permitted beyond that which is medically required. It is believed that any
touch might shorten his life, and we have no right to diminish this God-
given span by even a moment.

These last acts of kindness are performed traditionally by the men and
women of the "Holy Fellowship," the *Hevrah Kadishah,* a group of
people distinguished by their piety, who perform this service as a
voluntary act of free devotion, a true mitzvah, for which the departed
can render no thanks; only God may. When the man is dead, they then
place him on the earth (as symbol of his return to dust, whence he
came); later they wash him and dress him in the simple white linen
garments which he may have worn on Yom Kippur, and put a Tallit
around his shoulders. They make a simple wooden coffin and place him
in it.

Women have similar plain white garments; thus the equality of all in
death is visibly demonstrated. At the same time, the poor need not go
into expensive arrangements, which might be too hard on them. The
rabbis taught:

> Formerly, they used to serve in the house of mourning, the rich in crystal
> goblets, the poor in colored glasses. Formerly, they kept the faces of the
> rich uncovered, but covered those of the poor, which had been darkened
> from want; since the poor were thus put to shame, it was ordered that the
> faces [of the departed] be always covered, out of respect for the poor.
> Formerly, the rich were carried out on a specially made, bed-like coffin
> and the poor on a simple bier; since this put the poor to shame, it was
> ordered that all be carried on a simple bier. . . . Formerly, the funeral
> of the dead was harder on his family than his death [on account of the
> expense involved]; then Rabbi Gamaliel took action, ordering that he be
> treated in the plainest way, ruling that he be buried in linen garments.
> Thus the popular custom developed to bury the dead in linen garments
> (Talmud Moed Katan 27a, b).

The message seems to be particularly significant for our own time. No
ostentation is allowed. The departed is to be laid to rest as quickly as
possible. Embalming is to be avoided, unless the law requires it. Flowers
should not be sent; rather the money should be used for charitable
purposes in honor of the departed.

Friends dig the grave. After a brief eulogy and prayer, they lower the
coffin. Family and friends put the earth back. Thus does he return to the
earth whence he came, as the spirit returns to God who gave it.

(Cremation is not permitted in traditional Judaism.) At the moment of their bitterest grief, the mourners tear their garments. (Thus Judaism, in deep psychological insight, permits grief to be expressed freely, rather than be bottled up to lead to neuroses later on.) Then the children recite the Kaddish. As they leave to return home, they pass through the lines of their friends who greet them with the words, "May God comfort you."

Upon their return, the mourners receive their first meal as a gift of friends, lest, in their grief, they forget to sustain their bodies. For seven days they sit on low stools, receiving the consolations of their neighbors. Grief is expressed—it must be given an outlet to restore people to healthy living—and the friendship of their fellows sustains the mourners. After thirty days, life must return to normal, the period of mourning is over, except for parents, for whom it lasts a full year. Each morning and evening the sons join the congregation in worship and recite the Kaddish for eleven months. On the Sabbath eve service after their bereavement, the mourners are received at the door of the synagogue by the rabbi with the word of comfort: May God comfort you . . .

Funeral and mourning practices have been "modernized," in our time, not necessarily for the better. Our busy age has generally made the services of the professional undertaker mandatory, as volunteers are no longer available. I have personally found these men—whether Jewish or Christian undertakers—to be upright and honest men. They will readily comply with the wishes of the family if these wishes are clearly explained. It is the family itself that frequently decides to deviate from the sound psychological principles of Jewish tradition in order to follow generally accepted—though not necessarily desirable—practices of our environment. Caskets then become expensive, flowers abundant, the body of the departed may even be displayed during or before the service, the reality of death and grief is denied, and grief glossed over, lavish refreshments follow the return from the cemetery. The rabbi is frequently not consulted at all.

A return to the simplicity of the Jewish funeral is surely indicated. The family should indeed feel guilty at showing ostentation at the time of bereavement; the elaborate casket violates Jewish tradition, and the opening of it runs utterly counter to Jewish tradition: May the family and friends remember their dear ones as they had been in life, rather than by the made-up waxen figure in business suit, bedded in silk. May they be permitted to utter their grief and find solace in the true concern and ministration of friends who perform the Mitzvah of levayat hamet, accompanying the dead on his last journey, and who offer the first food to the returning mourners, as tradition commands, lest the mourners forget to eat in their sorrow. Let the service return to its simplicity, a psalm, a prayer, eulogy, Kaddish, and let the house of mourning become a place of quiet, friendly gathering, where friends truly comfort the mourners in quiet rehearsal of the departed's virtues and in meditation on God's merciful justice as they gather in worship during the days of *Shivah,* the seven days of mourning.

There is greatness in the uniformity of the Jewish service, its simplicity, the traditional robes for the dead, the wooden casket covered by its black shroud. In simplicity lies nobility and the source from which comfort springs.

As the years pass, the anniversary of the day of death is observed by the children. It is called *Yahrzeit* (from the German *Jahr,* year, and *Zeit,* time, meaning anniversary). A light is kindled for 24 hours, for the soul of man is a light of God. The children, in worship, fasting, and charity, reflect upon the lives of their dear ones, and emulate their example of *Tzedakah* (righteousness, charity). May their lives reflect true honor upon those who brought them up. This is the meaning of the Kaddish, recited at the burial, during the year of mourning, and on *Yahrzeit.* It is not a prayer for the dead, but an affirmation of faith, and as such is used in other parts of the service. How better can children demonstrate the faith and strength bequeathed unto them by their parents than by affirming God in the hour of their deepest loss? How better can they honor them than by declaring before the assembled congregation:

> Magnified and sanctified be His Great Name throughout the world which He has created according to His will. May He establish His kingdom during your life and during your days and during the life of all the House of Israel. To this say ye Amen [so be it].

And the people respond, uplifted by the faith of those who are bereaved:

> Amen. May His great Name be blessed for ever and ever.

The declaration of trust continues, to conclude with the words:

> May He who establishes peace in the heavens above, make peace for us also, and for all of Israel. To this say ye Amen.

And the people respond:

> Amen.

In this prayer (source of the Christian "Our Father") is enshrined the entire course of Jewish life, through days and seasons and years. It is appropriate that it conclude the lifetime of a Jew, linking it with those who come after him, for it is indeed the motto of Jewish life.

RETROSPECT AND PROSPECT 15

JEWS throughout the free world, but above all in America, consider themselves a religious group and are so regarded by their neighbors. This trend away from other definitions such as race and nationality is happily growing. Accepting this basic outlook, we shall endeavor to draw a necessarily brief balance sheet, centered about the forces which have shaped the character of the Jews.

Torah

The study of Torah, a keen desire to know the ideas and ideals of Judaism, is not widespread enough in modern Jewish life, although the concern seems to be growing and is stimulated by the national organizations. Yet out of the inbred love for learning, there has come the profound concern of Jews with intellectual pursuits. The number of Jews who go to college and of those who make teaching and research their life's vocation is proportionately extremely high. "The ignorant cannot be in fear of sin" is a rabbinic dictum and principle; that is, he who does not know the implications of sin cannot overcome it. In an extension of the principle, Jews have felt that the ignorant cannot be a decent citizen; he fails to make his contribution to the good society. By admonition, material sacrifices, and example, the Jews have therefore served the cause of education, sometimes as gadflies in their insistence that education be expanded, its opportunities extended to all, and that education must not merely mean training in specialization, but include the full spectrum of the arts. This perhaps explains why Jews have stood out in the arts as well, both as performers and patrons.

Torah teaches, "Thou shalt not hate thy brother in thy heart, thou shalt surely rebuke him" (Leviticus 19:17). Without this ideal, democracy is impossible and international cooperation inconceivable. Jews have internalized this injunction. They have been able and willing to work in friendship with those who only yesterday persecuted them. Taking their own experiences in other lands as a warning, they have

lived and toiled for democracy with deepest devotion, have raised their
voices whenever they felt it in the least threatened, have promoted it in
every way. It has been remarked that the synthesis of love of learning
and love of democracy has been so strong, that even the slum-dwelling
masses of Jewish immigrants—their status lowest on the scale—never
had delinquent children or violence-ridden sections in the metropolitan
communities in which they huddled, but produced future collegians and
dedicated Americans. They have shown that people can dwell together in
unity, each ethnic group making its contribution to the welfare of the
whole. If individuals can do it, so can nations, once they lose their
hatreds. Thus Jews have exemplified the possibility and value of the
building of bridges between groups and peoples. They have been bridge-
builders themselves.

The Torah holds out the vision of the future, and Jews have been firm
believers in it. They have been optimists throughout their existence, and
this optimism, based on faith in God as Master of History, has sustained
them. It was an optimism that always challenged them to be His co-
workers; the future will be a reality only if man works for it. Optimism
is task and duty, and without it, mankind will destroy itself, but with it
it can endure all its trials. This has been Jewish teaching, demonstrated
in the Jewish will to live.

The pursuit of this goal calls for integrity; expediency must yield to
principle, the immediate solution must be permeated by the vision of the
ultimate. Jews have shown it. In the pursuit of their goal, symbolized in
the messianic age, they withstood the blandishments of the peaceful life
here and now, that might have been granted them if only they gave up
their faith. The door of conversion was always wide open to them, but
very few entered it. By their historical experience they demonstrate the
value of integrity, of vision, and of a life of purpose, to the profit of all
mankind.

All these teachings of Torah have become internalized. Even the nonreligious Jew seems to be unconsciously aware of them; he may never
enter a synagogue, yet he does not leave his faith. How long this spirit
will prevail is a question, however. Franz Rosenzweig has once
compared modern Jewry to a diver in the sea, who lives by the previously
stored oxygen he finds in his tank; once it is gone, he must die. Only a
return to the sources of Judaism in Torah, to its life-giving air, can
sustain new generations. This is one of the great tasks the Jewish
community faces today. Indeed, the ideal and the real are often far
apart in Jewish communities and individuals. The "stubbornness" and
individualism, which sustained the will to live, have equally been the
cause of endless internal conflicts. Ignorance of tradition, escape from
commitment, and "adjustment" to the pressures and temptations of the
times are all too common.

God

Judaism is an intellectual religion. It has not been pressed into dogmas of belief. It leaves the individual free in his search for God, and in the definition of God he may find for himself. This same intellectualism holds the danger, however, that in our own time the existence of God itself may be doubted under the impact of science. Spinoza (1632–1677, a Dutch philosopher of Jewish background) pronouncing *amor dei intellectualis* (intellectual love of God) and arriving at a concept of God as the undergirding law of nature and as nature itself, deviated from Jewish teaching but expressed a Jewish trait. He also set a trend. Modern Jewish theologians are striving to find a definition acceptable to modern Jews, but many Jews have become "humanists," accepting the ideals of Torah without recognizing that they could never have come into existence without the belief in God. After all, men are not created equal. There are men and women, intelligent ones and mediocre ones; only in a God-related world does the idea of human equality make sense. Godless nations, such as the communist ones, have therefore discarded equality, replacing God by the state, and denying the inalienable dignity of man, who is then but a tool of the state to be discarded after use.

Leo Baeck, a contemporary rabbi, once pointed out that only to the degree that the Jewish God concept was spread throughout the world by Christianity and Islam has the lot of mankind improved. In those lands where it found no entry, in the sense of being truly applied to human relations, caste systems, serfdom, and even slavery have prevailed down to our age. The call to the individual to exert himself to the fullest in behalf of society springs from the Jewish messianic ideal, which is grounded in God. The elimination of God from modern society—as the power making for righteousness, love, social justice, and individual responsibility—thus holds a grave threat. Nations and individuals will seek material benefits in place of spiritual ones, and conflict becomes inevitable. Only under God is a balanced nationalism possible. "Holy Wars," fought throughout the ages and in many parts of the world, have indeed been a perversion of the faith which they were supposed to defend or advance. Behind the pious name there inevitably lurked the selfish motive of hatred, greed, political expansion, and imperialism. Even in those cases where the initial impulse may have been religiously motivated, these wars, without fail, became brutal struggles for power.

Only God can be the stabilizing element in a self-serving world. In order to be fully human, man must have the freedom of choosing good or choosing evil; only a God-centered Torah can produce the yardstick in this choice. To the degree that God has been eliminated, mankind has suffered from wars. The task of finding a concept of God acceptable to the modern Jews is extremely difficult and is occupying the best minds among modern Jewish theologians. Yet the search goes on, and in this search itself we have an affirmation of God.

Mitzvot

With the exception of the strictly Orthodox group, Jews have been negligent in the performance of Mitzvot. There are religious Reform Jews who have consciously discarded certain religious laws as irrelevant for our time. Generally there has been a widespread erosion in all branches of American Jewry. Attendance at worship is at a low ebb; perhaps people feel that God really is not too angry if they do not pray. To many Jews, the problems of God and the problem of worship are tied together. Prayers in their traditional form presuppose a God-concept which many Jews do not hold, hence they do not pray. Yet these prayers form the link with the millennia of Jewish history and generations and to change them is to break the link. This is a serious dilemma faced by the religious leaders. What modern Jews frequently forget is the fact that the praying congregation also reflects the unity of the Jewish people and is a source of mutual support and mutual dedication. As such, public worship has value beyond its aspects as a divine service. Another aspect, unhappily forgotten, is the fact that Mitzvot gave the Jew a feeling of constant response to God; hence they were increased during periods of humiliation. Mitzvot made manifest the Jew's closeness to God and His love. They helped the Jew to retain his mental balance and health. It is surprising that throughout the centuries Jews did not lose their emotional stability (though they may have become neurotics). They retained their mental health as a result of Mitzvot. They have demonstrated that the religious life is clearly an antidote to the strains, stresses, and anxieties of life in a disorganized world, both for the individual and for society.

In a wider sense, Jews have been faithful to Mitzvot; they have translated it into terms of social justice. The number of those who have gone to the South to help the Negroes gain equal rights as citizens has been proportionally very high. Jews did not mind jeopardizing their very lives in the performance of this Mitzvah. The wealthy Jew, schooled in Mitzvah by being called upon to perform an unequalled work of Tzedakah in rescuing his brethren from death in Europe, has consistently endorsed and fought for social legislation, even though it would affect him deeply in a material way. Undaunted by evidences of anti-Semitism in some Negro groups, they have remained active champions of civil rights and social justice for the Negro. Yet the comparison to the diver and his tank holds true here also. Social action is a universal task. Unless the Jew reaffirms his identity through Mitzvot, the reservoir may become depleted, which would be a universal tragedy.

The Land

The Land of Israel, however, has not been a diminishing but rather a growing influence on Jewry. Not that American Jews actually wish to go there. Considering themselves a religious group, they regard themselves as Americans and nothing else. What binds them to Israel is more than even kinship. Israel sprang out of the same motivations which gave the Jewish people the will to live. Though its society, too, is marred by many flaws, it offers at least an imperfect example of a community consciously striving for the prophetic ideal. Ben-Gurion, first prime minister of Israel (1948–1953 and 1955–1963), was once called "Messiah in a business suit." It is no accident, that Supreme Court Justice Louis Brandeis was a dedicated fighter for the Land of Israel, for this action sprang out of his dedication to social justice in general. It speaks well for America that it is possible for a Justice of the Supreme Court to give his love and ability to Israel without the slightest abridgement of his unconditional love for America, his country, and with his fullest identification with it. America understood that Brandeis was a fighter for a better society and that his concern for Israel sprang from it.

Israel can be a society of Mitzvah, of social justice. It can be a bridge between the nations of the undeveloped regions and the West. Were it permitted to do so it would gladly give the benefits of its know-how to the Arab nations. It has done so in connection with other countries in Asia and Africa, to whom it has sent agricultural and economic advisors, which—as a poor country—it can afford only as a result of this spirit of dedication to Mitzvah. In taking in refugees from all countries it has had to cope with problems of resettlement and of racial as well as ethnical animosities. It has been seriously engaged in finding ways of dealing with them which may be a help to us in America. Its people are truly considering themselves stewards of the land. Its cooperative settlements, *Kibbutzim,* demonstrate that people can live together and share together, if they are motivated by a goal higher than themselves.

The Israelis have established Torah not only by founding religious institutions, but also by creating a number of universities, fostering the arts and music, and building a hospital and medical center which is one of the greatest and most modern in Asia.

Only in Israel would an army chief of staff retire into Torah by becoming a leading archaeologist, as Yigael Yadin has done. Here the Torah is a textbook, and the words of the prophets the daily vernacular.

In their majority, the Israelis have not been "religious." As Martin Buber told me, his following was not very large. The "religious" element is powerful only politically, thus has the strength to enforce its demands on the state. This may have contributed to the alienation of the non-Orthodox from religion in general. Still the yearning for religion appears to exist, and new ways will have to be found. In Israel, the Land is the force. The late Chief Rabbi Kook once put it in parable form: The holy of holies of the ancient Temple was to be entered only by the high priest once a year in great awe; but when it was under construction, the workmen entered it in their work clothes, their tools, even their banter. The generations of today are the workmen of Israel, that can be a sanctuary, and they are aware of it.

It is for these reasons—Torah-Mitzvot-Land—that American Jewry has taken such pride in Israel. Actually, the Land has rejuvenated Jewry in the Diaspora (particularly in America), giving it new pride and self-respect. The Land is a spiritual force, and as such has made American Jews more dedicated and patriotic Americans.

The Future

The future of the Jew depends on two factors. The first is his function in the world. There can be no doubt about its significance, judging even by the few examples we have listed. The dispersion of the Jew has to be considered a permanent one, even as Jeremiah saw it. In free countries, Jews are full participants, hopeful that they may help alleviate flaws in social justice and promote the welfare of the country of which they are proud citizens. They hope for complete elimination of all prejudice against themselves and all minority groups and will fight for it. They wish to serve as an element of peace within the multitude of groups and peoples. In countries of oppression, they hold forth the image of a community which will not deviate from its goal because it is good and ethical and God-centered. This may increase their suffering, a situation they are willing to accept as price for their mission.

The second factor is their self-identification through specifically Jewish Mitzvot and through Torah. There is danger that in the free world this may weaken as a result of their equality. Such a spirit ultimately would indicate a wrong attitude toward Diaspora life; it is not a curse, but a blessing which can be shared by all mankind. The Jews are called to remember that their contribution depends on their survival, and that only by being themselves can they be contributing members of value in the human brotherhood. Then they will be *Am Olam,* a people of eternity, and a people of and for the entire world, for all of mankind. The word *Olam* means both.

BIBLIOGRAPHY

This bibliography is offered merely to provide the next step for the interested reader in his search. It generally lists paperbacks only; hard-bound books are marked by an asterisk.

UAHC stands for the Union of American Hebrew Congregations. JPS is the abbreviation for the Jewish Publication Society of America.

Introduction to Judaism; Jewish Ideas

Baeck, Leo, *The Essence of Judaism*. New York: Schocken Books, Inc., 1946.
———, *Israel and the World: The Meaning of Jewish Existence*. Philadelphia: JPS, 1965.
Buber, Martin, *Israel and the World*. New York: Schocken Books, Inc., 1948.
Cohon, S. S., *Judaism as a Way of Life*. Cincinnati: UAHC, 1948.
Epstein, I., *The Faith of Judaism*. New York: Penguin, 1954.
*Finkelstein, Louis (ed.), *The Jews: Their History, Culture, and Religion* (2 vols). New York: Harper & Row Publishers, Inc., 1960.
Herberg, Will, *Judaism and Modern Man*. Philadelphia: JPS, 1959.
Heschel, Abraham J., *God in Search of Man: A Philosophy of Judaism*. Philadelphia: JPS, 1954.
Jacobs, Louis, *We Have Reason to Believe*. London: Vallentine, 1957.
———, *Principles of the Jewish Faith: An Analytical Study*. New York: Basic Books, 1964.
*Kaplan, Mordecai M., *Judaism as a Civilization*. New York: The Macmillan Co., 1934.
*———, *The Meaning of God in Modern Jewish Religion*. New York: Behrman House, 1937.
Neher, André, "Jewish Religious Thought," in *Religions and the Promise of the Twentieth Century*, François Crouzet and Guy S. Metraux (eds.). New York: Mentor Books, 1965.
*Roth, Cecil (ed.), *The Standard Jewish Encyclopedia*. New York: Doubleday & Co., Inc., 1959.
Steinberg, Milton, *Basic Judaism*. New York: Harcourt Brace, 1947.
*Trepp, Leo, *Eternal Faith, Eternal People, A Journey into Judaism*. Englewood Cliffs., N.J.: Prentice-Hall, Inc., 1962.

History

Bamberger, Bernard J., *The Story of Judaism*. New York: UAHC, 1957.
Flannery, Edward H., *The Anguish of the Jews: Twenty-Three Centuries of Anti-Semitism*. New York: The Macmillan Co., 1965.
Margolis, Max L., and Alexander Marx, *History of the Jewish People*. Philadelphia: JPS, 1927; New York: Meridian Books, 1960.
*Noveck, Simon (ed.), *Great Jewish Personalities* (4 vols.). Washington: B'nai B'rith, 1960.
Roth, Cecil, *History of the Jewish People*. London: East and West Library, 1959.

Bible and the Biblical Period

Albright, William F., *Archaeology of Palestine*. New York: Pelican Books 1949.
——, *The Biblical Period from Abraham to Ezra*. New York: Harper & Row Publishers, Inc., 1963.
Bamberger, Bernard J., *The Bible: A Modern Jewish Approach* (2nd ed). New York: Schocken Books, Inc., 1963.
Buber, Martin, *Moses: The Revelation and The Covenant*. New York: Harper & Row Publishers, Inc., 1958.
——, *The Prophetic Faith*. New York: Harper & Row Publishers, Inc., 1960.
Gordis, Robert, *The Book of God and Man—A Study of Job*. Chicago: University of Chicago Press, 1966.
Heschel, Abraham, *The Prophets*. Philadelphia: JPS, 1962.
The Holy Scriptures (standard translation). Philadelphia: JPS, 1917.
The Torah (standard translation of the Pentateuch, revised). Philadelphia: JPS, 1962.
The Anchor Bible

Post-Biblical and Talmudic Periods

Adler, Morris, *The World of the Talmud*. New York: B'nai B'rith Hillel Foundations, 1959.
Baeck, Leo, *The Pharisees and Other Essays*. New York: Schocken Books, Inc., 1947.
Baron, Salo, and Joseph L. Blau, *Judaism in the Post-Biblical and Talmudic Period*. New York: Liberal Arts Press, 1954.
Flavius, Josephus, *The Jewish War*. Baltimore: Penguin, 1959.
Gaster, Theodor H., *The Dead Sea Scriptures*. New York: Doubleday Anchor Books, 1957.
Ginzberg, Louis, *The Legends of the Jews*. New York: Simon and Schuster, Inc., 1961.
Glatzer, Nahum, *The Rest is Commentary, A Reader in Jewish Antiquity*. Boston: Beacon Press, 1961.

Goldin, Judah, *The Living Talmud* (translation of "The Sayings of the Fathers"). New York: Mentor Books, 1957.
Herford, R. Travers, *The Ethics of the Talmud: Sayings of the Fathers.* New York: Schocken Books, Inc., 1962.
————, *The Pharisees.* Boston: Beacon Press, 1962.
Schuerer, Emil, *History of the Jewish People in the Time of Jesus.* New York: Schocken Books, Inc., 1961.
Strack, Herman L., *Introduction to the Talmud and Midrash.* Philadelphia: JPS, 1959; New York: Meridian Books, 1959.

Christianity

Anti-Defamation League of B'nai B'rith, Sins of Anti-Semitism: Statements by Christian Churches. Pamphlet reprinted from *Christian Friends Bulletin* (Dec.), 1965.
Baeck, Leo, *Judaism and Christianity.* Philadelphia: JPS, 1958.
Buber, Martin, *Two Types of Faith.* Chicago: Wilcox & Follett, 1951.
Carmichael, Joel, *The Death of Jesus.* New York: The Macmillan Co., 1962.
Flannery, Edward H., *The Anguish of the Jews.* New York: The Macmillan Co., 1965.
Isaac, Jules, *The Teaching of Contempt: Christian Roots of Anti-Semitism.* New York: Holt, Rinehart and Winston, Inc., 1964.
Klausner, Joseph, *Jesus of Nazareth.* New York: The Macmillan Co., 1953.
————, *From Jesus to Paul.* New York: Humanities Press, 1956; Boston: Beacon Press, 1961.
*Sandmel, Samuel, *A Jewish Understanding of the New Testament.* Cincinnati: Hebrew Union College Press, 1957.
*————, *The Genius of Paul.* New York: Farrar, Strauss, 1958; Boston: Beacon Press, 1961.
*————, *We Jews and Jesus.* New York: Oxford University Press, Inc., 1965.
Silver, Abba Hillel, *Where Judaism Differed.* New York: The Macmillan Co., 1956.
Zeitlin, Solomon, *Who Crucified Jesus?* New York: Bloch Publishing Company, 1964.

Medieval and Modern Periods

Abrahams, Israel, *Jewish Life in the Middle Ages.* Philadelphia: JPS, 1960.
Glatzer, Nahum N., *The Dynamics of Emancipation.* Boston: Beacon Press, 1965.
————, *Faith and Knowledge, a Medieval Reader.* Boston: Beacon Press, 1963.
Grayzel, Solomon, *A History of Contemporary Jews from 1900 to the Present.* Philadelphia: JPS; New York: Meridian Books, 1960.
Hay, Malcolm, *Europe and the Jews.* Boston: Beacon Press, 1960.
Katz, Jacob, *Exclusiveness and Tolerance.* New York: Schocken Books, Inc., 1962.

Marcus, Jacob R., *The Jew in the Mediaeval World*. New York: UAHC, 1938; Meridian Books, 1960.
Parkes, James, *Anti-Semitism*. Chicago: Quadrangle Book, 1964.
Sachar, Howard M., *The Course of Modern Jewish History*. New York: Dell Books, 1963.
Schwarz, Leo (ed.), *Memoirs of My People (Self-Portraits, Eleventh through Twentieth Centuries)*. New York: Schocken Books, Inc., 1963.
Silver, Abba Hillel, *A History of Messianic Speculation in Israel from the First to the Seventeenth Century*. New York: Harper Brothers, 1927; Boston: Beacon Press, 1959.

Jewish Philosophers

Bergman, Samuel H., *Faith and Reason: An Introduction to Modern Jewish Thought*. Washington: B'nai B'rith Hillel Foundations, 1963.
Buber, Martin, *Tales of the Hasidim; The Early Masters* (Vol. 1), *The Later Masters* (Vol. 2). New York: Schocken Books, Inc., 1947.
Glatzer, Nahum N., *Franz Rosenzweig, His Life and Thought*. Philadelphia: JPS, 1953.
*Guttman, J., *The Philosophies of Judaism*. Philadelphia: JPS, 1964; New York: Holt, Rinehart and Winston, Inc., 1964.
Herberg, Will, *The Writings of Martin Buber*. New York: Meridian Books, 1960.
Heschel, Abraham, J., *Who is Man?* Palo Alto: Stanford University Press, 1966.
Husik, Isaac, *A History of Medieval Jewish Philosophy*. Philadelphia: JPS; New York: Meridian Books, 1958.
*Kaplan, Mordecai, *The Purpose and Meaning of Jewish Existence* (a critique of Herman Cohen). Philadelphia: JPS, 1964.
Lewy, Hans, Alexander Altmann, and Isaac Heinemann (eds.), *Three Jewish Philosophers (Philo, Saadia, and Judah Halevi); Readings and Introduction*. Philadelphia: JPS; New York: Meridian Books, 1960.
Maimonides, Moses, *The Guide of the Perplexed* (abridged) transl. by M. Friedlander. New York: Dover, 1962.
Novek, Simon (ed.), *Great Jewish Thinkers of the Twentieth Century*. Washington: B'nai B'rith Hillel Foundations, 1963.
Sholem, Gershom, *Major Trends in Jewish Mysticism*. New York: Schocken Books, Inc., 1963.

Judaism in America

The American Jewish Year Book. Philadelphia: JPS, annual.
Blau, Joseph L., *Modern Varieties of Judaism*. New York: Columbia University Press, 1966.
*Davis, Mosheh, *The Emergence of Conservative Judaism: The Historical School in the Nineteenth Century*. Philadelphia: JPS, 1963.

Glazer, Nathan, *American Judaism*. Chicago: The University of Chicago Press, 1959.
*Gordon, A. I., *Jews in Suburbia*. Boston: Beacon Press, 1959.
*Handlin, Oscar, *Adventure in Freedom: Three-Hundred Years of Jewish Life in America*. New York: McGraw-Hill Book Company, Inc., 1954.
Heller, James G., *Isaac M. Wise, His Work and Thought*. New York: UAHC, 1965.
Herberg, Will, *Catholic, Protestant, Jew*. New York: Doubleday & Co., Inc., 1955.
Heschel, Abraham J., *The Insecurity of Freedom*. Philadelphia: JPS, 1966.
*Janowsky, A., *The American Jew, a Reappraisal*. Philadelphia: JPS, 1964.
Korn, Bertram W., *American Jewry and the Civil War*. Philadelphia: JPS, 1961.
*Learsi, Rufus, *The Jews in America*. New York: World, 1954.
*Plaut, W. Gunther, *The Rise of Reform Judaism*. New York: World Union for Progressive Judaism, 1963.
*———, *The Growth of Reform Judaism*. New York: World Union for Progressive Judaism, 1965.
*Schwartzman, Sylvan D., *Reform Judaism in the Making*. New York: UAHC, 1955.
*Sklare, Marshall, *The Jews, Social Pattern of an American Group*. Glencoe, Ill.: The Free Press, 1958.
*Wolf, Arnold J. (ed.), *Rediscovering Judaism*. Chicago: Quadrangle Book, 1965.

Zionism

Bein, Alex, *Theodor Herzl*. Philadelphia: JPS, 1940.
Hertzberg, Arthur (ed.), *The Zionist Idea*. Philadelphia: JPS; New York: Meridian Books, 1959.
Parzen, Herbert, *A Short History of Zionism*. New York: Herzl Press, 1962.
Spiro, Melford E., *Kibbutz, Venture in Utopia*. New York: Schocken Books, Inc., 1963.

Jewish Year in Worship and Art

Agnon, S. Y., *Days of Awe*. New York: Schocken Books, Inc., 1948.
Arzt, Max, *Justice and Mercy; Commentary on the Liturgy of the New Year and the Day of Atonement*. New York: Holt, Rinehart and Winston, Inc., 1963.
Gaster, Theodor H., *Festivals of the Jewish Year*. Philadelphia: JPS, 1953.
———, *Passover: Its History and Traditions*. Boston: Beacon Press, 1962.
*Idelson, A. Z., *Jewish Music*. New York: Tudor Publishing Company, 1944.
*Kampf, Avram, *Contemporary Synagogue Art*. Philadelphia: JPS, 1966.
*Millgram, Abraham, *The Sabbath, Day of Delight*. Philadelphia: JPS, 1944.
Prayer Books and *Haggadahs* by the various denominational groups.

*Roth, Cecil, *Jewish Art*. New York: McGraw-Hill Book Company, Inc., 1961.
Schauss, Hayyim, *The Jewish Festivals*. New York: UAHC, 1938.
*Wischnitzer, Rachel, *Synagogue Architecture in the United States*. Philadelphia: JPS, 1955.
————, *The Architecture of the European Synagogue*. Philadelphia: JPS, 1964.

Jewish Life

Brav, Stanley B., *Marriage and the Jewish Tradition*. New York: Philosophical Library, 1951.
*Cahnman, Werner J., *Intermarriage and Jewish Life*. New York: Herzl Press, 1963.
Levi, S. B., and S. R. Kaplan, *Guide for the Jewish Homemaker*. New York: Schocken Books, Inc., 1964.
Schauss, Hayyim, *The Lifetime of a Jew*. New York: UAHC, 1950.

SOME PERIODICALS

The various synagogue and rabbinical bodies have regular periodicals for their constituents. B'nai B'rith issues *The National Jewish Monthly*, which is popular in style and has wide appeal beyond the membership. *Judaism* is a scholarly quarterly. The *Reconstructionist* deals with many subjects from the Reconstructionist point of view. *Commentary*, a monthly magazine issued by the American Jewish Committee, holds high prestige among Jewish and non-Jewish readers. *Jewish Heritage* is the educational quarterly of B'nai B'rith. The national rabbinical and congregational organizations issue scholarly and popular journals. Other groups, as well as individual publishers, issue magazines and periodicals.

The larger Jewish communities have their own newspapers, usually dealing with local Jewish affairs, but often including wider coverage; they are usually weeklies and written in English.

GLOSSARY

Ab, ninth of—fast day commemorating the fall of the Temple.
Adonai—the Lord (speaking of God).
Aggadah—homiletic portions of the *Talmud*.
Alenu—concluding prayer of worship.
Amidah—prayer of petition, recited standing.
Ashkenasim—Jews living in Germany and France and later also in Poland and Russia.

Baal Shem (Master of the [Divine] Name)—name given to the founder of Jewish mysticism in Poland.
Bar Mitzvah—at age 13 a boy's coming of age as a responsible son of the *Mitzvah;* connected with a ceremony.
Bat Mitzvah—daughter of the *Mitzvah.*
B.C.E.—before the common era; used to designate dates preceding the Christian era.
Berakhah—the benediction or blessing; unit of prayer.
Bet Am—the House of the People.
Bimah—pulpit from which *Torah* is read; used also for "chancel" in the synagogue.
B'rit Milah—the act of circumcision.

C. E.—common era; designation of dates of the Christian era.
Cheder—(school) room; primary school for Hebrew study in Eastern European education system.

Diaspora—the dispersion or scattering of the Jews; Jewish community outside of Israel.

El—name of God; emphasizing His attribute of justice.
Elohim—name of God; as Sum of All power and justice.

Gedaliah, Fast of—fast day immediately after *Rosh Hashanah*, named for the Jewish governor of Palestine murdered by his fellow Jews at the time of destruction of the first Temple.
Gemara—record of the extensive discussions of the rabbis, based on the *Mishnah. Mishnah* and *Gemara* together form the *Talmud,* the compendium of learning.

Habdalah—prayer of separation (of the Sabbath and holy days from the days of the week).
Haftarah—portion of Prophets appointed to be read after the reading of Torah on holy days and special occasions.
Haggadah—text used at celebration of Passover *Seder*.
Halakhah—literally, "walk"; law; legal decisions of developers of Jewish law as guide of life.
Hallah—loaf of bread set on the table on the eve of the Sabbath and holy days.
Hallel—Psalms 113–118, Psalms of Thanksgiving.
Hametz—leaven; all items made with it must be removed from the house at the time of *Pessah* (Passover).
Hanukkah—midwinter festival of eight days commemorating the reconsecration of the Temple after the Maccabean revolt protesting desecration of the Temple by Antiochus IV, Epiphanes.
Hasidism—mystical movement, particularly that founded by Rabbi Israel Baal Shem (1700–1760).
Haskalah—enlightenment movement among Jews in Russia.
Hokmah—wisdom.
Huppah—the marriage canopy.

Kaddish—prayer of sanctification used in worship and also recited by mourners as evidence of their faith in God.
Kahal (Kehillah)—congregation.
Kashrut—kosher laws.
Kavanah—attunement of the heart.
Kedushah—sanctification of God in public worship (*Kodosh, Kodosh, Kodosh* . . . holy, holy, holy is the Lord of Hosts . . .).
Ketubah—marriage contract.
Ketubim—collected writings (e.g., Psalms, Job, etc.); third part of the *Tenakh*.
Kibbutz—cooperative settlement in Israel.
Kiddush—the blessing over the wine, in *sanctification* of Sabbath and holy days, part of the traditional Sabbath observance.
Kiddushin—sanctification of married life; wedding ceremony.
Kos—cup; from *kosas*, to measure out; in *Kiddush* becomes symbol of God's measured out destiny for man.
Kosher—all right; name given to foods and other items signifying that they are usable under Jewish law.

Maariv—the evening prayer.
Magen David—Shield of David; six-pointed Star; a symbol of Judaism.
Makom—place; a name of God, the Every-Place.
Malakh—angel.
Mappah—literally, the tablecloth; Rabbi Moses Isserles' annotations to the *Shulhan Arukh* of Joseph Karo.
Matzah—unleavened bread, "the bread of affliction" and of deliverance in bondage in Egypt; eaten at *Pessah* (Passover).
Menorah—the (seven-branched) candelabrum; a symbol of Judaism.
Messiah—the anointed one; the one who is forecast to bring peace and a perfect society.

Mezuzah—a small scroll containing selections of Scriptures including the *Shema*, placed on the doorposts of Jewish houses.
Midrash—search; i.e., search for meaning; a homiletic commentary on the Scriptures.
Minhag—custom and practice (plural: *Minhagim*).
Minhah—afternoon prayer.
Minyan—congregation; the quorum of ten constituting a congregation.
Mishnah—literally, review; the interpretations of the *Torah* passed along by word of mouth (Oral *Torah*) and finally written down c. 200 B.C.E. See *Talmud*.
Mitzvah—commandment.
Mohel—a pious man who performs the rite of circumcision.
Mussaf—additional prayer reflecting the significance of holy days.

Nabee—prophet.
Ne'eelah—the closing prayer on *Yom Kippur*.
Ne-vee-im—(the books of the) Prophets; second part of the *Tenakh*.

Olam haba—the world to come.

Pessah—festival of spring and rebirth marking freedom from bondage in Israel; Passover.
Pilpul—hairsplitting method of talmudic study.
Proseuche—early term for synagogue; the building where religious gatherings were held.
Purim—spring carnival feast (based on the story of Esther) in which getting drunk becomes a *Mitzvah*.

Rabbi—teacher, the ordained spiritual leader of a congregation. (Rabbi is a "degree" obtained in America after approximately five years of post-graduate studies in a Jewish theological school.)
Rashi—foremost commentator of Bible and *Talmud*.
Rosh Hashanah—New Year's Day, an autumn festival; beginning of a ten-day period of repentance.

Sanhedrin—the ancient Jewish Supreme Court and lawmaking body.
Seder—literally, order; the order of family service on *Pessah*.
Sefardim—Jews living in Spain.
Selihot—prayers for forgiveness.
Shabuot—the Feast of Weeks commemorating the giving of the Ten Commandments on Mt. Sinai.
Shaharit—morning prayer.
Shalom—peace; also a name of God meaning Absolute Perfection.
Shamosh—the "server"; name for the beadle in the synagogue; also used for the serving candle in the *menorah*.
Shebarim—a three-times-broken sound on the *shofar*, signifying the sobbing of a contrite heart.
Shema—"Hear," the first word of the affirmation of faith ("Hear, O Israel, the Lord Our God, the Lord is One," etc.), and hence standing for the whole affirmation.

Shivah—the seven days of mourning for the dead.

Shofar—ram's horn used as musical instrument.

Shohet—man trained in Jewish law who slaughters animals in the approved manner.

Shulhan Arukh—"The Well-Prepared Table," written by Joseph Karo, the authoritative code for Orthodox Jewish practices.

Siddur—the prayer book.

Sukkah—small hut or booth in which the family takes its meals during the holiday of *Sukkot*.

Sukkot—fall festival of Thanksgiving.

Synagogue—building where the congregation meets; also (formerly) the congregation itself.

Tallit—a four-cornered robe with tassels (*Tzitzit*) on it, worn to serve as a reminder of the constant presence of God.

Talmud—"compendium of learning" consisting of the *Mishnah* and *Gemara*.

Tannaim—the teachers, who speak in the *Mishnah*.

Tefillin—phylacteries; small containers in the form of a cube containing scrolls with several selections, including the *Shema;* one is worn on the head and the other on the left upper arm opposite the heart.

Tehillim—"praises," another word for the Psalms.

Tekiah—a long-drawn sound on the *shofar*, the awakening sound.

Tenakh—a Hebrew abbreviation for the Holy Scriptures; abbreviation of Torah, *N*evee-im, *K*etubim.

Teruah—a whimpering, nine-times-broken sound on the *shofar;* the weeping of a heart aware of its guilt.

Torah—"instruction," specifically, the Five Books of Moses, i.e., Genesis, Exodus, Leviticus, Numbers, and Deuteronomy; first part of the *Tenakh*, but used in wider connotation.

Tosafot—additions, written by Rashi's successors in explanation of his commentary.

Tzedakah—charity.

Tzitzit—tassels on the four-cornered robe, the *Tallit*.

Yeshivah—academy of advanced Talmudic studies.

YHWH—name of God: "I Am He Who Brings into Being," pronounced *Adonai*.

Yom Kippur—the Day of Atonement.

Zaddik—the righteous; also used as designation of leaders of the Hasidic movement.

NOTE: The Hebrew letters in the dedication are an abbreviation, standing for *Zikhronom le'brakhah:* "May their memory endure as a blessing."

INDEX

Aaron, 14; descendants of, 17
Ab, 9th of, day of mourning, 183
Abba Areka (Rab), 22
Academies: Cordova, 27; Mainz, 36; Nehardea, 22; Pumbedita, 22; Sura, 22; Worms, 36
Aggadah, 21, 120
Ahad Ha-Am (Asher Ginzberg), 52
Akiba, Rabbi, 21, 130
Albright, William F., 10, 107
Alexander the Great, 16, 17
American: Jewry, 6, 66–81
Amoraim (Speakers) and Gemara, 120
Amos, 8, 100, 109
Angels, 132–133
Antiochus IV, Epiphanes, 17, 173
Anti-Semitism, 52, 54–57, 64, 65, 78; Luther, 38, 56; theological, 56
Arabs, 23, 25–26, 61
Architecture: synagogue and temple, 149–151
Aristotle, 19, 23; and Maimonides, 30
Ark, 106, 107
Asceticism, 131
Asher ben Yehiel, 37
Ashkenasim, 25, 41; in Middle Ages, 32–39; Emancipation Period, 48–54
Assembly (Kallah), 23; Rabbinical, 73
Atonement, Day of, 166–168
Auto-Emancipation, 44, 52

Baal Shem, Rabbi Israel, 42
Babylonia: exile in, 12–15; Jewish center, 22; Jewish community of, 14, 22; return from Exile, 15–16; and Talmud, 22–23
Baeck, Leo, 57, 197
Balfour Declaration, 61
Bamidbar (Book of Numbers), 102–103
Bar Kokhba Rebellion, 18
Bar Mitzvah, 78, 188–189
Bat Mitzvah, 189
Basel: Jewish Congress (1897), 53

B.C.E.: defined, 12
Ben-Gurion, David, 199
Berakhah (Blessing) 141–142
Bereshit (Book of Genesis), 98–100
Beth Din (Court of Law), 121–122
Bible: See Torah
Black Death, 36, 40; Jews as scapegoats, 35
Blessing (Berakhah), 141–142
B'nai B'rith, 76, 79
"Book of Doctrines and Beliefs," 23
Brandeis, Louis, 76, 199: Brandeis University, 76
Brotherhood, 94
Buber, Martin, 57, 60, 83, 129; and Hasidism, 43; and religion in modern Israel, 200

Caftan, 40, 45
Caiphas, 20, 91–92
Calendar, Jewish, 160–162
Calonymus family, 33, 36
Cantor, 39
Caribbean Jews, 65
C.E.: defined, 12
Church, Roman Catholic, 38; Statement on the Jews, 83–90
Central Conference of American Rabbis, 69
Charlemagne and Jews, 32
Chazars, 26, 28
Cheder (school), 41
Chmielnicky Massacres in Poland, 41
"Chosenness," 7–8
Christianity 82–95; Jesus, 90–92, 93; banks established, 34; converts to, 31, 35, 78, 132, 186–187; conquest, 31; pogroms, denouncement of, 44; Jewish converts to, 16, 78; and Judaism, 76, 186–187; in Roman Empire, 18; trinitarian, 26, 93
Chronicles I and II, 117
"Chuzari," 28
Circumcision, 187–188

211